The Gateless Barrier

THE WU-MEN KUAN (MUMONKAN)

Translated and with a Commentary by

Robert Aitken

Illustrations by Sengai

North Point Press
Farrar, Straus and Giroux
New York

The paintings by Sengai are reproduced by
permission of The Idemitsu Museum of Arts.
Chapters of this book appeared in earlier versions in
Blind Donkey and *The Eastern Buddhist*, new series.

Designed by David Bullen
Second printing, 1995

LIBRARY OF CONGRESS

CATALOGING-IN-PUBLICATION DATA

Aitken, Robert, 1917–
    The gateless barrier : the Wu-men kuan
    (Mumonkan) / translated and with a
    commentary by Robert Aitken ; illustrations
    by Sengai.
        p.   cm.
    Includes bibliographical references.
    (pbk.)
        1. Hui-k'ai, 1183–1260. Wu-men kuan.
    2. Koan. I. Title.
BQ9289.H843A36   1990
294.3'4—dc20   90-48970

North Point Press
A division of Farrar, Straus and Giroux
New York

TO THE LIVING PRESENCE OF
YAMADA KŌUN-KEN RŌDAISHI

Bamboo shadows sweep the stairs
but no dust is stirred;
moonlight reaches to the bottom of the pond
but no trace is left in the water.
                                        Zenrinkushū

Contents

Illustrations

Acknowledgments

I could not even have dreamed of serving as a teacher of Zen Buddhism or of making this book if Yamada Kōun Rōshi had not guided me through Zen practice, both formally as a teacher and informally as a companion and friend. I am endlessly grateful to him for his compassion and wisdom.

My translation grew out of earlier versions made with Yamada Rōshi and Katsuki Sekida.[1] I owe a large debt to Yamada Rōshi and to Shibayama Zenkei Rōshi for their published commentaries on the *Wu-men kuan*, which have kept me on course.[2]

I am grateful to the abbots Reb Anderson and Mel Weitsman of the Zen Center of San Francisco, the staff and members of Green Gulch Zen Farm, and Yvonne Rand and William Sterling for their hospitality during a three-month sabbatical that gave me time and freedom from other responsibilities to work on my commentaries.

My old-time student Nelson Foster edited the outcome and brought a measure of coherence to my meanderings. Craig Twentyman and Anne Aitken read earlier drafts and made a great many helpful suggestions. Anne also took over many of my other responsibilities when I was glued to my desk.

Johanna Bangeman typed and retyped and helped with the appendixes. Carl Varady gave me technical assistance and suggested useful references.

Students at the Koko An Zendō, the Maui Zendō, and the Green Gulch Zen Farm offered useful ideas when I read parts of the manuscript to their classes. Others who helped in important ways were: David Chappell, Trish Dougherty, Shōkin Furuta, Glenn James, Barbara Newton, Shigeru Ohsuka, George Tanabe, Kazuaki Tanahashi, and Norman Waddell.

I am especially grateful to Jack Shoemaker, Dave Bullen, Barbara Ras, and the staff of North Point Press for their competence and creativity in making this book.

In citing quotations, I frequently refer to translations by D. T. Suzuki, Thomas Cleary, C. Y. Chang, Kazuaki Tanahashi, and others. I work from less accessible texts as well, however, and the translations often differ from those cited. These texts include some that are published with English translation, like Ruth Fuller Sasaki's *Recorded Sayings of Ch'an Master Lin-chi*,[3] and also such studies in Japanese as the *dokugo* of Yasutani Haku'un Rōshi,[4] the modernized *Shōbōgenzō* edited by the Honzanban Shukusatsu,[5] the various commentaries listed in the bibliography, works in the *Zen no Goroku* series,[6] as well as other Japanese scholarly studies, and manuscript translations prepared with Yamada Rōshi.

Palolo Zen Center
Spring Training Period, 1990

Introduction

The Gateless Barrier is a collection of stories and verses that present fundamental perspectives on life and no-life, the nature of the self, the relationship of the self to the earth—and how these interweave. Such stories and verses are called kōans, and their study is the process of realizing their truths. What may be known abstractly becomes personal, a vital experience of one's own. For example: the notion of transcendental oneness becomes a vivid experience of a shared and unbounded nature, and the thought of compassion is felt profoundly in a way that is consistent with its etymology: "suffering with others."

Classic kōans have proved effective over the centuries and millennia in recording—and evoking—especially illuminating experiences of such fundamentals.[1] Kōans are not riddles or puzzles whose trick is in their clever and obscure wording. They are the clearest possible expression of perennial facts which students grasp with focused meditation and guidance.

The original interactions that became kōans were challenges to students by their teachers (and vice versa) in old China. Hui-neng asked the head monk Ming about his original face, for example, and Ming realized something important.[2] Some one hundred and seventy-five years later, Kuei-shan asked Hsiang-yen about his original face before his parents were born. Hsiang-yen didn't understand the question at the time, but it cooked as a kōan in his psyche and later he too realized something important.[3] The question Hui-neng asked Ming was amplified a bit in the trial-and-error process of becoming a kōan. This process of amplifying and codifying along with creating new kōans continued down through the centuries to Sung times (960–1279), when several collections of kōans, including this one, were assembled and published.

Kōan study developed separately in the two great Buddhist traditions that became Rinzai and Sōtō Zen. Rinzai teachers, culminating with Hakuin, tended to systematize kōans into a kind of curriculum, while the Sōtō teachers tended to pick and choose kōans for each particular student. Today kōan study survives in the Rinzai school, but it is no longer used in the Sōtō. In the early part of this century, the Sōtō monk Harada Sōgaku (Dai'un) broke with his tradition by studying with the Rinzai master Toyoda Dokutan Rōshi. Returning to the Sōtō fold, he established his own way of kōan teaching which (after several generations) inspires this present translation and commentary. This way of teaching cannot be said to be either Rinzai or Sōtō, though it draws from each. It has been called the Harada–Yasutani school, after its first two teachers, and the Sanbō Kyōdan (Order of the Three Treasures).

Zen study as reestablished by Harada Rōshi begins with learning zazen (focused meditation), which I have discussed elsewhere in *Taking the Path of Zen* and which is also set forth in Yasutani Rōshi's "Introductory Lectures on Zen Training."[4] In consultation with a teacher, perhaps the student who has practiced zazen for a while will elect to begin work on one of the initial kōans—usually the word "Mu," set forth in Case 1, or possibly Bassui Tokushō's question, "Who is hearing?"[5] Such themes are pursued with a keen, inquiring spirit, and the process of resolving them may take a long time, many years in some cases. Finally, the student gains a degree of understanding and is ready for subsequent kōans to amplify, clarify, and deepen the original insight.

Through this process, we discover that life and death are the same as no-life and no-death; the other is no other than myself; each being is infinitely precious as a unique expression of the nature which is essential to us all. The inspired student seeks to live this reality within the home and outside, making each turn an occasion for further realization and practice of these fundamental facts—perhaps joining with like-minded people for an expression of broad social and environmental concerns. This life practice may have begun before the beginning of formal Zen study. It can continue throughout each of its steps, and there is no end.

My comments on the kōans, like those of my betters, including Wumen in the early thirteenth century, grew out of talks (teishōs) given during retreats—in my case to Diamond Sangha students in three cycles over a period of fifteen years. They have been much revised to function as essays while still retaining, I hope, their original flavor as teishōs: "presentations . of the shout."

I use Chinese names for Chinese personages and give Japanese equivalents in parentheses. I use certain Japanese terms like "Zen," "Mu," "teishō," "kōan," and "dōjō," for these are current and some even appear in modern English dictionaries. At the back of the book I offer a glossary of terms used throughout the text; to make the book more accessible, I have used translated forms of certain Japanese terms that are current in Western Zen centers. Familiar words from the Sanskrit like "nirvana" and "sutra" are given without diacritical marks. Accents that do not significantly affect the pronunciation of words for English readers are omitted. An acute accent over the letter *s* in Sanskrit words, as in Śākyamuni, is pronounced *sh*. The macron over a vowel in Sanskrit and Japanese gives emphasis and length to that syllable, as in *dāna*.

Chinese pronunciations are difficult, and neither the traditional Wade-Giles nor the modern pinyin romanizations do the original much justice. Here I have used the Wade-Giles system, as it is more familiar, and give the pinyin version in the Equivalency Tables (Appendixes II and III). When the two are compared, an approximation of the true pronunciation can emerge.

The Lineage Charts (Appendix I) are arranged to show teachers by generation, and the important names in the Equivalency Tables are keyed to the charts to show generation numbers. Suggested readings and references are provided in the Bibliography. Many of them are out of print—try your library and if necessary request an interlibrary loan. Reading supplements instruction and can provide important help in the absence of a teacher.

The Gateless Barrier

Preface

The Buddha mind and words point the way; the Gateless Barrier is the Dharma entry. There is no gate from the beginning, so how do you pass through it? Haven't you heard that things which come through the gate are not the family treasure? Things gained from causal circumstances have a beginning and an end—formation and destruction.

Such talk raises waves where there is no wind and gouges wounds in healthy flesh. How much more foolish are those who depend upon words and seek understanding by their intellect! They try to hit the moon with a stick. They scratch their shoes when their feet itch.

In the summer of the first year of Shao-ting,[1] I was head of the assembly at Lung-hsiang in Tung-chia. When the monks asked for instruction, I took up kōans of ancient teachers and used them as brickbats to batter at the gate, guiding the monks in accord with their various capacities. I recorded these cases and thus, without my intending it, they have become a collection. I did not arrange the kōans in any particular order. There are forty-eight cases in all, and I call the collection The Gateless Barrier.

The person of courage unflinchingly cuts straight through the barrier, unhindered even by Nata, the eight-armed demon king. In the presence of such valor, the twenty-eight Indian ancestors and six Chinese ancestors beg for their lives. If you hesitate, however, you'll be like someone watching a horse gallop past a window. With a blink, it is gone.

WU-MEN'S VERSE

The Great Way has no gate;
there are a thousand different paths;
once you pass through the barrier,
you walk the universe alone.

Wu-men (Mumon) Hui-k'ai was a Sung period master of the Lin-chi (Rin-zai) school who lived from 1183 to 1260. He worked on the kōan "Mu" ardently for six years, sometimes, it is said, pacing the corridors at night and knocking his head intentionally against the pillars. One day he heard the drum announcing the noon meal—and suddenly, like the Buddha seeing the morning star, he had a profound experience of understanding. His poem on that occasion reads:

A thunderclap under the clear blue sky;
all beings on earth open their eyes;
everything under heaven bows together;
Mount Sumeru leaps up and dances.

After receiving transmission from his master, Yüeh-lin (Gatsurin), Wu-men wandered as a teacher from temple to temple, never settling long in one place. Toward the end of his life, he retired to a hermitage but was regularly disturbed by visitors seeking guidance.

An unconventional Zen master in many respects, Wu-men let his hair and beard grow and wore old soiled robes. He worked in the fields and carried his own slops. Called "Hui-k'ai the Lay Monk," he is a wonderful archetype for us monkish lay people in the West.[2]

Wu-men's Preface is straightforward and needs little comment: "Things which come through the gate" are those, as the next line indicates, that have a beginning and an end—fame and fortune, for example. These are not the family treasure.

What is the family treasure? I think Wu-men is talking about human vision and human fulfillment, not anything grandiose. In Stevenson's "The Poor Thing," a fisherman proposes marriage to the daughter of an earl by saying, "Come, behold a vision of our children, the busy hearth, and the white heads. And let that suffice, for it is all God offers."[3] Zen practice shows us how to cherish what we are and what we have—and what the earth is and has.

"You'll be like someone watching a horse gallop past a window. With a blink it is gone." Quick as a wink, you'll find that life has passed you by—grasp the chance before you *now*!

Wu-men's verse begins: "The Great Way has no gate"—as broad as the world, with no barriers!

"There are a thousand different paths"—every event is a path on that Great Way: the advice of a friend, the song of the thrush in the early morning, the smell of rain in dusty fields.

D. T. Suzuki translates the last line "in royal solitude you walk the universe," which adds a word to the original and indicates the pleasure of such solitude.[4]

Wu-men said that he did not arrange the cases of his book in any particular order, but the order he did choose is well established after all this time, and my commentary builds from case to case. It is all right to skip around on first reading, of course, but eventually, to gain the most from the book, I think it would be best to begin at the beginning and persevere chapter by chapter.

Chao-chou's Dog

THE CASE

A monk asked Chao-chou, "Has the dog Buddha nature or not?"
Chao-chou said, "Mu."[1]

WU-MEN'S COMMENT

For the practice of Zen it is imperative that you pass through the barrier set up by the Ancestral Teachers. For subtle realization it is of the utmost importance that you cut off the mind road. If you do not pass the barrier of the ancestors, if you do not cut off the mind road, then you are a ghost clinging to bushes and grasses.

What is the barrier of the Ancestral Teachers? It is just this one word "Mu"— the one barrier of our faith. We call it the Gateless Barrier of the Zen tradition. When you pass through this barrier, you will not only interview Chao-chou intimately. You will walk hand in hand with all the Ancestral Teachers in the successive generations of our lineage—the hair of your eyebrows entangled with theirs, seeing with the same eyes, hearing with the same ears. Won't that be fulfilling? Is there anyone who would not want to pass this barrier?

So, then, make your whole body a mass of doubt, and with your three hundred and sixty bones and joints and your eighty-four thousand hair follicles concentrate on this one word "Mu." Day and night, keep digging into it. Don't consider it to

PLATE 1: *A Dog and Its Buddha Nature.* Courtesy of
The Idemitsu Museum of Arts. (Case 1)

Dog, Buddha Nature.
Don't say he doesn't have it!
Don't say Mu!
A stiff spring wind has risen,
rattling the gourds on the east wall.

Trans. by Norman Waddell

be nothingness. *Don't think in terms of "has" and "has not." It is like swallowing a red-hot iron ball. You try to vomit it out, but you can't.*

Gradually you purify yourself, eliminating mistaken knowledge and attitudes you have held from the past. Inside and outside become one. You're like a mute person who has had a dream—you know it for yourself alone.

Suddenly Mu breaks open. The heavens are astonished, the earth is shaken. It is as though you have snatched the great sword of General Kuan. When you meet the Buddha, you kill the Buddha. When you meet Bodhidharma, you kill Bodhidharma. At the very cliff edge of birth-and-death, you find the Great Freedom. In the Six Worlds and the Four Modes of Birth, you enjoy a samādhi of frolic and play.

How, then, should you work with it? Exhaust all your life energy on this one word "Mu." If you do not falter, then it's done! A single spark lights your Dharma candle.

WU-MEN'S VERSE
Dog, Buddha nature—
the full presentation of the whole;
with a bit of "has" or "has not"
body is lost, life is lost.

Here at the outset of *The Gateless Barrier* we meet Chao-chou (Jōshū), whose kōan "Mu" is the foundation of our kōan study. He had the longest and one of the most unusual careers of any Zen master. Born in 778, he came to study with Nan-ch'üan (Nansen) when he was only eighteen years old and remained until his old teacher died forty years later. After two years of mourning he set out on a pilgrimage to visit the many eminent teachers of his time. On his departure he is said to have vowed: "If I meet a hundred-year-old person who seeks my guidance I will offer the best teaching I can to that venerable person. If I meet a seven-year-old child who can teach me I will become an ardent disciple of that child."[2] Contrast this vow with Confucian attitudes toward age and youth that prevailed in Chao-chou's time. At age sixty he had freed himself of cultural constrictions as much as anyone can, and had regained his beginner's mind.

Chao-chou maintained his vow for the next twenty years. Wandering from teacher to teacher, he invited them to probe his mind, checking them as well, deepening and clarifying understanding throughout the Zen world. Finally, at eighty, he settled down in a small temple and for the next forty years guided disciples from his wonderfully seasoned understanding, passing away in his hundred and twentieth year.

Throughout his long career Chao-chou taught in a simple manner with just a few quiet words. It is said that a light seemed to play about his mouth as he spoke. Dōgen Kigen, who freely criticized many of his ancestors in the Dharma, could only murmur with awe, "Jōshū, the Old Buddha."[3] Forty generations of Zen students and more since his time, Chinese, Korean, Vietnamese, Japanese, and now people everywhere, have breathed his one word "Mu," evoking the living presence of the Old Buddha himself.

Thus Mu is an arcanum—an ancient word or phrase that successive seekers down through the centuries have focused upon and found to be an opening into spiritual understanding.[4] When you join that stream you have joined hands with countless pilgrims, past, present, future.

In everyday usage the word "Mu" means "does not have"—but if that were Chao-chou's entire meaning, there wouldn't be any Zen. As I mentioned in my comment to his Preface, Wu-men worked hard on Mu for six years. Though he declares that he did not put the cases of his book in any particular order, it nonetheless seems significant that he chose his own first kōan as the first for his book. In many Zen Buddhist temples, including our own, the first teishō of every sesshin (retreat) is devoted to Mu. This single syllable turns out to be a mine of endless riches.

The monk's question is about Buddha nature, and Chao-chou's "Mu" in response is a *presentation* of Buddha nature. Buddha nature is the fundamental subject of Buddhist teaching. It is the nature of our being. Dōgen establishes this at the outset of his essay titled "Buddha Nature": "All beings without exception have Buddha Nature. The Tathāgata abides without change. This is the lion roar of our great teacher Śākyamuni, turning the Wheel of the Dharma, and it is the head and eyeballs of all Buddhas and all Ancestors."[5]

"Tathāgata" is another term for Buddha nature, or simply Buddha. This is the essential nature of all beings and, indeed, the universe itself. It is completely empty, yet it is potent with infinitely varied and dynamic possibilities. The monk sitting before Chao-chou cannot acknowledge his own Tathāgata. At a very deep level he is asking, "Do I really have Buddha nature as they say?" Chao-chou presents his affirmation with a single word of a single syllable: "Mu."

In his quiet way Chao-chou is also showing the monk how to practice. He is just saying "Mu." This you can take as guide, inspiration, and model. This is your path and, breath by breath, you will realize the Buddhahood that has been yours from the beginning. *"Muuuuuu."*

Wu-men unpacks Chao-chou's "Mu" for us most compassionately in his comment, giving one of the few expositions in classic Zen literature of the actual process of zazen up to and including realization. Phrase by phrase it opens the Way. "For the practice of Zen," he begins, "it is imperative that you pass through the barrier set up by the Ancestral Teachers." The oldest meaning of "barrier" in English, and in Chinese and Japanese as well, is "checkpoint at a frontier." There is only an imaginary mark on the earth to distinguish, say, the United States from Canada, yet our two countries have placed checkpoints along its length. There is no line in your essential nature to distinguish insight from ignorance, but in Zen Buddhist practice someone in a little house by the road will say: "Let me see your credentials. How do you stand with yourself? How do you stand with the world?" You present yourself and are told: "Okay, you may pass" or "No, you may not pass."

The barrier is an archetypal element of human growth—an obstacle to be surmounted by heroes and heroines from time immemorial. It is said that Bodhidharma, revered as the founder of Zen in China, faced the wall of his cave in zazen for the last nine years of his life, though he had long ago found that wall, that barrier, to be altogether transparent. For his part, the Buddha saw through his barrier when he happened to glance up and notice the morning star. Down through the ages there have been countless Buddhas whose barrier turned out to be wide open after all. You too face that barrier. Confirm it as your own.

"For subtle realization," Wu-men continues, "it is of the utmost importance that you cut off the mind road." This is not an injunction to cut off thoughts. As Yasutani Haku'un Rōshi used to say, "It is probably possible to control the brain so that no thoughts arise, but that would be an inert state in which no creativity is possible."[6] Wu-men's point is that if you try to cut off thoughts and feelings you might be able to reach a dead space as Yasutani Rōshi suggests. Or, more likely, thoughts and feelings will defeat your efforts and come flooding through, and you'll be desperately trying to plug the dike. Such an endeavor brings only despair. Inevitably you notice that you are thinking something as you sit there on your cushions in zazen. Remember Mu at such a time. Notice and remember; notice and remember—a very simple, yet very exacting, practice.

Of course, this practice is not intended as a denial of thoughts and feelings. Even anger can be positive and instructive if it is simply a wave that washes through. Thoughts and feelings have a positive role in zazen, too, for they serve as reminders, just like bird song. Quoting Tung-shan Liang-chieh (Tōzan Ryōkai):

> The song of the cuckoo
> urges me to come home.[7]

And you begin again. Noticing and remembering, noticing and remembering, gradually you become big with Mu—all things become big with Mu. Fantasies, plans, and sensations become absorbed in Mu. Mu breathes Mu. The whole universe breathes Mu.

Thoughts will come back. But no matter how important and instructive they may seem, ignore their content and significance, and persevere with your Mu. Let thoughts or sounds or sensations remind you to come back to Mu. Pay attention to Mu the way you would to a loved one, letting everything else go.

The barrier is Mu, but it always has a personal frame. For some the barrier is "Who am I really?" and that question is resolved through Mu. For others it is "What is death?" and that question too is resolved through Mu. For me it was "What am I doing here?" For many students it is Śākyamuni's question, "Why should there be suffering in the world?" The discursive words in such questions just take the inquirer around and around in the brain. With Mu—the single word of a single syllable—the agonizing interrogatives "who?" "why?" and "what?" are not answered in any literal sense, but they are certainly resolved.

"If you do not pass the barrier of the ancestors," says Wu-men, "if you do not cut off the mind road, then you are a ghost clinging to bushes and grasses." The ghost is one who can't let go. "Bushes" and "grasses" are shorthand for the many fixations that provide the ghost with identity—such as money and possessions, old resentments, and persistent habits of thought. We are all ghosts after all!

"What is the barrier of the Ancestral Teachers? It is just this one word 'Mu'—the one barrier of our faith. We call it the Gateless Barrier of the Zen tradition." Beyond the Zen tradition, a single word of a single syllable is a perennial theme of focused meditation. The author of *The Cloud of Unknowing*, a fourteenth-century manual of Christian mysticism, declares, "Short prayer pierces Heaven." Cry out "Mu" in your heart the way you would cry "Fire!" if you awakened with your house ablaze. In *The Cloud of Unknowing* we find:

> And just as this little word "fire" stirs and pierces the Heavens more quickly, so does a little word of one syllable do the same when it is not only spoken or thought, but secretly intended in the depths of the spirit. This depth is height, for spiritually all is one, height and depth, length and breadth. It pierces the ears of Almighty God more than does any psalter thoughtlessly muttered in one's teeth. This is the reason it is said that *short prayer pierces Heaven*.[8]

Buddhists might not resonate with "Almighty God" as a useful metaphor. One of my students complained to me that his Alcoholics Anonymous program required him to place his trust in a higher power. "As a Buddhist, how can I do that?" he asked. We were standing at the window of the Castle Memorial Hospital in rural O'ahu where he was undergoing treatment. I pointed out the window at the Ko'olau Mountains towering above the hospital. Mountains have stupendous power, the power of things-as-they-are. The one who cries out "Fire!" in a burning house is gathered and all of a piece—like a mountain, like the cardinal that celebrates itself from the telephone wires, or the gecko who calls from the rafters, or the Zen student who breathes "Mu" with skin, flesh, bones, and marrow.

"When you pass through this barrier," Wu-men continues, "you will not only interview Chao-chou intimately. You will walk hand in hand with all the Ancestral Teachers in the successive generations of our lineage—the hair of your eyebrows entangled with theirs, seeing with the same eyes, hearing with the same ears." In this experience, we discover the original realm where we not only practice with our Dharma ancestors, we practice with all beings.

When people write to me from a place where there are no Zen centers and where it is impossible to find even a single Zen friend, I advise them, "Just sit with the awareness that you are sitting with us in the Diamond

Sangha. Just sit with the awareness that you are sitting with everyone and every being in the whole universe, past, present, and future." We may not realize it, but we are all of us dwelling together in the original realm—sitting here in the Koko An Zendō, flitting around in the mango-tree branches outside, blowing and spawning in Lahaina Roads, and so on out through a vast multidimensional net of unknown magnitude.

This multidimensional net is not static but exquisitely dynamic—the mutual interdependence of all things and their mutual intersupport, the nature of our world. As philosophy this net forms a beautiful coherence. As experience it is the containment of all beings by me, by the *me* of you, and there are countless numbers of us. This experience is called "realization," and it is also called "intimacy"—the two words are synonyms in Zen Buddhist literature. You tangle eyebrows with the many ancestors of our lineage and find that you yourself are their mind, the mind which Dōgen said is "the mountains, rivers, the earth, the sun, the moon, and the stars."[9] You find that you include them or that they contain you. There is no barrier!

The word "intimate" is *ch'in-ch'ieh* in Chinese, pronounced *shinsetsu* in Japanese. Its primary meaning is "apposite" or "to the point." But "having intimate connections" is the significance, and in everyday usage the term means "kind" or "generous" or "warmhearted." If you are invited to someone's home in Japan and you take along a little gift, your hostess will say you are very *shinsetsu*—you are very kind and your conduct is just right. But implicit in that word is the message that you are intimate. So you can see, through etymology, how the Buddha Dharma of Interbeing is manifested in daily life. Wisdom and intimacy are actually the same thing.

As a Zen student you are challenged to find this intimacy in the ordinary, workaday, confrontive society you live in. How can you see with another's eyes, or hear with another's ears, across space and time or even face to face at the post office? If you steadfastly breathe "Mu" right through all feelings of anxiety when you are on your cushions, and if you ignore distractions and devote yourself to the matter at hand on other occasions, you will be like Pu-tung (Fudō) holding fast in the flames of hell.[10] Those flames are the distressing aspects of your life, and in persevering you will surely enter the original realm.

"Won't that be fulfilling? Is there anyone who would not want to pass this barrier?" Wu-men is inviting his ponies with a carrot. Be careful. Mu is only the first of the kōans, and passing all thè kōans is only a good beginning. One peep into essential nature is a great release and a great encouragement, but if you take it as be-all and end-all, you'll drop straight back into hell.

"So, then, make your whole body a mass of doubt, and with your three hundred and sixty bones and joints and your eighty-four thousand hair follicles concentrate on this one word 'Mu.' " When students asked Yamada Kōun Rōshi, "What is the 'great doubt' that Zen teachers are always urging upon us?" he said, "Great doubt is the condition of being one with Mu." Very simple. There's no need to manufacture doubt or to create it from outside. It's right here: What is Mu?

Wu-men uses Sung dynasty terms to convey this point. "Three hundred and sixty bones and joints and eighty-four thousand hair follicles" may not be accurate modern physiology, but as metaphors they illumine the Tao of complete physical and mental absorption in Mu. This Tao is a perennial human process found here in Zen—a path to understanding that is sought one direction or another in all world religions.

"Day and night, keep digging into it." Wu-men was speaking to monks in a monastery who can carry Mu with them day and night throughout the year—at least theoretically. We lay people can do the same during retreats. And like the accountant monk and the cook, we can find ways to keep digging into it in our daily life as well. I suggest that you commit yourself at home and in your workshop or office to practice Mu for single breaths at a time—at intervals between one task and another, when you are waiting for an appointment or for your children to fall asleep. You can do this without attracting undue attention to yourself. When your other responsibilities permit, you can practice on your cushions.

"Don't consider it to be nothingness. Don't think in terms of 'has' or 'has not.' " Mu is not nothingness or somethingness. Fixed notions of "nothing" bar you from true intimacy. After all, there's very little to be intimate with there! "Has" and "has not," like self and other, arise with the concept of the human skin as some kind of armor. Actually your skin is as porous as the universe. Each particle of its substance is vastly separate from the next, and all beings pass through.

"It is like swallowing a red-hot iron ball. You try to vomit it out, but you can't." Sitting there, big with Mu, letting Mu breathe Mu, you are completely caught up in your zazen. This is the red-hot iron ball that you can neither swallow nor spit out—a metaphor that can be precise at times and inexact at others. You might feel the heat, or you might just feel a great lump. Your whole abdomen might seem to be a great basketball. Whatever it seems, let it breathe Mu.

"Gradually you purify yourself, eliminating mistaken knowledge and attitudes you have held from the past. Inside and outside become one. You're like a mute person who has had a dream—you know it for yourself alone." Focusing on this single word "Mu," you become its intimate and all things become its intimate. You are no longer self-centered. The thrush calls "Mu," the gecko cries "Mu," the fly buzzes "Mu," the crisp crack of the monitor's staff is Mu. These are not separate from your own breath and your own heartbeat. The self-centered preoccupations that kept you separate all these years simply fall away. You are like a fish in the water or a bird in the air—completely harmonized with your habitat. But you are not yet awakened in your habitat, for you are unable to express who or where you are.

"Suddenly Mu breaks open. The heavens are astonished, the earth is shaken." Well, first experiences of the original realm certainly differ. Some are full of emotion; some are mild. Kenshō, the term used for this experience, simply means "seeing nature"—that is, seeing into essential nature. How you react is your peculiarity. But if your vision is genuine, you are hand in hand with all the ancestors.

"It is as though you have snatched the great sword of General Kuan." General Kuan was a heroic warrior who helped establish the Han dynasty. Here he is Mañjuśrī, the incarnation of wisdom, who wields an exquisitely sharp sword that cuts off delusions and self-centered tendencies. Now at last the sword of Mañjuśrī is your own sword, and you are mounted on his lion.

"When you meet the Buddha, you kill the Buddha. When you meet Bodhidharma, you kill Bodhidharma." Of course, there is no need to kill the Buddha in one sense—he isn't around at all. Bodhidharma, our revered ancestor, is nowhere to be seen either. But Wu-men was not speaking so loftily. Swing Mañjuśrī's sword and cut off the mind road, he is saying, even it is occupied with the Buddha himself. Cut off the Three Poisons of greed, hatred, and ignorance. What remains? Only the beautiful song of the thrush singing to the overcast sky.

"In the Six Worlds and the Four Modes of Birth, you enjoy a samādhi of frolic and play." These worlds and modes are Sung dynasty metaphors for all realms. The Six Worlds are those of devils, hungry ghosts, animals, titans, human beings, and angels—realms through which we migrate every day. The Four Modes of Birth are the womb, the egg, the water, and the metamorphosis. Samādhi means "absorption" or "oneness." In short, wherever you are and whatever you are, you are not just yourself anymore. You include all. This is the great life of the Sambhogakāya, the Body of Bliss. You are immersed in frolic and play because children, lambs, and birds are frolicking in your own blood.

"How, then, should you work with it? Exhaust all your life energy on this one word 'Mu.' If you do not falter, then it's done!" Wu-men recaps his comment with this line. Give yourself to Mu. Let Mu breathe Mu. Don't give energy to anything except Mu. Don't feel that you are faltering because you don't realize it. When you do falter, come back to Mu at your first chance. With all your faltering, don't falter.

"A single spark lights your Dharma candle." Those sparks are always going off. You are not floating alone in a sensory-deprivation bath. As you lose yourself in Mu, you are open. Your body is no other than the sounds of the world. As you focus on Mu, let it be open. Let the buzzing fly put an end to "has" and "has not." Let the cry of the gecko put an end to birth and death. Let somebody's cough put an end to ignorance and realization.

That's Wu-men's comment. Yamada Rōshi used to say that he read it constantly, and each time found something new. This is a hint about Mu as well, for this kōan is not a raft you discard when you finally make it your own. I am still working on Mu, a great mystery, though it is no longer alien.

Wu-men's verse is equally important in its own way: "Dog, Buddha nature . . ." Moving on from Mu, the basic kōan of our practice, Wu-men sets forth the first of subsequent kōans and brings us back to the dog—and indeed to all beings.

"The full presentation of the whole." That's another arcanum. With Mu you gathered yourself. With Wu-men's verse you allow the world to gather itself. The world gathers you. You gather the world. The great gathering!

"With a bit of 'has' or 'has not' / body is lost, life is lost." Wu-men is very concerned about this point. In his comment he cautions us: "Don't consider it to be nothingness. Don't think in terms of 'has' or 'has not.'"

Be diligent with your total being—don't let yourself be confined by your skull.

If, however, you are preoccupied with "has" and "has not," that is, if you cultivate thoughts about attaining something, you cut off your head, or rather you cut off your body. You cut off the whole world. Preoccupied with brooding, fantasy, memory, or whatever, you are unable to hear the thrush in the avocado tree or smell the *kahili ti* in the early evening. What a loss!

Pai-chang's Fox

THE CASE

Once when Pai-chang gave a series of talks, a certain old man was always there listening together with the monks. When they left, he would leave too. One day, however, he remained behind. Pai-chang asked him, "Who are you, standing here before me?"

The old man replied, "I am not a human being. In the far distant past, in the time of Kāśyapa Buddha, I was head priest at this mountain. One day a monk asked me, 'Does an enlightened person fall under the law of cause and effect or not?' I replied, 'Such a person does not fall under the law of cause and effect.' With this I was reborn five hundred times as a fox. Please say a turning word for me and release me from the body of a fox."

He then asked Pai-chang, "Does an enlightened person fall under the law of cause and effect or not?"

Pai-chang said, "Such a person does not evade the law of cause and effect."

Hearing this, the old man immediately was enlightened. Making his bows he said, "I am released from the body of a fox. The body is on the other side of this mountain. I wish to make a request of you. Please, Abbot, perform my funeral as for a priest."

Pai-chang had a head monk strike the signal board and inform the assembly that after the noon meal there would be a funeral service for a priest. The monks

PLATE 2: *Pai-chang and the Fox*. Courtesy of The Idemitsu
Museum of Arts. (Case 2)

Not falling into cause and effect can bring the wild
   fox to life;
not obscuring cause and effect kills him stone dead.
If you still don't understand
why don't you go to the foot of the north cliff and
   take a look at him.

                          Trans. by Norman Waddell

talked about this in wonder. "All of us are well. There is no one in the morgue. What does the teacher mean?"

After the meal, Pai-chang led the monks to the foot of a rock on the far side of the mountain. And there, with his staff, he poked out the body of a dead fox. He then performed the ceremony of cremation. That evening he took the high seat before his assembly and told the monks the whole story.

Huang-po stepped forward and said, "As you say, the old man missed the turning word and was reborn as a fox five hundred times. What if he had given the right answer each time he was asked a question—what would have happened then?"

Pai-chang said, "Just step up here closer, and I'll tell you." Huang-po went up to Pai-chang and slapped him in the face.

Pai-chang clapped his hands and laughed, saying, "I thought the Barbarian had a red beard, but here is a red-bearded Barbarian."

WU-MEN'S COMMENT

"Not falling under the law of cause and effect." Why should this prompt five hundred lives as a fox? "Not evading the law of cause and effect." Why should this prompt a return to human life? If you have the single eye of realization, you will appreciate how old Pai-chang lived five hundred lives as a fox as lives of grace.

WU-MEN'S VERSE

Not falling, not evading—
two faces of the same die.
Not evading, not falling—
a thousand mistakes, ten thousand mistakes.

This kōan appears in several collections of Zen stories. Its origin, like that of all folklore, is obscure. If you have read studies of myths and folktales by Heinrich Zimmer and Joseph Campbell, you know that the deepest function of the stories is to present configurations of the human psyche. You understand the story of Pai-chang and the fox to the degree that you understand yourself.

Pai-chang (Hyakujō) had been a student of the great Ma-tsu (Baso), who was, more than any other teacher, responsible for the efflorescence of Zen in the T'ang period (618–922). The occasion of Ma-tsu helping Pai-chang to deepest understanding is well known:

Once when Great Master Ma and Pai-chang were walking together,
a·wild duck flew up. The Great Master said, "What is that?"
  Pai-chang said, "A wild duck."
  The Great Master said, "Where did it go?"
  Pai-chang said, "It flew away." The Great Master laid hold of Pai-chang's nose and gave it a twist. Pai-chang cried out in pain.
  The Great Master said, "When did it ever fly away!"[1]

Pai-chang was thereafter intimate with himself and the world, and he
went on to a career of teaching that affected the entire course of Zen history. He is ancestor of the Lin-chi school and revered as the founder of the
monastic schedule of work, services, and zazen that Zen centers maintain
with modifications to the present time.

Like most other Zen teachers, Pai-chang was named for his place—in
his case the nickname of his mountain (One Hundred Leagues). In this
story a former abbot of a monastery on that mountain, who of course was
also known as Pai-chang, appears and the two exchange words about
karma and essential nature.

Old Pai-chang and the present Pai-chang met transcending time. Zen
is not magic but ordinary fact. Once you establish that hundred-league
mountain as yourself, you can meet them too as Wu-men has assured you:
"The hair of your eyebrows entangled with theirs, seeing with the same
eyes, hearing with the same ears."

"Once when Pai-chang gave a series of talks, a certain old man was always there listening together with the monks. When they left, he would
leave too. One day, however, he remained behind." I am not sure what ritual accompanied the teacher's talks in the old days. In Japanese monasteries today, the monks gather in the zendō (hall of focused meditation); then
on signal from a big drum they file into the Main Hall and seat themselves.
The drum continues to beat in a syncopated rhythm, and at a certain point
the rōshi enters with his attendant.[2] After the teishō there are closing sutras, and the rōshi exits as the sutras are ending. It seems reasonable to suppose that this style derives from the Chinese monastic ritual, which Pai-
chang himself is believed to have set up. Possibly the old man stepped forward at a certain point, and so Pai-chang remained behind also.

There's something very evocative here—coming and going each day in
a series of teishōs, probably during a sesshin. And then one day, there is no
coming and going. Everything stops.

Pai-chang asks him, "Who are you, standing here before me?" The old man explains that he is not a human being and then tells his story, harking back to a far distant past, the time of Kāśyapa Buddha. This Kāśyapa Buddha should not be confused with Mahākāśyapa, the successor of Śākyamuni, the historical Buddha. Kāśyapa Buddha lived a very long time ago indeed. He was the sixth of the Ancient Seven Buddhas, preceding Śākyamuni by a kalpa or so.

In that zone of mythic time, the old Pai-chang had an exchange with a monk about karma and realization. When asked if a fully realized person would fall under the law of karma, he replied that such a person would be free of karma. With this answer, he was subjected to five hundred rebirths as a fox.

This was a drastic outcome. The fox is everything in Asian folklore that it is in Western folklore—tricky, dishonest, and unreliable. Even more, in the East the fox is the familiar of the witch—like the black cat in our culture, but more dangerous. There is something occultly nasty about an oriental fox. It can possess you, as it possessed Pai-chang the Elder. To this day there are fox shrines everywhere in Japan. Foreigners suppose that people worship the foxes, but this is not the case. They go to the shrines and make offerings to the fox spirits to keep them happy. "Leave us alone," they say in effect, "let us live in peace." Without such inducement, they believe, the spirits might bring them illness and misfortune.

From the very beginning of Buddhism the effort of the believer has been to purify all past karma. Attaining such liberation, one has no residual cause for a return—there is no further rebirth, no further suffering. Such a realized Buddha has harmonized completely with essential nature. This has been, and still is, an important tenet of most Asian Buddhism.

But far from being liberated, Pai-chang the Elder had been enslaved. What was wrong with his answer? Or was he wrong? If he was wrong, then haven't our Ancestral Teachers and sutras been wrong too?

This matter of rebirth poses difficulty for Westerners. Rebirth has been a heresy in Christianity since at least the fourth century, and the idea of a human becoming a fox is thus likely to seem quite weird. But if you are preoccupied with heresies or any other kind of concept, you cannot see the intent of this kōan.

In effect, the monk in mythological times was asking the old Pai-chang about the two worlds of karma and essential nature. Is the person who has fully realized essential nature free from the laws that govern phenomena? Yamada Rōshi always insisted that the two worlds are the same—"not even one," he would say. But there are no absolutes here. I remember fifteen years or more ago when Kalu Rinpoché came to Maui and gave a public talk before two hundred people. In the question period, a young man stood up and asked, "Does the person of complete realization fall under the law of cause and effect or not?"

Kalu Rinpoché said, "No, such a person does not fall under the law of cause and effect." There in a row we Zen students were nudging each other, enjoying a family joke.

The Rinpoché's response, and that of Pai-chang the Elder, can be construed in two ways: the literal and the essential. The literal view is the belief that there really can be Buddhas who are harmonized perfectly with essential nature. Then there is the essential view: the integral purity of all beings from the very beginning. As the Buddha himself said, "All beings are the Tathāgata." But he added, "Their delusions and preoccupations keep them from testifying to that fact."[3] All this bears directly on the problem faced by the two Pai-changs and the way they ultimately handled it.

The old man appealed to Pai-chang, "Please say a turning word for me and release me from the body of a fox. Does an enlightened person fall under the law of cause and effect or not?"

Pai-chang said, "Such a person does not evade the law of cause and effect." Hearing this the old man was immediately enlightened. "Turning words" are expressions that turn one to realization. Sometimes these can be casual words; sometimes they can be specific presentations of deepest truth.

In many Zen stories, a topic is raised on two or more occasions. Sometimes the interval between them is brief, perhaps just overnight, or it may be a very long time—in the present case, an entire kalpa elapsed. The point is that during the hiatus the people involved have matured to some extent. When the topic is picked up again, perhaps something can happen.

It seems that Pai-chang the Elder was now ready. His successor remarks, "Such a person does not evade the law of cause and effect." What is he saying here? On the one hand, Buddha nature is steady and serene; it does not come or go, it is always at rest. On the other hand, everything depends upon everything else. Karma and no karma are inextricably mixed. Life and death, no-life and no-death—these only seem to be separate matters.

The old man was enlightened by Pai-chang's response. Making his bows he said, "I am now released from the body of a fox. My body is on the other side of this mountain. Please perform my funeral ceremony." So after the meal Pai-chang led the monks around to the back of the mountain and there poked out the dead body of a fox from under a rock and performed the ceremony of cremation.

A thousand years later Hakuin challenged Pai-chang on this act of cremation: "What are you doing, old Pai-chang, performing a funeral for a fox as though it were a priest?"[4] The priest with his neatly pressed robes and clean-shaven face and head is the embodiment of essential nature itself. As to the fox, well, you know about foxes. Hakuin is challenging Pai-chang: "Aren't you making a mishmash of the Dharma? Isn't a priest irrevocably a priest and a fox irrevocably a fox?"

Hakuin is teasing Pai-chang here, of course. But more fundamentally, he is teasing you and me. He is really saying, "Hey, wait a minute now! Don't just go skipping over the cremation ceremony." He is raising an important point, perhaps as important as the dialogue between the two Pai-changs. See through his irony. What is his inner message?

Finally that evening Pai-chang gave the monks a full account of how he had met with the old man and agreed to perform the funeral rites. Huang-po stepped forward and said, "The old man missed the turning word and was reborn five hundred times as a fox. Now what if he had given the right answer every time?" What would have resulted from such good causes?

Shibayama Rōshi says that Huang-po means, "Sentient beings and insentient beings all have Buddha nature."[5] Can you see what he and Huang-po are driving at here?

Pai-chang said, "Come here and I'll tell you." Pai-chang was a gnarled old priest. Huang-po was a giant of a man seven feet tall and built in proportion—a very imposing figure. He stepped forward and slapped his old teacher's face, or at least he mimed slapping. For the sake of the story, he slapped him.

Huang-po was head monk of Pai-chang's monastery. Was he fit to become a true teacher? Maybe that was a question in Pai-chang's mind. With Huang-po's astute action, however, the matter seems to have been cleared up: Pai-chang laughed and clapped his hands, exclaiming, "I thought the Barbarian had a red beard, but here is a red-bearded Barbarian."

This exclamation refers to Bodhidharma, the twenty-eighth successor of the Buddha Śākyamuni. It was he who introduced the stream of Buddhism that became Zen to China from India and Central Asia. The Chinese, like others in other times, called foreigners "barbarians." Chinese Buddhists revere Bodhidharma profoundly but maintain the disparaging nickname to keep him human. There are no saints among our Ancestral Teachers.

Pai-chang was, of course, acknowledging Huang-po, who indeed went on to a great career of teaching. But it is important to see into Pai-chang's profound expression of approval.

Wu-men comments: " 'Not falling under the law of cause and effect.' Why should this prompt five hundred lives as a fox? 'Not evading the law of cause and effect.' Why should this prompt a resumption of human life?" Why indeed!

"If you have the single eye of realization, you will appreciate how old Pai-chang lived five hundred lives as a fox as lives of grace." When I was living in La Crescenta, California, attending Senzaki Nyogen Sensei's Zen meetings in East Los Angeles, on weekends I used to walk up a dirt road into the national forest. One day I came upon a fox—or a fox came upon me—where the road bent around a little ridge. She had come trotting down from above, and I appeared from below. We both stopped and looked at each other. At that moment the wind came up and blew a large piece of newspaper around and around on the road in a miniature cyclone. The fox jumped on this piece of paper and looked at me with a merry look in her eye. Then she stepped off the newspaper and it began to blow around again. She jumped on the paper again and looked at me, just as though she were inviting me to laugh at her great game. Suddenly conditions changed, and she ran back up the road. This encounter was truly an experience of grace.

When you take up Zen study, your task is to personalize such grace in your own body. As Yamada Rōshi used to say, the function of Zen is the perfection of character. We are not merely solving intellectual riddles. Examine Wu-men's comment carefully. He is not suggesting that old Pai-chang merely made a virtue of necessity. He did not simply make the best of things as he was sniffing around.

Wu-men's verse upholds the main points of the story: "Not falling, not evading—/ two faces of the same die." The cube is the same, but different numbers of dots appear on each side. Can you paraphrase Wu-men here in a personal way—in the context of the kōan?

"Not evading, not falling—/ a thousand mistakes, ten thousand mistakes." What is the error in Pai-chang's response to the old man? What is the error in old Pai-chang's response to the monk? Yamada Rōshi suggests that both responses might be taken conceptually.[6] But what is it about concepts of karma and essential nature that can be so mistaken?

Chü-chih Raises One Finger

THE CASE

Whenever Chü-chih was asked a question, he simply raised one finger. One day a visitor asked Chü-chih's attendant what his master preached. The boy raised a finger. Hearing of this, Chü-chih cut off the boy's finger with a knife. As he ran from the room, screaming with pain, Chü-chih called to him. When he turned his head, Chü-chih raised a finger. The boy was suddenly enlightened.

When Chü-chih was about to die, he said to his assembled monks: "I received this one-finger Zen from T'ien-lung. I used it all my life but never used it up." With this he entered into his eternal rest.

WU-MEN'S COMMENT

The enlightenment of Chü-chih and the boy has nothing to do with the end of a finger. If you can realize this, then T'ien-lung, Chü-chih, the boy, and you yourself are all run through with a single skewer.

WU-MEN'S VERSE

T'ien-lung made a fool of old Chü-chih
who cut the boy with a sharp blade,
just as the deity Chü-ling raised his hand,
and Hua-shan, with its many ridges, split into two.

Chü-chih (Gutei) lived about the same time as Lin-chi (Rinzai), around the ninth century, and was his second cousin in the Dharma. We don't have his dates of birth and death; in fact, we don't even know his family name. Chü-chih was a nickname taken from the title of the dhāranī: *Ch'i-chü-chih-fu-mu-hsin*. I am not familiar with that dhāranī, but apparently he was always reciting it.

He began this practice in conjunction with his zazen when he was a young monk living in a little hut by himself. Solitary practice is not so unusual. From time to time I meet people like Chü-chih who at a certain phase of their lives prefer to do zazen alone. It is, as Chü-chih himself learned, just a phase.

One day toward evening a nun named Shih-chi (Jissai) appeared at his hut. Yamada Rōshi translates her name as "True World," an interpretive rendering that is quite interesting. The Chinese ideographs could mean either "True Encounter" or "True Boundary," so Yamada Rōshi is implying that Shih-chi presents the most vital quality of human life as well as its extent.

True World did not knock or call out when she arrived, but just walked in. It was probably a one-room cottage—traditionally such cottages were just ten feet square—and there was Chü-chih, sitting in zazen, right in the center. Without taking off her sedge hat, she walked around him three times and then stood before him, saying, "If you can say an appropriate word, I will take off my hat."

Circumambulation is a ritual found in traditional societies all over the world.[1] In Zen Buddhism, it is an act of self-presentation by a pilgrim to a teacher.[2] It is then followed by three bows to the floor and other procedures. True World did not observe the proper ritual, however, and Chü-chih was unable to respond. He seemed dumbstruck.

So True World walked around him three times again, stood before him, and said, "If you can say an appropriate word, I will take off my hat." Again he was unable to speak. She repeated her performance still a third time. Silence. So she turned on her heel and walked out.

When Chü-chih finally came to himself, he went to the door after her and called out, "It will be dark soon. Why don't you stay the night?" She turned around and said, "If you can say an appropriate word, I will stay the night." He still couldn't say a word, so she left.

Chü-chih was downcast. He felt he had been defeated by True World and thought, "I'm going about this matter of finding realization the wrong way. I need a good teacher." He packed his gear and then, because it was dark, sat nodding over his pack, waiting for the dawn. Suddenly, the tutelary deity of the mountain appeared there in the dark and said, "Don't leave. A great Zen master will come here soon and you can consult with him." So Chü-chih unpacked his gear and waited. Sure enough, in a couple of days, T'ien-lung appeared.

T'ien-lung was a Dharma successor of Ta-mei (Daibai), whose kenshō story is found in Case 30. Though almost unknown to us now, he was, we can be sure, an eminent master of his time. Chü-chih told him the whole story, and T'ien-lung raised one finger. With this Chü-chih was enlightened to the dimensions of the true world.

We can learn from Chü-chih's mistake. He had probably fantasized: "I will attain the heights with my own genius and inspiration. I won't be bothered with trying to deal with the world of contradictions—the world of malice and misunderstanding, difficult personalities, and arguments. I am just going to sit here in purity and recite my dhāranī and do my zazen and let the world go by."

The world would not go by. It intruded, in fact, and he couldn't deal with it. He realized, to his credit, "I've been making a mistake. I see now that I must interact and through interaction I can find realization. I must search out a good teacher. I must reenter the world."

With that decision, he was abruptly assured from his own inner depths that a teacher would come to him. He made himself available, and sure enough T'ien-lung appeared. That was the second visit of the true world. He engaged T'ien-lung in a crucial dialogue and was enlightened.

Chü-chih was right in wanting to devote himself to his practice. We need zazen, lots of zazen. When I assure people that ten minutes of zazen a day is the minimum, I am speaking with some irony. But Chü-chih's mistake was in supposing that lots of zazen is enough in itself. It is not. Even a small amount of zazen can be bondage if it is a device for avoiding the world. It is in engagement that we find our true nature—the true nature of the universe.

This is the fact of mutual interdependence, the teaching of the Buddha Śākyamuni. Some Zen students, who have come from other religious paths, listen for the "inner voice." This can be a great delusion. Lots of people are in prison or in asylums because they made a practice of listening to their inner voice. Chü-chih's finger is much more reliable.

Our text says that he "always" raised one finger, but of course this should be understood as almost always. He dealt drastically with a young attendant who understood it to be always! Other teachers are well known for their distinctive actions. Lu-tsu, a brother of Pai-chang and Nan-ch'üan in the Dharma, was famous for just turning around and facing the wall when a student came to him for instruction.[3] Bankei Yōtaku is famous for uttering the single word "unborn."[4] But few teachers, it seems, were as singular in their method as Chü-chih. Yet did he actually make the *same* gesture all his life?

Yasutani Rōshi loved Chü-chih. When he gave teishōs on this case, he would raise his thumb rather than his forefinger. I used to think it was the longest thumb I ever saw. Everything would come to a complete stop. Everything would be completely silent.

But be careful. Don't be casual about that one finger. Not only your own finger, but your life, your vitality, your hopes, your inner riches—all will be dissipated by superficial imitation. You must express Chü-chih's mind clearly. What do you do? What do you say? If you can respond, then, as Wu-men says in his comment, you and T'ien-lung and the boy will all be run through with a single skewer.

The story of Chü-chih cutting off the boy's finger, like Nan-ch'üan killing a cat,[5] Mu-chou breaking Yün-men's leg,[6] Te-shan's stick,[7] Lin-chi's shout,[8] and so on, give Zen a bad name in some quarters. Literalists turn to something milder. Yet look closely. Read religion as parable, as folklore, as poetic presentation of your own history and nature. Put yourself back on Grandmother's ample lap, listening to her read "Jack and the Bean-stalk," and you'll shiver again with those awesome words, "I'll grind his bones to make my bread!"

"When Chü-chih was about to die, he said to his assembled monks: 'I received this one-finger Zen from T'ien-lung. I used it all my life but never used it up.' With this he entered into his eternal rest." Chü-chih took delight in the Tathāgata treasure, and here he brings it forth and enjoys it with his monks for the last time.

T'ien-lung's finger and then Chü-chih's finger reveal the marvelous extent of the world and ourselves. Chü-chih's life reveals the importance of accepting the world at the outset of practice. Only by accepting can we come to appreciate its true boundaries. My way cannot be my exclusive way. It is the Tao of the universe or it is vain. This is the Great Way of the Mahayana.

Wu-men comments: "The enlightenment of Chü-chih and the boy has nothing to do with the end of a finger." He is cautioning you that even though Chü-chih devoted himself to his presentation of one finger throughout his life, his realization and yours don't depend upon that specific gesture. Here Wu-men is making a fundamental point. Zen Buddhism is not shamanism, though shamanic elements come up here and there in its folklore—the tutelary deity appearing to Chü-chih, for instance. If the Buddha had been a shaman, his spiritual way might have been linked with the morning star in particular, as traditional seers are often linked to the beings that appeared in their visions. Wu-men is saying that even Chü-chih, enlightened by and teaching with a single finger, is not using his finger as a totem.

"If you can realize this, then T'ien-lung, Chü-chih, the boy, and you yourself are all run through with a single skewer"—and all Buddhas and Ancestral Teachers too, seeing with the same eyes, hearing with the same ears. Actually, you are already run through. But you must know that steel for yourself.

Wu-men's verse begins: "T'ien-lung made a fool of old Chü-chih, / who cut the boy with a sharp blade." I have heard it said by way of comment on the first line that T'ien-lung fooled Chü-chih into raising one finger for the rest of his life. As Yüan-wu, editor of *The Blue Cliff Record*, is forever saying, "Fortunately, that has nothing to do with the matter."[9]

"Just as the deity Chü-ling raised his hand, / and Hua-shan, with its many ridges, split into two." Chü-ling (Korei), the deity of the mountain Hua-shan (Kasan), was very concerned that every year the Yellow River would overflow its banks and flood the farmers' fields in the uplands, drowning crops and people, so he raised his hand—and the mountain impeding the river split into two and the Yellow River rushed through. Not only did it split into two, it crumbled to the plains. Lots of things crumbled for Chü-chih and for his attendant in turn, when the long finger went up.

Huo-an's Beardless Barbarian

THE CASE

Huo-an asked, "Why has the Western Barbarian no beard?"

WU-MEN'S COMMENT

Practice must be true practice. Satori must be true satori. Once you see the Barbarian's face intimately, at first hand, you have it at last. But when you explain this experience, you immediately fall into dualism.

WU-MEN'S VERSE

Don't discuss your dream
before a fool—
Barbarian with no beard!
That obscures the clarity.

Huo-an (Wakuan) was a Southern Sung teacher about whom we know very little. He died four years before Wu-men was born and was grandson in the Dharma of Yüan-wu, editor of *The Blue Cliff Record.*[1]

Even if this case were the only one known relating to Huo-an, it would be clear that he was a great teacher. We also have his death poem, however, confirming this excellent impression:

> An iron tree in bloom;
> the rooster lays an egg;
> seventy-two years—
> the cradle has fallen.[2]

The first two lines are in the realm of infinite possibilities, like the lines of Fu Ta-shih (Fu Daishi):

> Empty-handed, yet holding a hoe;
> walking, yet riding a water buffalo.[3]

"The cradle has fallen"—only at death do we lose the human confines of our birth.

Huo-an's question belongs in that same realm, though it is deceptively simple: "Why has the Western Barbarian no beard?" Bodhidharma, the Western Barbarian, was widely respected when he was living, and later he was elevated to a position of highest esteem. But this high position is not in any way remote. Many Japanese homes and shops display him in folk-art sculpture.

On our altar at the Koko An Zendō, Bodhidharma makes his appearance without a single hair, but ordinarily he is depicted with a big red beard, as we gather from the way Pai-chang approved of Huang-po in Case 2. Huo-an is not merely denying the archetypal image. His question is itself the point. The "why" is everything, as Wallace Stevens makes clear in "Questions Are Remarks":

> His question is complete because it contains
> His utmost statement. It is his own array,
> His own pageant and procession and display.[4]

Like Stevens' two-year-old grandson, Huo-an's pageant and procession are his "why?" In his comment on this case, my teacher Nyogen Senzaki used to say, "Bodhidharma not only has no beard, he has no eyes, no nose, no skin, no teeth." Very true, but somehow that doesn't really answer the question. The "why" resonates like the sound of a great bell.

I understand that some teachers will accept a response that begins with "because." That won't do, I think. Not enough pageant, I would say. Take up this "why." Your insistence upon the question itself will turn your ordinary world on its ear and you'll be two years old again. You will be "like a fish, like a fool,"[5] deep in the question.

In Zen practice, the "why" of Bodhidharma appears again and again. A stock question in the literature is "Why did Bodhidharma come from the West?" He came from India, or perhaps Central Asia, which is, of course, west of China. But "West" also carries overtones of Lotus Land, the Western Paradise—the Kingdom of Heaven, in Christian terms. What is the *meaning* of his coming from the West? What is the essence he and other founding teachers have conveyed?

> A monk asked Shih-t'ou, "What is the meaning of Bodhidharma's coming from the West?"
> Shih-t'ou said, "Ask that post over there."
> The monk said, "I don't understand."
> Shih-t'ou said, "My ignorance is worse than yours."[6]

Shih-t'ou is saying, "My not-understanding is greater than your not-understanding." Still, the post is rather beside the point from Huo-an's perspective. He is asking about something much more spirited—Bodhidharma specifically.

> Emperor Wu asked Bodhidharma, "What is the first principle of the Holy Teaching?"
> Bodhidharma said, "Vast emptiness, nothing holy."
> The Emperor said, "Who is this confronting me?"
> Bodhidharma said, "I don't know."[7]

The emperor didn't understand, so Bodhidharma gathered himself and crossed the Yellow River and went on to northwestern China, where he took up zazen in a cave behind a ruined temple. Gradually a few disciples gathered about him, and the end is not in sight. What a potent Beardless Barbarian he was!

> A monk asked Lin-chi, "What is the meaning of Bodhidharma's coming from the West?"
> Lin-chi said, "If you find any meaning, you will not save even yourself."
> The monk asked, "If there is no meaning, what did the Second Ancestral Teacher [Hui-ko] attain?"
> Lin-chi said, "What is called attainment is really not attainment."
> The monk persisted and asked, "If so, what is the meaning of not-attained?"

Lin-chi said, "Your mind is always running after the objects that present themselves and cannot restrain itself. An old teacher called this 'seeking to place another head over your own.' If you turn your light within and reflect intimately there and stop seeking external things, you will realize that your own mind and those of the Buddhas and Founding Teachers do not differ from one another."[8]

These points are tests of your ability to settle on a question and remain there. Settle on Huo-an's "why" and remain there.

Wu-men says in his comment: "Practice must be true practice." The true practice of zazen is a matter of bringing the mind into focus so there is nothing but the object of your concentration before you. Your mind becomes quieter and quieter. External events become harmonized with your breathing. Self-concern subsides. It is a matter of making Huo-an's rumination your own. Yasutani Rōshi called his written commentaries "musings."[9] When you are working on Huo-an's question, you no longer seek peace or absorption yet you find yourself peacefully absorbed in the question: "Why has the Western Barbarian no beard?"

Wu-men continues, "Satori must be true satori." This is a literal translation. No explanation is necessary. No fakes permitted. Not only must you see Bodhidharma's face, you must come forth with Wu-men's voice. Each kōan must be personalized in this way.

Wu-men continues, "Once you see the Barbarian's face intimately, at first hand, you have it at last." I am grateful for Wu-men's daring words. He is presuming to say there is something to attain—fully aware that Lin-chi, for one, would disapprove. But really there is such a thing.

Then Wu-men concludes, "But when you explain this experience, you immediately fall into dualism." Talk is dualistic: attainment and nonattainment, beard and no-beard. Yet our language is set up that way, and so is the human cortex. We must use dualistic words. The question is: "How should we use them?" If you see from within the world—that is, if "you and I" is just a convenient expression and you really know that "I" and "I" (all of them very different) are the true pronouns—then the way will be clear and you can use dualistic language freely without stumbling.

Wu-men's verse begins: "Don't discuss your dream / before a fool." These two lines are a natural continuation of the last sentence in Wu-men's comment: "When you explain this experience, you immediately fall into dualism." This is not a logical construct about a beard—don't be foolish!

Or, better, be completely foolish in your devotion to Huo-an's fine point. It will guide you unerringly.

"Barbarian with no beard! / That obscures the clarity." Indeed. Wumen is saying that everything is clear from the beginning. Just as you see, just as you hear. The hedge is full of hibiscus flowers after our recent rains. The thrush sings sharp and clear this cloudy morning. What is all this about beard and no-beard?

Hsiang-yen: Up a Tree

THE CASE

The priest Hsiang-yen said, "It is as though you were up in a tree, hanging from a branch with your teeth. Your hands and feet can't touch any branch. Someone appears beneath the tree and asks, 'What is the meaning of Bodhidharma's coming from the West?' If you do not answer, you evade your responsibility. If you do answer, you lose your life. What do you do?"

WU-MEN'S COMMENT

Even if your eloquence flows like a river, it is all in vain. Even if you can expound cogently upon the whole body of Buddhist literature, that too is useless. If you can respond to this dilemma properly, you give life to those who have been dead and kill those who have been alive. If you can't respond, you must wait and ask Maitreya about it.

WU-MEN'S VERSE

Hsiang-yen is just blabbing nonsense;
his poisonous intentions are limitless.
He stops up the monks' mouths,
making his whole body a demon eye.

Hsiang-yen (Kyōgen) was a cousin of Lin-chi in the Dharma. His dates of birth and death are unknown, but it seems that he was active in the ninth century. His teacher was Kuei-shan (Isan), cofounder of the Kuei-yang school of Zen.[1]

When Hsiang-yen was a young monk, he studied under Pai-chang, and it was only when Pai-chang died that he became a disciple of Kuei-shan. He was an intellectual and, like many intellectuals, had a hard time with the practice at first. One day Kuei-shan said to him: "I am told that you have been under my late master Pai-chang and also that you have remarkable intelligence. But the understanding of Zen through this medium necessarily ends in intellectual and analytical comprehension which is not of much use. Yet you may have some insight into Zen. Let me have your view as to your own being before your parents were born."[2]

Hsiang-yen couldn't respond. He retired to his room and looked through all his notes of Pai-chang's teishōs, but he could not find anything suitable. Returning to Kuei-shan he said, "I have failed to find a response to your question. Please teach me the essential point."

Kuei-shan said, "I really have nothing to teach you. And if I tried to express something, later you would revile me. Besides, whatever understanding I have is my own and will never be yours." Hsiang-yen thereupon burned his notes and determined that he would be just "a rice-gruel monk" and face Kuei-shan's profound question moment by moment, rather than trying to resolve it by means of intellectual research. Hearing that the tomb of Nan-yang (Nanyō) was being neglected, he asked Kuei-shan's permission to go there and serve as caretaker.[3] Kuei-shan approved, so Hsiang-yen built a small hut near the tomb and spent his days cleaning the grounds, absorbed in his kōan.

One day while sweeping up fallen leaves, his bamboo broom caught a stone and it sailed through the air and hit a stalk of bamboo with a little sound. *Tock!* With that *tock!* he was awakened. Hurrying to his hut, he bathed and then offered incense and bowed in the direction of Kuei-shan's temple, crying out aloud, "Your kindness is greater than that of my parents. If you had explained it to me, I would never have known this joy."

Like the Buddha whose preparation under the Bodhi Tree invited the morning star, Hsiang-yen's deep absorption in Kuei-shan's kōan set the stage for the little stone to do its work. Practice makes kenshō possible— and then an unexpected intervention breaks the spell of time and space.

PLATE 3: *Hsiang-yen Sweeps the Grounds*. Courtesy of
The Idemitsu Museum of Arts. (Case 5)

One *tock!* and knowledge is forgotten;
what kind of sound is that?
At once a bit of rubble
turns itself into gold.

It is significant that Hsiang-yen's experience came during *tso-wu* (*samu*)—"work ritual." This Chinese Buddhist tradition carried over into Korea and Japan and is maintained today in Western Zen as part of our natural rhythm of practice: zazen, work, rest, recreation. When zazen is the ground, all other activity is practice too.

Hsiang-yen packed up and returned immediately to Kuei-shan, and showed him a poem he had composed about his understanding:

> One *tock!* has made me forget all my previous knowledge.
> No artificial discipline is needed at all.
> In every movement, I uphold the ancient Way
> and never fall into the rut of mere quietism.
> Wherever I walk, no traces are left,
> and my senses are not fettered by rules of conduct.
> Everywhere those who have found this truth
> all declare it to be of the highest order.[4]

Kuei-shan was very pleased with this poem, but his senior disciple, Yang-shan (Kyōzan), was not satisfied. So Hsiang-yen wrote another poem:

> My poverty last year was not true poverty;
> this year it is the real thing.
> Last year a fine gimlet could find a place;
> this year even the gimlet is gone.[5]

Yang-shan said, "You have attained Tathāgata Zen all right, but you don't even have an inkling of Ancestral Zen." These categories aren't particularly significant in themselves. The point is that Yang-shan was not yet confident of his brother's insight. So Hsiang-yen wrote still another poem:

> I have a single potential;
> it can be seen in a solitary twinkle.
> If you still don't understand,
> call the acolyte and ask him about it.[6]

Call the little-boy monk and ask him. Surely this transcends even Zen itself! And, indeed, Yang-shan approved at last.

Thereafter Hsiang-yen resumed monastery life, but as an independent teacher, and found an important place in the golden age of Zen in the T'ang period. His teachings are very clear:

> A monk asked Hsiang-yen, "What is Hsiang-yen's mind?"
> Hsiang-yen said, "Plants and trees are not abundant."[7]

The original realm is vividly apparent!

Another time a monk asked him about the invisible inward power that is transmitted during ordination. He replied, "I will tell you when you become a layman again."[8] "Come off it," Hsiang-yen seems to be saying, "let's keep to our plain, original nature!"

One day Hsiang-yen took the high seat[9] before his assembly and said, "It is as though you were up in a tree, hanging from a branch with your teeth. Your hands and feet can't touch any branch. Someone appears beneath the tree and asks, 'What is the meaning of Bodhidharma's coming from the West?' If you do not answer, you evade your responsibility. If you do answer, you will lose your life. What do you do?"

A similar parable is found in classical Buddhist literature and has been adapted by Zen teachers. One version appears in Nyogen Senzaki's "101 Zen Stories":

> A man traveling across a field encountered a tiger. He fled, the tiger after him. Coming to a precipice, he caught hold of the root of a wild vine and swung himself down over the edge. The tiger sniffed at him from above. Trembling, the man looked down to where, far below, another tiger was waiting to eat him. Two mice, one white and one black, little by little began to gnaw away the vine. The man saw a luscious strawberry near him. Grasping the vine with one hand, he plucked the strawberry with the other. How sweet it tasted![10]

The mouse metaphor is the key to understanding this parable in terms of your own condition. One mouse was black as night, the other white as day. Night and day pass, gnawing at the root, as terrible tigers threaten from every direction. Hanging there as your hair turns gray and then white, this is your dilemma. In his comment to Case 1, Wu-men says: "At the very cliff edge of birth-and-death, you find the Great Freedom." The man threatened by tigers illustrates this point clearly. How delicious that strawberry is! Clinging to the vine is sweet life itself.

In Hsiang-yen's kōan, however, you can't pick a strawberry, and you have no support system at all. Moreover, in your desperate situation you remain responsible to your fellow beings. Someone appears under the tree and asks, "What is the meaning of Bodhidharma's coming from the West?" A life-or-death question in a life-or-death predicament!

I read somewhere that an old man wrote a friend saying, "I feel like a young man who has something the matter with him." This is the dilemma of old age. I am seventy-three this year. Some people my age can't get in or out of bed without help, and I know I will probably reach that condition before long. How will I resolve this dilemma? Everybody is in a dilemma. Act within the dilemma, and you will be true to Hsiang-yen.

Yasutani Rōshi used the "Dry Well" kōan to check students who had recently gained some insight into Mu. "Suppose," he would say, "you were at the bottom of a two-hundred-foot well that had completely smooth sides. What would you do?" This is not quite the same as being up a tree and hanging there with your teeth, since no one is pestering you with impossible questions. But the point is similar.

The priest Hsiang-yen and Yasutani Rōshi echo the Buddha's First Noble Truth, *duhkha*, the dissatisfaction one feels about the circumstances of life. The most difficult of these circumstances are evanescence and interdependence. Everything passes away, and everything depends upon everything else. Permanence and independence are simply not possible, any more than release from the dry well or the tree is possible. But *duhkha* itself can be melted, as the Buddha said, and this is Hsiang-yen's purpose.[11]

The parables of hanging in the tree and hanging over the cliff are instructive at many levels. And it is zazen that lies at the heart of the metaphors—no going forward, no going back. This dilemma can give rise to the "red-hot iron ball" of Wu-men in Case 1, the "dark night of the soul" of San Juan de la Cruz, the "valley of the shadow of death" of David the Psalmist. The parables dare us to persevere through stuckness, to grin right back at *duhkha*.

Wu-men comments: "Even if your eloquence flows like a river, it is all in vain." Not only is it in vain, it gets in your way. Kuei-shan was a great teacher who taught by not explaining. Hsiang-yen, like Te-shan, burned all his notes in the process of his Zen training—Hsiang-yen before his realization, Te-shan afterward.[12] These are symbolic acts of transcending dogma, though it is not necessary to imitate them literally.

Wu-men comments: "If you can respond to this dilemma properly, you give life to those who have been dead and kill those who have been alive." Who is dead? Ghosts clinging to bushes and grasses, I would say. Giving life to those who are dead means, I think, that you can encourage people to accept their dilemmas—to suffer them—and get on with their practice of wisdom and compassion.

Offering permission is not passivity. If circumstances permit me to dodge a truck bearing down on me, I will do so. I won't just stand there and declare it to be my karma, or the will of God, that I should be struck down. But if circumstances don't permit me to dodge, I will open myself as best I can to the accident itself—and to the succor of the medic as we ride to the hospital.

At the same time, I am engaged with others in the world of dilemmas. I am a medic too, in my fashion, riding with patients whom I encourage to be patient. And if the system of healing is faulty, I'll raise my voice to encourage corrections. Accepting one's lot is also a matter of accepting the pain of others and taking responsibility for their healing. In political terms, the one who asks the question in Hsiang-yen's parable is the importunate beggar at the marble portals of the World Bank.

"You kill those who are alive" makes the same point: those living in a state of preoccupation can be encouraged to die to that condition. I think Wu-men is referring to those who spend their lives in undisciplined conjecture and who are, in Stephen Leacock's words, "riding off in all directions." This tendency must be cut off. "If you meet the Buddha, kill the Buddha." If you are working on Mu, and your mind wanders off to our great Founding Teacher—kill, kill!

I will sometimes say to a student, "You have slid past the point." If you try to go beyond Mu, beyond Huo-an's question about Bodhidharma's missing beard, beyond the condition of hanging by your teeth or sitting in a dry well, you fall straight into tangled weeds. Only when you focus directly on the question will you realize its truth and the emancipation it holds.

Wu-men says further: "If you can't respond, you must wait and ask Maitreya about it." You'll have to wait around, that is, for the Future Buddha who is due to appear 5,670,000,000 years after the death of the Buddha Śākyamuni—5,669,997,625 years from now, approximately. That's how long speculation will take you. Maitreya will save you in the end, but it will take forever. It is better to take up the matter in your zazen and in your daily life, in this one *nien* (*nen*), this one thought-breath.

As to Wu-men's verse: "Hsiang-yen is just blabbing nonsense; / his poisonous intentions are limitless." Hsiang-yen's topic doesn't make sense. It panders to all the stereotypes about dangerous, unreasonable Zen. Not only is Hsiang-yen poisonous, he is murderous. Or so it seems. In fact, Wu-men is fiddling with metaphors here. See if you can play his game.

"He stops up the monks' mouths, / making his whole body a demon eye." The monks are struck dumb, and Hsiang-yen stares around with all his energy gathered in his piercing eyes. What do you think he might be saying?

The World-Honored One
Twirls a Flower

THE CASE

Once, in ancient times, when the World-Honored One was at Mount Grdhrakūta, he twirled a flower before his assembled disciples. All were silent. Only Mahā-kāśyapa broke into a smile.

The World-Honored One said, "I have the eye treasury of right Dharma, the subtle mind of nirvana, the true form of no-form, and the flawless gate of the teaching. It is not established upon words and phrases. It is a special transmission outside tradition. I now entrust this to Mahākāśyapa."

WU-MEN'S COMMENT

Gold-faced Gautama insolently degrades noble people to commoners. He sells dog flesh under the sign of mutton and thinks it is quite commendable.

Suppose that all the monks had smiled—how would the eye treasury have been transmitted? Or suppose that Mahākāśyapa had not smiled—how could he have been entrusted with it?

If you say the eye treasury can be transmitted, that would be as if the gold-faced old fellow were swindling people in a loud voice at the town gate. If you say the eye treasury cannot be transmitted, then why did the Buddha say that he entrusted it to Mahākāśyapa?

WU-MEN'S VERSE

Twirling a flower,
the snake shows its tail.
Mahākāśyapa breaks into a smile,
and people and devas are confounded.

First the dramatis personae. The World-Honored One is the Buddha Śākyamuni. In the Mahayana account of his birth, it is said that he took seven steps in each of the cardinal directions, raised one hand and pointed to the heavens, lowered the other and pointed to the earth, and proclaimed: "Above the heavens, below the heavens, only I, the World-Honored One."[1] As D.T. Suzuki says, "That voice reaches to the furthest edge of the chiliocosm, and all beings . . . share in the joy of the Buddha's birth, realizing that they too are destined to be Buddhas."[2] Mahākāśyapa, one of the Buddha's senior disciples, was responsible for organizing the great council that codified the Buddha's teachings after his death. He is remembered especially for his presentation of the precepts as the ground of the religious life.

The story of the Buddha twirling a flower before his assembly, like the story of the baby Buddha taking seven steps in each of the cardinal directions, need not be taken literally. The first account of his transmitting the Dharma to Mahākāśyapa is set forth in a sutra of Chinese origin that is dated A.D. 1036, fourteen hundred years after the Buddha's time.[3] This was the Sung period—a peak in the development of Chinese culture when great anthologies, encyclopedias, and directories were being produced. Myth, oral tradition, and sectarian justification all played a role in this codification. The fable of the Buddha twirling a flower filled a great need for connection with the founder, and it was picked up immediately and repeated like gospel. The "Four Principles" attributed to Bodhidharma were also formulated during the Sung period, some six hundred years after Bodhidharma's time, using some of the same language attributed to the Buddha: "A special transmission outside tradition—not established on words or letters."[4] The Sung teachers were making important points with their myths.

During World War II, I asked a Catholic priest who was interned with us, "What if it could be proved that Jesus never lived?" He replied, "It would destroy my faith." That priest was very young at the time. I wonder what became of him, and what he might be saying on the subject now. Something a little different, I would suppose. I too was young at the time, but I felt there was something wrong with his answer. I still think so. I don't believe it is very important whether Jesus and Buddha and Moses were historical figures. True religious practice is grounded in the nonhistorical fact of essential nature. "The World-Honored One Twirls a Flower," "Pai-chang's Fox," and all the other fabulous cases of Zen literature are your stories and mine, intimate accounts of our own personal nature and experience.

The setting of this story is Mount Grdhrakūta, Vulture Peak, so called for the shape of its summit. The geographical Vulture Peak is in Maghadā, India, where the Buddha was enlightened and gave many of his teishōs. Hermits made their camps there in caves and under trees. The mythic Vulture Peak is the temple where countless Buddhas, śrāvakas, pratyekas, bodhisattvas, devas and demons, and you and I gather to hear the Dharma.

The story reflects the South Asian custom of bringing flowers to temple images and to monks and nuns. Someone had presented a single flower to the Buddha before he was to speak. He held it up and looked around, twirling it gently, waiting for a response. Many of the Buddha's successors made similarly simple presentations. Chao-chou said "Mu," Chü-chih held up one finger, Nan-ch'üan presented a sickle:

> Once when Nan-ch'üan was working in the garden, a monk asked him, "What is the way to Nan-ch'üan?"
>
> Nan-ch'üan held up his sickle and said, "This sickle cost 30 cents."
>
> The monk said, "I didn't ask about a sickle. I asked about the way to Nan-ch'üan."
>
> Nan-ch'üan said, "I can use it with pleasure."[5]

The presentational mode of communication is very important in Zen Buddhist teaching. This mode can be clarified by reference to Susanne Langer's landmark book on symbolic logic called *Philosophy in a New Key*.[6] She distinguishes between two kinds of communication: "Presentational" and "Discursive." The presentational might be in words, but it might also be a laugh, a cry, a blow, or any other kind of communicative action. It is poetical and nonexplanatory—the expression of Zen. The discursive, by contrast, is prosaic and explanatory. The sentence "Nan-ch'üan was indicating that his way was embodied in the sickle" would be discursive (and also mistaken). The discursive has a place in a Zen discourse like this one, but it tends to dilute direct teaching.

In a single gesture, and a few words, Nan-ch'üan expressed the eye treasury of the right Dharma. The Buddha expressed it with a simple, silent action. I don't know how the monk responded to Nan-ch'üan after he said he could use it with pleasure, but no one could understand the Buddha except Mahākāśyapa, who broke into a smile. The original says "cracked his face," the way we would say "cracked a smile." The implication is that he was trying to be serious and sober, but couldn't help smiling. The question is: "Suppose you were Mahākāśyapa there, smiling in the crowd. What might you be saying under your breath?"

Anne Aitken and I once saw a compelling image of Mahākāśyapa in the Kamakura Museum in Japan. Almost life-size, he was standing with hands upraised and clasped, a gesture more common in Christianity than in Buddhism, bending slightly forward, his face lifted as though he were looking at the Buddha on his high seat. His face was quite lined, for according to tradition Mahākāśyapa was older than the Buddha. He was smiling with his mouth slightly open, and we could feel his awe and hear his breath. Ah!

The World-Honored One said, "I have the eye treasury of right Dharma." This is *Shōbōgenzō* in Sino-Japanese, the term used by Dōgen for the title of his great collection of teishōs.[7] Right Dharma is what the Buddha expressed before the assembly and Mahākāśyapa expressed with his smile. Sometimes a person will come into the interview room with that smile. It is unmistakable. Though I think to myself, "There is no need to check," of course I do check, and inevitably it is indeed right Dharma. No mistake.

"The subtle mind of nirvana" is the mystery of the universe that is your mind and my own. This mind is obscured when you are centered upon yourself, limited to your sole self, a regrettable condition considering the circumstances: the true Dharma of no separation in the vast universe. It is when one is preoccupied with *me* that the mind is obscured, a phase through which all human beings pass. The subtle mind of nirvana stood forth when the Buddha announced himself as an infant. It comes forth once again when he twirls a flower. The whole universe is in awe.

"The true form of no-form" is found in Zen practice:

> With form that is no-form,
> going and coming, never astray.[8]

It is karma, yet no karma—the message of Pai-chang in his story of the fox. Throughout the Mahayana, throughout perennial religion, throughout the universe, essential no-form reveals itself in every word and gesture and movement—though in the Buddha's assembly and elsewhere there are few who notice.

"The flawless gate of the teaching" is the Way of the Buddha: nothing has any substance of its own, all things depend upon each other, everything is completely its own reason. Joy in these verities can be attained with certain upright attitudes and actions. The Buddha is the "king of doctors,"[9] teaching us how to escape our despair over evanescence and dependency. "Here is the Way!" he announces, holding up a flower, twirling it gently.

"It is not established upon words and phrases. It is a special transmission outside tradition." The words and phrases of the *Diamond Sutra*, for example, present the Way of the Buddha explicitly and profoundly. But the *Diamond Sutra* is not the exclusive source of truth, nor is any sutra or kōan, including this one. The great genius of Śākyamuni, Chao-chou, Chü-chih, and the other great worthies in our stream is to present the truth directly, to present something that is potent with the universe—a flower, a word, a finger.

> A monk asked Yün-men, "What is the discourse that transcends Buddhas and Ancestral Teachers?"
> Yün-men said, "Rice cake."[10]

This too is outside meaning and tradition. It erases time and space—like the temple bell that the haiku poet Bashō heard while absorbed in his enjoyment of cherry flowers at his cottage on the Sumida River:

> A cloud of flowers—
> was that the bell at Ueno
> or Asakusa?[11]

Only that deep, resonating sound! It swallows up the great temples in all the many directions at once.

The old teachers created folklore, but they were vigorous in resisting the human tendency to cling to it. Referring to the story that the baby Buddha stepped off in the four directions and pronounced himself honored, Yün-men said: "If I had been there, I would have cut him down with my staff and fed his body to the dogs, so that peace could prevail all over the world."[12]

Wu-men is in the same mood when he comments: "Gold-faced Gautama insolently degrades noble people to commoners." Images of the Buddha are covered with gold leaf, an honorific that extends back to his person. Honored or not, he singles out Mahākāśyapa and makes the other Buddhas, śrāvakas, pratyekas, bodhisattvas, demons, and devas look like fools. "All beings by nature are Buddha."[13] How is it that the Buddha himself is mixed up with concepts of "enlightened" and "not enlightened"?

"He sells dog flesh under the sign of mutton and thinks it is quite commendable." Under the sign of a sheep, he sells you meat that most people disdain. All this talk of the "right eye of the Dharma and the subtle mind of nirvana"—come on! Isn't that just the act of sitting down at the table and unfolding a napkin? Wu-men is suggesting, with perhaps only a little irony, that it isn't commendable at all to put such ordinary activities into such glorious language.

Then Wu-men takes up the central matter: transmission. If everybody had smiled, or if Mahākāśyapa had not smiled, what then? Suppose Mahākāśyapa had never lived, even in folklore? Who would Ānanda have studied with? Wu-men leads us down the garden path of conjecture to the gate of penetrating inquiry.

What is transmission, after all? Certainly it is not a heavenly decree. Even excellent teachers have made mistakes and named disgraceful successors. If transmission is set forth as some kind of occult sanctification, then Buddhas, śrāvakas, and the rest of us are betrayed. It is all a hoax, as Wu-men says. The World-Honored One would be no better than a swindler at the town gate hawking tin jewelry dipped in gold paint.

The point is that transmission is not identifiable by any set of fixed criteria. The Buddha himself cannot be distinguished by any particular features or qualities.[14] Nonetheless, something happened there at Mount Grdhrakūta—and that something continues to happen in upright Zen programs everywhere. Yasutani Rōshi criticized with the most penetrating language the Buddhist teachers who declare that realization is something that our ancestors might have attained but is beyond our reach to-day.[15] I am confident that he would have berated those who deny transmission, as well.

In any case, the realization experience is itself a kind of transmission. This story of the Buddha twirling a flower is an archetype for the unity of these two kinds of transmission: first the message of the flower and second the acknowledgment of the Buddha. The flower is one of the myriad things that advance from nowhere and confirm the self.[16] Confirmation by a sense experience of the world, confirmation by the master, and, finally, confirmation by the Buddha Sangha—these are the three transmissions. All three are transformational experiences, and no one can teach unless each of them is in place.

In his verse Wu-men reviews the main point of the case: "Twirling a flower, / the snake shows its tail." This imagery comes from a folkloric account of the Buddha under the Bodhi Tree, protected by a hydra, a nine-headed cobra. On one of our Diamond Sangha altars, he is sitting on the coils of the hydra with the nine hoods spread over him. Turn the figure around, and there is the little tail. When you see the tail, you know the snake is there. When you see horns over a hedge, you know an ox is there.[17] It is just like Nan-ch'üan and his sickle; with one gesture he shows the whole Tao of his heritage.

"Mahākāśyapa breaks into a smile"—perfect communication! "And people and devas are confounded." The Buddha was communicating with his entire assembly and all students down through the centuries, not just with Mahākāśyapa. He was presenting his realization and sharing it with everyone when he twirled a flower, but only Mahākāśyapa perceived it and smiled. Earlier the morning star in its own way had presented itself there in the sky of Magadha. It was the Buddha who noticed it, but it is there for us to notice, too, just as the cardinal sings for our notice and our transmission.

The experiences of the Buddha and Mahākāśyapa were potent with responses. The Buddha sat absorbing his new understanding for a while, but at last he got up and sought out his five companions of earlier times and preached to them on the Four Noble Truths. He then went on for almost forty years giving sermons that still echo in our hearts. In turn, Mahākāśyapa smiled at the Buddha's presentation and the Buddha heartily acknowledged him. On and on goes this transmission, as Mahākāśyapa called out to Ānanda, as Ānanda tugged at Śānakavāsa's robe, as Śānaka-vāsa clarified body and mind for Upaguta, down through eighty genera-tions and more in countless lines of succession.[18] These incidents of trans-mission are communications that transcend time. They stand out as arcana—points for us, as modern-day heirs of these old worthies, to reflect upon and enter for direct transmission.

Chao-chou: "Wash Your Bowl"

THE CASE

A monk said to Chao-chou, "I have just entered this monastery. Please teach me."
Chao-chou said, "Have you eaten your rice gruel?"
The monk said, "Yes, I have."
Chao-chou said, "Wash your bowl." The monk understood.

WU-MEN'S COMMENT

Chao-chou opened his mouth and showed his gallbladder, his heart, and his liver. I wonder if the monk really heard the truth. I hope he did not mistake the bell for a jar.

WU-MEN'S VERSE

Because it's so very clear,
it takes so long to realize.
If you just know that flame is fire,
you'll find your rice has long been cooked.

Chao-chou is the master of Zen masters. He appears seven times in the forty-eight cases of *The Gateless Barrier* and twelve times in the hundred cases of *The Blue Cliff Record*. Reflect on the thousands of teachers remembered from ancient days, and you'll appreciate the veneration Wu-men and his colleagues felt for him.

In Case 1, Chao-chou utters the single word of a single syllable that becomes an arcanum for the ages. Here he speaks a few more well-seasoned words, heart to heart, to a new monk and to you and me. The monk enters Kuan-yin-yüan (Kannon-in), Chao-chou's monastery, and presents himself to the teacher. It is a precious opportunity: Young Buddha meets Old Buddha—the pattern of all teaching. Our interview practice is a dream of Kuan-yin-yüan. We reenact Chao-chou's engagement with his monks in each of our encounters. Since each person comes forth differently, the dialogue that makes up this case is unique—special to the student, to Chao-chou, and to the circumstances. Like our own dialogues it was a chance to turn the Dharma Wheel and change the world. This is a chance found outside the temple, too, in conversations between spouses, friends, coworkers, and strangers. Use your chance well.

Often a new student will wait for the teacher to speak first. Commonly I will say, "We are just getting acquainted. Please tell me about yourself." This is where the divergence among students begins. Not only will the story be special, the selection of biographical data will be unique. Sometimes the student begins with age, marital status, and occupation, sometimes with an account of a spiritual path. And sometimes, as in the present case of Chao-chou and the new monk, teacher and student launch directly into essential matters.

Almost any presentation will do as a start. In fact, almost any honest presentation will do at any phase of practice. It will be your state at that time. If your teacher is worthy, you will find yourself tossing the Buddha Dharma about before long.

Here a monk enters the monastery and makes a polite request: "Please teach me." Couched in humble language, this is nonetheless a challenge. "Here I am, a new student. What do you have to teach me?" Although the monk was new to Kuan-yin-yüan, he was apparently already well along in his practice. A person completely accomplished in the Tao, for example, might have framed his first words to Chao-chou in such a way. It was a seasoned presentation—an offer to enter into a conspiracy with Chao-chou to establish something only the two of them could create.

Chao-chou responds, "Have you eaten your rice gruel?" Rice gruel, with a few pickles, is the traditional breakfast at Asian monasteries. Superficially, Chao-chou is politely asking if the monk has been fed. Fundamentally, however, he is offering a challenge in response to a challenge—an essential question.

Tan-hsia asked a monk, "Where have you come from?"
    The monk said, "From down the mountain."
    Tan-hsia asked, "Have you eaten your rice?"
    The monk said, "Yes, I have."
    Tan-hsia said, "What sort of fellow would bring you rice? Did he have open eyes?" The monk could say nothing.[1]

Tan-hsia (Tanka), a contemporary of Chao-chou, is clearly severe, but Chao-chou is exacting, too, in his kindly way. There is more to Tan-hsia's dialogue, but this is enough to draw the parallel to the present case. Like Tan-hsia and all Zen teachers, Chao-chou finds nothing more interesting and enjoyable than sitting there in the little house by the gateless barrier and examining the people who appear before him. "Are you in order? How do you stand with yourself? How do you stand with the world?"

"Have you tasted the plain but delicious food of our ancestors?" The monk replies, "Yes, I have." What do you think of this response? I find it not too bad. The monk is just getting his bearings, after all. Perhaps he is thinking, "Let's see what the Old Boss will do."

Sometimes a student will come to me from another Zen group and yell "Mu!" or "Kats'!" at the outset of our first conversation. I just shake my head. Too noisy. It is inappropriate to make a big show over something as ordinary as rice gruel. Moreover, it usually turns out that *show* is all it is.

Many years ago when a certain American passed his first kōan, he went to see Dr. D. T. Suzuki and announced excitedly that he had experienced kenshō. Dr. Suzuki gave him short shrift, and the student didn't understand why. *Zen kusai* is the epithet for such announcements: "Zen stink"—the stink of spiritual materialism.

Yamada Kōun Rōshi points out that one might feel pleased with oneself on discerning the essential world. It is a rare experience, after all. However, the rōshi goes on, "If that pride swells, one becomes afflicted with what is known as Zen sickness. It is manifested by certain esoteric mannerisms, such as an excessive use of Zen terms, which ordinary people don't understand. . . . The truly great Zen person, who has experienced deep enlightenment and has extinguished all illusory feelings after ken-shō, should be indistinguishable from the ordinary person, at least in externals."[2]

Yamada Rōshi lived up to his own homily. I remember once when Anne Aitken and I were living in Kamakura, I was returning from the station by bus after a train trip to Tokyo. Suddenly, one stop before my own, someone clapped me on the shoulder as he was getting off. It was the rōshi himself, returning from his work in the big city. We had been on the same train, and now we were on the same bus, but I had not noticed him. In his dark blue suit and his fedora, nothing set him off as a Zen master.

It is pride that shows. I have always encouraged people to keep the details of their practice to themselves and thus avoid setting themselves apart. In following my suggestion, some keep quiet about their kōan study but purvey the bad smell of Zen simply by the way they walk or laugh. The human urge to stand out from the crowd is not necessarily put to rest by a preliminary experience. Work ahead! This is the way to get the most out of kōan practice, and indeed out of life. Dwelling on accomplishments is putrefaction.

The monk in this story is open to the teaching, but most teachers are critical of his response: "Yes, I have." A dull reply, they say, revealing in one short answer that he may have a bit of an eye but is rather self-conscious about it. In his place, how would you reply?

The monk's response set up Chao-chou's final riposte: "Wash your bowl!" That's the blow that killed Buddha! It has no beginning, no end, no cause, and no purpose. Yet it is instructive in our everyday world. As Yamada Rōshi has said, each kōan must be grasped in its essential spirit, but there may also be an aspect relating to step-by-step training which deserves comment.[3] The essential is called the Standpoint of the Original Element. The dimension of training is called the Aspect of Practice and Verification. The two are in fact inseparable, but for purposes of clarification they can be picked apart temporarily. This case of Chao-chou and the new monk is a superb example of the two aspects as one.

I got instruction in the practice aspect one evening when I was in the bathhouse of Ryūtaku Monastery with Nakagawa Sōen Rōshi. He told me about a remark attributed to the great nineteenth-century statesman and swordsman Yamaoka Tesshū. In Tesshū's time, new Western imports like soap were beginning to replace traditionally Japanese things like pumice.

He said, "Zen is like soap. First you wash with it, and then you wash off the soap."

In discussing Chao-chou's "Wash your bowl," R. H. Blyth writes: "If Chao-chou had asked the monk if he had washed his bowl, and said, 'Then put some rice in it,' there is no difference."[4] He means that such a sequence would present the same point as the original case, and he seems to be suggesting that symmetry and balance are the tests of a Zen dialogue. This is correct as far as it goes. But "Wipe it away!" is very different from "Fill 'er up!" As D. T. Suzuki used to say, Zen has *noetic* implications—implications of knowledge. Zen dialogues are not just "Where did you go?" "Out." "What did you do?" "Nothing." Chao-chou's words are charged with power for both practice and experience.

In his comment, Wu-men keeps to the essential ground. He praises Chao-chou and wonders about the monk's realization. The Old Buddha opened his mouth and showed his gallbladder, his heart, and his liver. But maybe the monk didn't really hear the obvious. He might have mistaken the bell for a jar, poor fellow.

Chao-chou's gallbladder, heart, and liver cry out, "Wash your bowl!" Nothing missing! Nothing left over! It is like a great temple bell: *BONGGG!* But it is possible to overlook that clear signal. It is possible to reduce its sound to explanation. Of course, Wu-men is speaking to his students, to all of us. Don't mistake the bell for a jar! Don't mistake the fact of essential nature for the ordinary injunction to clean up your idea of realization. The light playing about Chao-chou's mouth is extinguished if your understanding is limited to the practice aspect. The kōan becomes flat, and "skulls appear in every field."[5]

The first morning of my first visit to Ryūtaku Monastery in November 1950, Sōen Rōshi instructed me in "outside cleanup"—the practice of sweeping up leaves and pulling up the tiniest weeds in the temple compound. "When you sweep the leaves," the rōshi said, "you are sweeping your own mind." I was already familiar with this notion, and felt he was being rather obvious. I thought, "Well, I know that already." I could not hear any echo of Chao-chou. "Sweep the leaves!" There, too, training and essence were the same, though I hadn't a glimmer.

Wu-men's verse begins: "Because it's so very clear, / it takes so long to realize." Leaves are green, hibiscus flowers are red, robes are black—there they are! If you suppose that there is some symbolic significance in the deep black of Zen robes, your appreciation for that blackness is put off.

Sometimes students from the Vajrayāna tradition visit us and complain about our somber robes and cushions. They much prefer their own maroon robes and crimson cushions. I want to say, "The very black of my robe— that's it! The very red of your cushion—that's it!" The leaves fallen from the Bodhi Tree are brown, the plumeria flowers are yellow. Completely clear! We are always slipping off the facts into associations, on and on, along an infinite number of by-paths, ignoring the black, the brown, the red, the yellow that bespeaks itself—totally itself. But when I say "totally itself" you might be inclined to imagine something, and Chao-chou's good karma is put off.

"If you just know that flame is fire," Wu-men continues, "you'll find your rice has long been cooked." Flame is fire—as obvious as Chao-chou's liver and gallbladder. But if you deviate into causes and effects, properties and features, temperature and intensity, realization and wiping it away, you are denying yourself unnecessarily. This is the teaching of all the Buddhas:

> Every day, the master Chin-niu himself came to the zendō with the rice bucket, danced and laughed loudly, calling out, "Little Bodhisattvas, come and eat your rice!"[6]

Hsi-chung Builds Carts

THE CASE

The priest Yüeh-an said to a monk, "Hsi-chung made a hundred carts. If you take off both wheels and the axle, what would be vividly apparent?"

WU-MEN'S COMMENT

If you realize this directly, your eye is like a shooting star and your act is like snatching a bolt of lightning.

WU-MEN'S VERSE

Where the wheel revolves
even a master cannot follow it;
the four cardinal half-points, above, below,
north, south, east, west.

First the priest Yüeh-an (Gettan): he was a teacher in the Lin-chi line who flourished during the late eleventh or early twelfth century, a great-grandfather of Wu-men in the Dharma. We do not have his dates of birth and death, nor any biographical data, but judging from this case he must have been a most creative and exacting teacher.

He said to a monk, "Hsi-chung made a hundred carts." Hsi-chung

(Keichū) was the inventor of the wheel and the cart according to Chinese mythology. ("Wheel" and "cart" are written with the same Chinese ideograph, just as American slang equates "wheels" to an automobile.) The key term in Yüeh-an's statement is "carts 100 *fu*." *Fu* means "spoke," and Shibayama Rōshi renders the line "[Hsi-chung] made a cart whose wheels had a hundred spokes."[1] Yamada Rōshi interprets the word *fu* as a counter for carts—literally, a hundred spoke of carts, as we would say a hundred head of cattle.[2] I have followed this latter translation, but both versions pose difficulties, and I can't be sure which is correct. But it doesn't matter. The kōan concerns the question about taking off the wheels and axle.

Yüeh-an had a purpose in invoking Hsi-chung from the mythological past. By pointing to the Adam of the cart, he is calling to the depths of the monk's own psyche. He sets the scene, so to speak, in that monk's mythos, and in ours, saying, in effect, I am going to ask you a question about the original person and the original cart. Ready? Okay, suppose you take that cart and remove the wheels and axle. What would be perfectly clear?

Some people answer "A box," meaning just the top part of the cart. An innocent response. But Yüeh-an really means, "What if we took all the pieces away? The front part, the back, the cargo box, the seat, the wheels, the axle—everything! Then what would be vividly clear?" If you say "Nothing," that won't do either. Yüeh-an is not being one-sided.

We don't see many carts in Western society these days, but we do have pickups and cars. So suppose you take a pickup. You remove the body, the wheels, the axles, the headlights, the seats, the dashboard, the floorboards, the chassis, the cargo box, the steering mechanism, the suspension system, the engine, the transmission, the gas tank—then what will be crystal clear? Don't say, "A pile of parts." That isn't Yüeh-an's point either. He is not just giving lessons in mechanics.

I tell beginning students that zazen is like learning to ride a bicycle. You have to steer, pump, keep your balance, and watch our for pedestrians and other vehicles—all at once. You are riding a pile of parts with your pile of parts. After you learn to ride, however, what then? You are free of those parts, surely. You are one with the bicycle, and the bicycle keeps its own balance. It steers and pumps itself, and you can enjoy your ride and go anywhere, to the store, to school, to the office, to the beach. You have forgotten sprockets and handlebars. You have forgotten that you have forgotten. Likewise, when Hsi-chung made those carts he was lost in cutting and fit-

ting. We can say that he did not cut and he did not fit. The same is true of
any artist. In D. H. Lawrence's well-known account of his first experience
as a painter, he describes how he scraped off the dull paint from someone's
used canvas, set it up on an easel, dipped his brush into fresh paint, and
then disappeared into the canvas.[3]

I must add a word of caution here. The oneness of rider and bicycle, the
oneness of Lawrence and his canvas, and the unity of Hsi-chung and his
carts may be quite wonderful. But they are not the fundamental matter.
You can enter into the deepest spiritual union with your loved one; you can
float harmoniously through a rigorous game of tennis; you can enter into
profound samādhi on your cushions so that twenty-five minutes flash by in
a moment; you can walk on hot coals without a scar and suspend your an-
imation for days at a time. Yet all this is not the ultimate point. The yogi
needs a good kick in the pants. Come off the top of that hundred-foot pole!

Yamada Rōshi frequently warned his students about this matter, and he
was joined by Shibayama Rōshi and other true teachers.[4] Archery, Aikidō,
Tai-chi, Tea Ceremony, and a thousand other creative skills are wonderful
samādhi devices. But don't suppose that *Zen in the Art of Archery* is really
Zen. It is not. It is archery, raised to an exquisite point, and it stops there.
Oneness is a trap for a tiger! Even great musicians or painters have to realize
the main fact if they are to meet Yüeh-an face to face.

Oneness doesn't do it. You must become intimate, and this means taking all the parts away. In working on Mu, let everything else go. The best
ideas, the most profound psychological insights, the dearest memories,
Chao-chou himself, his encounter with the monk, the dog whose Buddha
nature is under question, concepts of form and emptiness, birth and
death, Buddha nature itself—all fall away. Like sexual intimacy, the practice of seeing into your own true nature is a naked encounter. Not two, not
even one. Only Mu. That is true intimacy.

Some years ago, Christmas Humphreys wrote a piece for *The Eastern
Buddhist* in which he suggested that Westerners cannot handle kōan work
the way Asians can—Westerners need "more meat on the bone."[5] Well,
besides the unfortunate metaphor, I disagree with the intent of his statement. The more meat on the bone, the more parts to the cart, the more
thought in the zazen.

Take off all those parts. Take off all that meat; take away the gristle, the
fat, the marrow, the protein, the vitamins, the calcium, the phosphorus,

the atoms, the electrons, the neutrons, the protons—and what is crystal clear? (*Crack!*)[6]

This is the lesson of the *Diamond Sutra*: There is no formula by which the Buddha attained anything. Buddhists of all traditions set a lot of store by the Thirty-two Marks of the Buddha, and they are still listed in Buddhist dictionaries: flat feet, webbed fingers, and so on.[7] Ridiculous! Material characteristics are not material characteristics. The Thirty-two Marks of the Buddha do not identify the Buddha.[8] Wipe them away! Throw away the dictionary itself—now what is vividly clear about that Buddha?

Wu-men said, "If you realize this directly, your eye is like a shooting star and your act is like snatching a bolt of lightning." Pay close attention to Wu-men's words. He and Yüeh-an are prompting the thunderbolt of Samantabhadra, the Bodhisattva of Great Action. Let's see it and hear it! The whole universe is watching and listening.

Wu-men says in his verse: "Where the wheel revolves / even a master cannot follow it." Wu-men calls his book *The Gateless Barrier*, but he is erecting solid barriers everywhere. Here is another one. How is it that even a true maestro cannot follow the music and an expert wheelwright cannot follow a wheel's course? When the wheel turns, *nobody* can follow it— that's the truth of it, expert or no expert.

"The four cardinal half-points, above, below, / north, south, east, west." In the original, *szü-wei* (*shiyui*) refers to the four half-points of the compass: northeast, northwest, southeast, and southwest. Together with above and below and north, south, east, and west, the half-points form the Ten Directions—used in Chinese, that most concrete of languages, to mean "everywhere." *Szü-wei* also means the four cardinal virtues: propriety, righteousness, integrity, and modesty. This meaning is an overtone in Wu-men's verse, suggesting the nobility of the master. Thus in those final two lines of his verse Wu-men is really pointing to you as the noble master. In effect he is asking you, "Where does that wheel turn? Where does that cart go?"

Don't say "nowhere." Even a stone goes somewhere. Don't say "everywhere." Even the air is still. Where does that cart go? Samantabhadra knows.

Ch'ing-jang's
Nonattained Buddha

THE CASE

A monk asked the priest Ch'ing-jang of Hsing-yang, "The Buddha of Supremely Pervading, Surpassing Wisdom did zazen on the Bodhi Seat for ten kalpas, but the Dharma of the Buddha did not manifest itself and he could not attain Buddhahood. Why was this?"

Ch'ing-jang said, "Your question is exactly to the point."

The monk said, "But he did zazen on the Bodhi Seat; why couldn't he attain Buddhahood?"

Ch'ing-jang said, "Because he is a nonattained Buddha."

WU-MEN'S COMMENT

I approve the Old Barbarian's realization, but I don't approve his understanding. If an ordinary person realizes, he or she is thus a sage. If a sage understands, he or she is thus an ordinary person.

WU-MEN'S VERSE

Better than knowing the body is knowing the mind in peace;
when the mind is realized, the body is no longer anxious.
When body and mind are fully realized,
the saintly hermit declines to become a noble.

Ch'ing-jang of Mount Hsing-yang (Seijō of Mount Kōyō) was a disciple of Pa-chiao (Bashō), who is represented in Case 44 of this text. Ch'ing-jang's dates of birth and death are not known, but it seems that he lived in the tenth century or thereabouts, perhaps contemporary with Yün-men or a little later. He was a great-grandson in the Dharma of Yang-shan, co-founder of the Kuei-yang school of Zen, a school best known for the gentle spirit of its Dharma encounters.

I should perhaps pause here for a word about the schools of Zen. The Lineage Charts (Appendix I) trace five schools, all of them rising within the T'ang period or soon thereafter. Only two survive today: the Ts'ao-tung (Sōtō) and Lin-chi (Rinzai). The others, the Kuei-yang, Yün-men (Unmon), and Fa-yen (Hōgen), disappeared after only a few generations or combined with the Lin-chi school.

These schools of T'ang period Zen were distinguished after the fact. Until about the beginning of Sung times (A.D. 960), there was not much to identify them and monks would freely seek instruction across what now seem to be sectarian lines. Today we find Rinzai and Sōtō to be very different indeed, though occasionally students still shift from one to the other.

I suppose there were a variety of reasons for the demise of the Yün-men, Fa-yen, and Kuei-yang traditions, but in the case of the Kuei-yang school, Yamada Rōshi liked to point out that whereas the Lin-chi people are very demanding of students, consistently denying their attainment and pressing them forward, Kuei-shan, Yang-shan, and their followers were quite mild, sometimes even expressing approval at the end of a dialogue.[1] "The Kuei-yang teachers were easy on their students, and perhaps this is one reason their stream dried up," Yamada Rōshi used to remark. In the present case, Ch'ing-jang is quite firm but he cannot be called severe. Perhaps Wu-men included his amiable teaching in *The Gateless Barrier* to balance the shouts and disorderly conduct found in some of his other stories.

In any case, one day a monk asked Ch'ing-jang, "The Buddha of Supremely Pervading, Surpassing Wisdom[2] did zazen on the Bodhi Seat for ten kalpas, but the Dharma of the Buddha did not manifest itself and he could not attain Buddhahood. Why was this?" This question comes from a parable in Chapter Seven of the *Lotus Sutra*, an elaborate account of a profoundly devout king and his sixteen sons who all eventually attained supreme enlightenment. The Buddha Śākyamuni, in this story, was the youngest of these sons.[3] The case involves a portion of the story and is modified and taken out of context. Lin-chi explains "Supremely Pervading, Surpassing Wisdom" like this: " 'Supremely Pervading' refers to the one who personally penetrates everywhere into the ten thousand dharmas [phenomena], which have no nature and no form. 'Surpassing Wisdom' refers to the one who has no doubts anywhere and does not attain a single thing. Buddha is the one whose clear light shines throughout the Dharma world."[4]

According to the *Lotus Sutra*, this great Buddha did not achieve the true way, though he sat cross-legged with body and mind motionless for ten kalpas. In the Indian Buddhist tradition, eternity can be measured by minor kalpas, medium kalpas, and major kalpas. One minor kalpa is the period of time described as the interval involved in emptying a container that is a mile wide, a mile long, and a mile high, full of poppy seeds, by removing a single poppy seed every three years or, alternatively, the interval required for a celestial lady to wear away an iron block, likewise a mile on each side, if she descends and brushes it with her ethereal garments once every three years. Medium kalpas and major kalpas require even larger cubes.

"He did zazen on the Bodhi Seat" all that time! "Bodhi Seat" is a translation of the Sanskrit *bodhimanda*, which refers to the ground under the Bodhi Tree where the Buddha Śākyamuni sat in zazen. Hence it is the spot or place of *bodhi*, enlightenment. The Sino-Japanese for this term is *dōjō*, a word we commonly use to designate the room where we do zazen. *Dōjō* has become secularized to some extent and is commonly the name for the gym where people practice Kendō or Aikidō. Notice the conduct of the players in that gym, however. They bow on entering and leaving, and in good dōjōs they maintain a devotional spirit while working out. It is still a sacred place. When I watched the 1988 Olympics on television, I noticed swimmers from the People's Republic of China bowing on entering and exiting the pool area. Even though they might have been without overt religion, that pool was nonetheless their dōjō.

Lin-chi gives an explanation of the final part of the monk's question: " 'Sat on the Bodhi Seat for ten kalpas' refers to the practice of the Ten Pāramitās. 'The Dharma of the Buddha did not manifest itself' means that the Buddha is in essence not born, and the Dharma does not pass away. 'He did not attain Buddhahood'—the Buddha cannot become Buddha again."[5]
The Ten Pāramitās are the ten ways of perfecting oneself as a human being:

by generosity, morality, patience, zeal, meditation, wisdom, conduct and speech appropriate to the truth, resolve or will, strength, and spiritual knowledge. Lin-chi is saying that zazen is not just a matter of squatting on cushions. It is the entire person engaged in the Buddha Way—a way that includes meditation, wisdom, and upright conduct too. You may be a Zen teacher, but if you are not considerate and decent then Lin-chi will show you his stick.

Perhaps the monk who posed the question thought zazen was a magic device that could transport him into nirvana. This is an error all Zen students know about. Most of us have complained in interviews with our teacher, "It has been ten kalpas since I began my practice, and I don't have a single glimmer. I am sitting hard, attending every sesshin I can, but I haven't attained anything. Why is this?"

Ch'ing-jang gives us the answer: "Your question is exactly to the point." Your question is its own response, as we learn when working on Huo-an's question about the Beardless Barbarian. The point upon which you focus is exactly the question itself. There your practice unfolds and things become clear.

But the monk persists: "He did zazen on the Bodhi Seat; why couldn't he attain Buddhahood?" Poor fellow. He couldn't see the nose on the end of his face.

So Ch'ing-jang gives the coup de grace: "Because he is a nonattained Buddha." By this time perhaps you see the point, even if the monk did not. But do you see it intimately? What is your own attainment of nonattainment?

Wu-men comments, "I approve the Old Barbarian's realization, but I don't approve his understanding." "Old Barbarian" refers to Bodhidharma,[6] and if we give this statement the Zen parse, we come up with, "I approve realization, but not understanding." And Wu-men goes on to say, "If an ordinary person realizes, he or she is thus a sage. If a sage understands, he or she is thus an ordinary person."

Wu-men distinguishes clearly between the monk's understanding and Ch'ing-jang's realization. The monk *understood* that practice promotes realization, but Ch'ing-jang *realized* that the two are not separate. A contemporary folk story may clarify this difference and identity: It seems that a freighter suffered through a bad storm near the coast of South America. Its water kegs were smashed, and the crew was parched with thirst. Encountering another vessel, the captain signaled a request for water. To his surprise, the signal came back, "Let down your buckets." He did so, and found the seawater was fresh. For though he was out of sight of land, the ship was off the mouth of the Amazon River, where the water was sweet for many miles.

Let down your buckets where you are. At a conference I attended several years ago, a psychologist had his subjects close their eyes and repeat their first names silently for a few moments. When he asked one young woman for comments, she said the game had made her feel uncomfortable. When pressed further, she said it had made her feel guilty. It seems she felt guilty about being herself. This is not at all uncommon, but it was good that she could verbalize it. The monk in this present case may also have had doubts about himself—another distraction! Do you have such a distraction? Take comfort in remembering that you share the nature of the Buddha Śāk,a-muni—he had a hard time too. Settle into Mu and persevere there. You'll find that your skin is not your outer limit, and that you too penetrate the formless beings everywhere.

When Wu-men says he does not approve of understanding, he means that he does not approve of the monk's intention in asking the question. The monk was engaged in examining the process, rather than riding the process itself. I enjoy citing the example of my friend Flora Courtois, who turned herself over to her process. For years she suffered deep anxiety about life's purpose, and then one day her anxiety matured. While she was gazing idly at a little desk, the universe turned on its axis and she found to her joy that she was all right—that everything is all right from the beginning-less beginning.[7] Supremely Pervading, Surpassing Wisdom herself was all right.

People sometimes ask me, "How long will it take?" My answer is, "No time at all." The question is in the dimension of understanding—as contrasted, in Wu-men's expedient dichotomy, with realization. Disengage yourself from any concern about how the process works. That is a by-road that can lead you into elaborate speculations, charts, and statistics. I don't approve. "But I have been doing zazen for ten years—why isn't anything happening?" Exactly: nothing is happening, though your realization of that fact may be evolving.

Ch'ing-jang was encouraging this process of no-process. I wonder if the monk was far enough along on the path to take the hint. Readiness may be all, but how does one get ready? This must have been as big a problem for monks in the T'ang period as it is for students today. Sometimes it's hard to take even the first step. If the flames of one's own hell are too hot, a single period of zazen may be excruciating. I daresay that many monks, nuns, and lay people in the past fell from the Dharma path because their neuroses or even psychoses made it impossible for them to practice. Fortunately we in the West can deal with these flames with psychological methods that were unknown to our ancestors. A wise therapist, or a Zen teacher wise in therapy, can help to turn down the flames and make it possible to sit still without getting burned.

This is an expedient use of understanding, but it cannot replace realization, as Wu-men says in his verse: "Better than knowing the body is knowing the mind in peace." Understanding problems of the body, past traumas, interpersonal matters, financial matters, career matters, can be greatly beneficial. But at last one must realize the mind, which Yamada Rōshi renders as "heart-mind," since the Chinese word means both mind and heart.

"When the heart-mind is realized, the body is no longer anxious." Correct. I am reminded of the aphorism attributed to G. K. Chesterton: "The reason angels can fly is that they take themselves so lightly." To realize the mind is to find that everything is all right. Of course we must work hard at our practice and at encouraging growth among our friends and within our social structures to make clear what has been true from the beginning. I hope we can also see the joyous implications of the Rings of Saturn. When worlds turned to dust there, what a great blast it must have been! More than all right!

"When body and mind are fully realized, / the saintly hermit declines to become a noble." When we are truly realized, there is no progression. The saintly hermit, the Buddha of Supremely Pervading, Surpassing Wisdom, and indeed you and I—we are just fine as we are. But the monk's question remains: "Why don't I get it?"

Ch'ing-shui: Solitary
and Destitute

THE CASE

*A monk said to Ts'ao-shan, "I am Ch'ing-shui, solitary and destitute. Please give
me alms."*

Ts'ao-shan said, "Venerable Shui!"

Ch'ing-shui said, "Yes, sir!"

*Ts'ao-shan said, "You have already drunk three cups of the finest wine in
China, and still you say that you have not moistened your lips."*

WU-MEN'S COMMENT

*Ch'ing-shui is submissive in manner, but what is his real intention? Ts'ao-shan
has the eye and thoroughly discerns what Ch'ing-shui means. Tell me, where and
how has Ch'ing-shui drunk wine?*

WU-MEN'S VERSE

With the poverty of Fan-tan
and the spirit of Hsiang-yü,
though he can hardly sustain himself,
he dares to compete with the other for wealth.

Ts'ao-shan (Sōzan) was a disciple of Tung-shan Liang-chieh and together they are sometimes credited with cofounding the Ts'ao-tung (Sōtō) Zen school in the ninth century.[1] He composed an important commentary on the "Five Modes of the Universal and the Particular," an overview of Zen originally formulated by his teacher Tung-shan.[2] As for Ch'ing-shui (Seizei), we don't have any details of his biography, but he must have been widely known in his time—otherwise he would not be mentioned here by name. By framing his question so profoundly, he reveals commendable insight.

The question is: "I am solitary and destitute—won't you give me alms?" A world of meaning lies within these words. Wu-men challenges you to see into that world of religious solitude and poverty as well as Ts'ao-shan did.

"Everything is totally without meaning or purpose. The whole universe is nothing but a vast desert without a blade of grass or drop of water. There's no significance, no merit, no virtue in my life. I feel completely lost." Thus have students of all religions described their "dark night" experiences. Not only do students of religion encounter this fearsome valley, people everywhere sound its depths, a condition sometimes laughed off by their friends as a "midlife crisis."

This bleak state of spirit was called "accidie" by the early Christian teachers, a word that means "spiritual sloth" according to the dictionary. "Slothful," however, implies being lazy on purpose, and there is nothing intentional here. David the Psalmist called this condition "the valley of the shadow of death." William James called it "the sick soul." Though it has negative names and a bad reputation, it is actually a very promising condition—an essential phase of spiritual evolution.

Once I consulted Father Thomas Hand, a Jesuit retreat master, about accidie. He said that people passing through this phase should be careful—first to keep their schedule of religious practice and second to stay in touch with their spiritual guides. We can understand by this advice that it is important not to turn back at such a crucial point in one's development.

When the Scottish philosopher David Hume reached a place like this in his intellectual quest, he found it frightening and turned for solace to his merry friends and a good game of backgammon.[3] But Ch'ing-shui pressed on. He is a more courageous model for us. Instead of giving himself up to the comfort of chess or a game of cards with his friends, he presents himself

fully to Ts'ao-shan. "This is where I am. What should I do now?" Most
commendable.

We must be clear about Ch'ing-shui's position. Yamada Rōshi says,
"He is trying to examine the state of [Ts'ao-shan's] consciousness to
fathom the depth of his realization."[4] This is exactly to the point, but it
must not be interpreted to mean that Ch'ing-shui was already aware that
his poverty and solitude were complete fulfillment. From the depths of his
poverty, he examined his teacher as his own practice.

Ts'ao-shan, with marvelous directness, rises immediately to Ch'ing-
shui's urgent request and calls out, "Venerable Shui!" Ch'ing-shui replies,
"Yes, sir!" That's a splendid presentation too. So Ts'ao-shan says, "You
have already drunk three cups of the finest wine in China, and still you say
that you have not yet moistened your lips." The original says: "You have
drunk three cups of wine of the House of Pai of Ch'ing-yüan." Most commentators note that Pai (Haku) was a famous company of winemakers in
the district of Ch'ing-yüan. It probably was, but I wonder if there aren't
some Zen puns at play here. *Ch'ing-yüan* is written with the same ideographs as the ancestor of Ts'ao-shan's line, Ch'ing-yüan (Seigen). Moreover, *pai* means "white," and in Asia "white" also connotes "no color." Let
me play with this a little. Bashō has the haiku:

> Whiter than the stones
> of Stone Mountain—
> the winds of autumn.[5]

The stones of Stone Mountain are white, but the winds are even whiter.
Look again at Ts'ao-shan's words: "You have drunk three cups of wine from
the House of No Color in Ch'ing-yüan, but still you say you have not
moistened your lips." We can carry the point about white as the absence of
color even further. "Color" and "form" are the same ideograph in Chinese.
So the "wine of the House of Pai" can be read as the "wine of the House of
No Color and No Form."[6] *That* is the wine we keep looking for deep in our
cellars.

It is interesting to see what Meister Eckhart has to say about spiritual
poverty and realization. From his point of view, Ch'ing-shui might not
have been truly poor when he came to Ts'ao-shan. Perhaps he was still looking for something. You must, the *alte Meister* said, be as free from your
creature will as you were when you had not yet been born: "For, by the ev-

erlasting truth, as long as you will to do God's will, and yearn for eternity and God, you are not really poor, for he is poor who wills nothing, knows nothing, and wants nothing.'" So long as you seek peace of mind and Buddhahood, you cannot realize the peace which is true poverty of spirit. You cannot acknowledge the Buddhahood of your own original nature which wills nothing, knows nothing, wants nothing. Our ancestors in the Dharma sweated blood in their practice, but they were caught up in the process. They were not visualizing how it would be when it was over.

This is like any intensive period of change in human development. Adolescents, for example, do not constantly hold in mind the attainment of adulthood. They too are caught up in the process, struggling within the present. It is not, experientially, becoming or attaining. Externally it may be viewed as such, but internally it is not. Learn from your teenagers. Let your concepts of becoming and attaining go, and you will be truly poor— free to give your full attention to Mu.

Wu-men comments: "Ch'ing-shui is submissive in manner, but what is his real intention?" He could not have been more humble, but his words were a cry from his heart that challenged Ts'ao-shan's competence. In Kendō, the Way of the Sword, there are three stances: high, middle, and low. In the high stance, the player assumes a threatening position. In the middle stance, the player holds the sword straight forward. In the low stance, the sword points downward. But high, middle, or low—each is a stance of challenge. Ts'ao-shan easily parried Ch'ing-hui's humble stance and flashed a trenchant response.

"Ts'ao-shan has the eye and thoroughly discerns what Ch'ing-shui means." Of course. Ts'ao-shan could see clearly the desert place that is the original garden itself, where Ch'ing-shui sat comfortably beneath the tree of life, luxuriating in every delight imaginable.

"But just tell me, where and how has Ch'ing-shui drunk wine?" This is the key point. If you truly appreciate Wu-men here, then you, Wu-men, Ts'ao-shan, and Ch'ing-shui too, are all sloshed together.

Wu-men's verse begins: "With the poverty of Fan-tan / and the spirit of Hsiang-yü . . ." Fan-tan (Hantan) and Hsiang-yü (Kōu) are folkloric figures of China, probably historical personages originally. Fan-tan was obliged by circumstances to give up a civil service career. He trundled his wife and children about in a pushcart, eking out a living as a fortune-teller. As Yamada Rōshi observes, fortune-tellers are not generally so wealthy, though they may be clever in talking about fortune.⁸ So Fan-tan and his family barely kept themselves alive eating the poorest food imaginable and dressing in the most ragged, hand-me-down clothing. Hsiang-yü was a great general of the third century B.C. Though he was defeated in a battle that led to the founding of the Han dynasty, he was renowned for his valor. His horse Chui (Sui), equally courageous, and his beautiful mistress, Yü (Gu), have roles in his famous story. With defeat imminent, he sat carousing in his tent and singing the song that has been sung down through the ages:

> Strength to drive through a mountain!
> spirit to cover the whole Earth!
> but the time is unfavorable;
> Chui doesn't want to go forth.
> Yü! Oh, Yü! what will be your fate?⁹

Ch'ing-shui, Wu-men is saying, had the poverty of Fan-tan and the spirit of Hsiang-yü. Without such a spirit, poverty is despair. I often hear people speak of the ideal of poverty, but rarely of its spirit. The New Age of the sixties and seventies, when we rejected the mores of our political leaders, realized little of its potential because we never completed the rejection: we clung to ourselves, to our own aggrandizement. In those days there were a number of people wandering around Maui with no money in their pockets and very little food in their backpacks. One day when a group of us were going to the beach, we picked up a woman dressed in white who asked for a ride. She said she was a member of the Christ Family and had taken a vow of complete poverty with her sisters and brothers. We learned afterward that they were applying to the county for transportation back to the Mainland. Like the rest of us, they were not yet completely poor. True poverty means really giving up acquisition and status, and this requires a resolute spirit that can drive through mountains and cover the earth. "Blessed are the poor in spirit." Read Dominique Lapierre's *The City of Joy* to find that blessedness in the bowels of Calcutta.¹⁰

"Though he can hardly sustain himself, / he dares to compete with the other for wealth." Realization sometimes emerges in Dharma exchanges, and this is the competition Wu-men refers to here. It is not the effort to overpower another. Ch'ing-shui finds himself in original poverty. He has nothing at all. What does he do? Well, he certainly doesn't appear and say, "I have nothing to show." That's what I did with Yasutani Rōshi for more years than I care to remember—weak-spirited and irresolute. If you can see into Wu-men's lines and take them to your heart, then your spirit, too, covers the whole earth.

Chao-chou and the Hermits

THE CASE

Chao-chou went to a hermit's cottage and asked, "Anybody in? Anybody in?" The hermit lifted up his fist.

Chao-chou said, "The water is too shallow for a ship to anchor." And he left.

Again he went to a hermit's cottage and asked, "Anybody in? Anybody in?" This hermit too lifted up his fist.

Chao-chou said, "Freely you give, freely you take away, freely you kill, freely you give life." And he made a full bow.

WU-MEN'S COMMENT

Both held up their fists in the same way. Why did Chao-chou approve one and not the other? Tell me, what is the core of the complication? If you can give a turning word on this matter, you will realize that Chao-chou's tongue has no bone in it. He is free—now to raise up, now to thrust down. Be that as it may, can you realize also that Chao-chou was seen through by the two hermits? Furthermore, if you say that one hermit was superior to the other, you do not yet have the eye of reflective study. And if you say there is no difference between them, you do not yet have the eye of reflective study.

WU-MEN'S VERSE
Eye like a shooting star;
activity like lightning;
the sword that kills;
the sword that gives life.

Here we meet Chao-chou again. Shibayama Rōshi suggests that this incident took place while Chao-chou was on his long pilgrimage, visiting many teachers to deepen his own realization.[1] However, we know that Chao-chou engaged in Dharma dialogues with people outside his monastery even after he settled down in Kuan-yin-yüan. Case 31, for example, tells the story of his visit to a tea seller whose comments to monks had intrigued him.

Thus we can't be sure when he met the hermits; in fact, we can't even be sure that two of them were involved. I have translated it that way, but some teachers, including Senzaki Sensei, say there was only one hermit.[2] The Chinese is not clear on this point. Fortunately, for kōan purposes it doesn't matter.

There are two words in Chinese that can be translated "hermit." One is *hsien*, literally "man of the mountains," a Taoist term that implies "saint" or "wizard"; the other is *an-chu*, as in this case, literally meaning "master of a hermitage." *An-chu* refers to a monk who has completed his training under a teacher and is living alone in a little hut to polish his wisdom through further zazen. This was the custom in T'ang Buddhist times, though today in those Asian countries where Buddhism is still tolerated the *an-chu* usually finds himself in a village or neighborhood conducting memorial services and kindergarten supervision.

The hermit's cottage in this case is surely rustic and very tiny, a one-room hut, open to the elements. Nothing could be concealed there, but Chao-chou walks in, calling out, "Anybody in? Anybody in?" as if there were room to doubt. In classical Japanese this salutation is *"Ariya? Ariya?"* I can still hear Yasutani Rōshi calling out in his teishō *"Ariya! Ariya!"* and then his inimitable laugh. "Are you there? Are you there?"

The hermit lifted up his fist.[3] Chao-chou responded, "The water is too shallow for a ship to anchor." What's happening here? Yamada Rōshi suggests that Chao-chou did not leave without a glance at the hermit to see his response to this abuse.[4] It was indeed abuse, but it was abuse beyond aspersion. Chao-chou was scolding the Buddha on the monk's altar, as well as the monk himself.

Chao-chou liked to test the depth of the water. Here he tries it with Chia-shan (Kassan):

> Chao-chou went to Chia-shan's monastery and entered the Dharma Hall with his staff in his hand. Chia-shan asked, "What's the staff for?"
> Chao-chou said, "To test the depth of the water."
> Chia-shan said, "There isn't a drop of water here. What can you test?" Chao-chou leaned on his staff and went away.[5]

No doubt chuckling, "Quite right, quite right!" as he walked away.

Back to our story. Chao-chou again went to a hermit's hut and walked in, calling *"Ariya? Ariya?"* This hermit too, or again, lifted his fist. Chao-chou said, "Freely you give, freely you take away, freely you kill, freely you give life." And he made a full bow.

Yamada Rōshi says that Chao-chou must have glanced at this hermit's face as well, to see how he responded to the praise.[6] Yes, it was praise, but it transcended commendation. The Old Master was really mumbling to himself, I think. Your task is to overhear him after all this time.

Wu-men gives rather an extended comment to this case, and when we examine it closely we find several themes. First, he says, "Both held up their fists in the same way. Why did Chao-chou approve one and not the other? Tell me, what is the core of the complication?" The core of the complication, if any, is that Chao-chou really didn't approve one and not the other. Both held up their fists in the same way, and Chao-chou's teishō came out one way the first time and another way the second. "Comparisons are odious," says the old proverb. Keep it clean! If you are clear about the fists, you will also see Chao-chou clearly.

Wu-men then goes on to say, "If you can give a turning word on this matter, you will realize that Chao-chou's tongue has no bone in it. He is free—now to raise up, now to thrust down." Wu-men is playing along with Chao-chou's little game. The fact is that Chao-chou is free to expound point *A* in his putdown and point *B* in his praise. He is like an image of the

Buddha Śākyamuni ticking off the categories of the Four Noble Truths. He is like a bamboo grove that clatters when the wind comes up and is silent when the wind dies down.

Then Wu-men takes another approach. "Be that as it may," he says, "can you realize also that Chao-chou was seen through by the two hermits?" What did the first one see in Chao-chou's response to his upraised fist? What did the second one see? Suppose you were the first hermit, how would you respond to Chao-chou? And if you were the second hermit? These two old fellows surely knew what Chao-chou was up to. Otherwise, they might better have returned to their home monasteries and taken up Mu again as beginning students.

There are important overtones to this case that relate to everyday life. When you make a presentation and it is put down, what is your response? When you make a presentation and it is praised, how do you react? How do you view the critic? We are not doing intellectual tricks with these kōans. If they had no connection to daily affairs, we would be simply an esoteric cult engaging in mutual ego trips to show our superiority to the world.

Without a certain measure of emotional maturity it is difficult even to begin Zen practice. You tend to take the rōshi's suggestions as personal criticism and end up on your cushions with paranoid thoughts revolving in your head. Or you take his approval as personal praise and make yourself unbearable to your friends. But as you become emotionally mature you can handle praise or blame with equanimity.

Such moral overtones can be abstracted and played separately as Buddhist ethics, but in this process don't neglect the primordial themes of the Tathāgata. In this case avatars of the Buddha are seeing through one another. To see through others is to breathe in their own inspiration. To allow others to see through you is to inspire them in turn.

You meet avatars of the Buddha at every turn. In one of our sutra dedications, the leader recites the words, "Our friends and family members guide us on the ancient path." Out of the mouths of babes comes wisdom, and out of spouses' mouths too, and from people on the street.

The other day at the McKinley Car Wash I switched off my car radio as one of the Samoan workers was preparing to vacuum the seats. We were anticipating a typhoon, and he asked if I had heard news about it. I said, "It seems to be just sitting there south of us." He said, "Well, maybe it's waiting for us to make our move." There you have the Buddha's doctrine of interdependence from the least doctrinaire corner of our society.

Returning to Wu-men, we find him taking still another tack. "Furthermore, if you say that one hermit was superior to the other, you do not yet have the eye of reflective study." Yes, that would be like saying there is no difference between old and young or between Chao-chou and yourself. Yamada Rōshi calls this the trap of pernicious equality. Female and male are the same, parent and child are the same, student and teacher are the same. "It's all God." Deliver us from this infernal snare!

Wu-men's verse begins: "Eye like a shooting star; / activity like lightning." The shooting star and the lightning are suddenly present, then suddenly gone. This is the nature of things, and Chao-chou is entirely of that nature himself. His presentations flash in the sky of no meaning. Nothing remains behind.

The verse continues: "The sword that kills; / the sword that gives life." This is Chao-chou: altogether appropriate to the circumstances—now setting up, now pushing down, forthrightly expounding the Dharma. It is also an echo of his words to the second hermit, "Freely you give, freely you take away, freely you kill, freely you give life," as well as a comment on his teaching to both of them. What is the implication of "killing"—and how does it relate to Chao-chou's words?

In the Chinese, Wu-men uses a synonym for "sword" in the fourth line. But the sword that kills and the blade that gives life are both wielded by Chao-chou, and in the hands of this great teacher the blade and the sword are one. Is their function the same as well?

If it were not for Chao-chou, we would none of us be practicing zazen, I am sure. It behooves us to study his words and his manner with minute closeness, beginning with his handiest sword of all, the one that has killed many and brought many to life:

"Muuu."

Jui-yen Calls "Master"

THE CASE

The priest Jui-yen called "Master!" to himself every day and answered himself "Yes!"

Then he would say "Be aware!" and reply "Yes!"

"Don't be deceived by others!"

"No, no!"

WU-MEN'S COMMENT

Old Jui-yen buys himself and sells himself. He brings forth lots of angel faces and demon masks and plays with them. Why? Look! One kind calls, one kind answers, one kind is aware, one kind will not be deceived by others. If you still cling to understanding, you're in trouble. If you try to imitate Jui-yen, your discernment is altogether that of a fox.

WU-MEN'S VERSE

Students of the Way do not know truth;
they only know their consciousness up to now;
this is the source of endless birth and death;
the fool calls it the original self.

Jui-yen (Zuigan) was a disciple of Yen-t'ou (Gantō) and a cousin in the Dharma of a large number of other T'ang period luminaries. We don't know his dates of birth and death, but we can determine that he was active at the end of the ninth century, forty years or so after Lin-chi.

Jui-yen's teacher, Yen-t'ou, was a very interesting figure, a talented Zen master about whom I will say more in the next case. Jui-yen was his only successor of any prominence.

> Jui-yen came to Yen-t'ou and asked, "What is the original and everlasting truth?"
> Yen-t'ou said, "It moved."
> Jui-yen said, "What about when it moves?"
> Yen-t'ou said, "You don't see the original and everlasting truth."

This is an intriguing dialogue which you may study someday in the *Book of Serenity*. Jui-yen's persistence in following up Yen-t'ou's first response was commendable, but after Yen-t'ou's second reply he fell silent. Yen-t'ou continued: "If you affirm this, you are not yet rid of the root of defilement. If you do not affirm it, you are immersed in endless births and deaths."[1]

It's all there in Yen-t'ou's wise words. We can be sure that Jui-yen examined them deeply in his zazen. "What is the original and everlasting truth? Isn't it in the moving? Isn't emptiness form? Why did Yen-t'ou say that I don't see it? How is it that my affirmation would show the root of defilement? And my silence would be a matter of relativity?"

His ultimate resolution of these doubts is reflected in his custom of calling "Master!" to himself and responding "Yes!" "Be aware!" "Yes!" "Don't be deceived by others!" "No, no!"

We know that Jui-yen did not just use this calling and answering as private practice. He would actually take the high seat before his assembly and go through the recital by way of a teishō.[2] Yamada Rōshi remarks that Jui-yen hit upon a truly enlightened way to maintain his practice after his deep realization.[3] In fact, Jui-yen is anticipating Dōgen's well-known words in the *Genjō Kōan*:

> To study the Buddha Way is to study the self. To study the self is to forget the self. To forget the self is to be confirmed by the myriad things. To be confirmed by the myriad things is to cast off body and mind as well as those of others. No trace of realization remains and this no-trace is continued endlessly.[4]

Jui-yen calling to his master is the final step in Dōgen's sequence. With his practice of calling, his body and mind dropped away. He was not simply indulging in ethical self-correction, as when you muse at the end of the day on the awkward things you said or did and resolve to do better tomorrow. A few moments of such contemplation are very useful, but Jui-yen had a different purpose.

You might assume that Jui-yen was just talking to himself. Zen teachers, as I learned in my long apprenticeship, often talk to themselves while packing a suitcase or arranging a room for a meeting. This is an uninhibited projection of what would otherwise be an inner narrative. Perhaps it is all right to say that Jui-yen was talking to himself—if you really know what the self is. The ideograph for "self" in this case is pronounced *tzu* in Chinese, *ji* in Japanese. This is the same *tzu* of Kuan-tzu-tsai (Kanjizai), the bodhisattva of the *Heart Sutra*, "The One Who Perceives the Unfettered Self." *Tzu* or *ji* is thus the "self" that is the source of all words and deeds. As an element in compound words it means "auto-" as in the Japanese word for automobile: *jidōsha*, "self-moving vehicle." It sometimes is used to translate the Sanskrit term *atman*, "self" or "soul." For the Buddhist, however, there is no self and no soul as an enduring entity. Then who is the one who perceives such an unfettered self? Who is it that stands up and sits down? Pai-chang, I would say, answered this question a hundred years earlier:

A monk asked Pai-chang, "What is the matter of special wonder?"
Pai-chang said, "Sitting alone, Ta-hsiung Peak."[5]

Ta-hsiung Peak is also called Mount Pai-chang.[6]

Yasutani Rōshi comments on this dialogue: "The universe has entered his belly in this sitting alone. He lies down alone at Ta-hsiung Peak. He walks alone at Ta-hsiung Peak. Wherever, no one accompanies him. He goes out alone. He returns alone. He is all alone. This is not 'the four cardinal half-points, above, below, north, south, east, and west'—it is instead: 'Above the heavens, below the heavens, only I, the World-Honored One.'"[7]

This sitting alone is not everywhere, Yasutani Rōshi is saying, it is not the dimension of "pervading the whole universe." It is not the interdependence of all things. Rather it is the fact expressed mythically by the infant Buddha when he pointed above and below and said that he was the only one anywhere, alone and revered, and that he was altogether at ease about it.

In the dedication of certain of our Diamond Sangha sutras, the leader reads, "Buddha nature pervades the whole universe, existing right here now." This is true, but you do not live everywhere, or *within* the void. You are as free as Kuan-tzu-tsai, now calling, now answering, never astray. You have the modest confidence of the Buddha that you are in touch with the mystery.

Senzaki Sensei says: "Some of you have passed the kōan 'the sound of one hand,' and you enjoy the voice of silence, glancing at it once in a while. You are playing at banking your own money, postulating the debtor and creditor, just for fun. Jui-yen was playing in the same way."[8]

Shibayama Rōshi quotes an earlier teacher: "The dragon enjoys its jewel."[9] The dragon in Buddhist imagery always holds a jewel in one of its claws. Dragon Jui-yen plays with his jewel and flashes its light directly in your face. "Who is calling? Who is answering? Who are the others?" These are the questions to ponder.

Senzaki Sensei used to advise us, "When you are with your friends, and everyone is talking loudly and you feel distracted, just close your eyes for a moment and you will find your treasure is right there." This is Right Recollection, the seventh part of the Eightfold Path, a way to enjoy your jewel of Mu in daily living.

There are many such ways. Recently I have been suggesting to students that they list the natural breaks that occur in the course of their waking hours—moments when they can remember to call to themselves and take one breath of Mu. While Jui-yen's practice is appropriate after realization, the inventory method is designed for people who are not quite that far along. Still, the two ways are essentially the same practice. Here is a sample inventory of the first part of the day for someone who works outside the home:

> Getting out of bed.
> Using the toilet.
> Washing my hands.
> Stepping into the shower.
> Stepping out of the shower.
> Drying my body.
> Brushing my teeth.
> Brushing my hair.
> Getting ready to dress.
> Opening the door.

Sitting down for zazen.
Exhaling each breath.
Rising from zazen.
Walking to the kitchen.
Getting ready to prepare breakfast.
Starting to set the table.
Sitting down to breakfast.
Taking up my spoon.
Putting down my spoon.
Standing up to clear the table.
Getting ready to put things away.
Getting ready to leave the house.
Stepping into the open air.

When you stand up, "Mu." When you sit down, "Mu." Notice that these are moments of routine activity or the intervals between. At this stage of your practice, you can't include moments of social interaction with your spouse or children. Deliberately going back to Mu during conversations would divide you from your loved ones or from your friends and colleagues. At times of interaction, your practice is to listen and respond with full attention. You can't include moments of exacting work either, for again, at this stage, you would be separating yourself. During anything more than the most routine activity, your practice is to give full attention to what you are doing.

There is a lot of leftover time, however, as you will find when you develop your inventory. Make suggestions beside your entries. Alongside your words "Getting out of bed," for example, you can note for yourself: "Sit there for a moment." Write out your inventory of potent moments for your entire day, and then revise and refine it after you try it out, for you will find intervals that hadn't occurred to you at first.

Your practice of breathing Mu at these hinges of your day will not be noticeable, though your family members and close associates will be influenced by your measured manner. My grandmothers knew about this way of moving through their lives. When they felt under stress, they would sigh deliberately and return to themselves.

The practice of identifying routine tasks and intervals and then reminding yourself to breathe Mu at such moments may seem rather mechanical, a kind of time-motion routine. It would not be necessary for someone like Flora Courtois or Bankei Yōtaku who had the question nat-

urally in mind at all times. For the rest of us, the inventory program serves
as a good reminder that the practice is there to be cultivated.

Eventually, you will find yourself practicing in the presence of Mu
throughout the day. There will no longer be any need for an inventory.
This is an important eventuality, but the future is not the present. For a
good while you will have to do it deliberately. After all, it took Brother
Lawrence ten years of hard practice to find the presence![10]

The "Pure Conduct Chapter" of the *Avatamsaka (Hua-yen) Sūtra* is devoted to gāthās, cautionary verses that monks and nuns memorized to remind themselves about protecting and enlightening all beings, including
themselves. It was in fact their act of protecting and enlightening—very
like Jui-yen's way of calling "Master," very like our way of coming back to
Mu. Dōgen quotes the following "Pure Conduct" gāthās for brushing the
teeth:

> Taking my toothbrush in hand
> I vow with all beings
> fully to realize the subtle Dharma
> and at once attain purity.

> When I brush my teeth
> I vow with all beings
> to have the eye teeth to conquer demons,
> and bite through all afflictions.[11]

Thich Nhat Hanh advises his students to write their own gāthās for
daily practice. I know of some students who do this. It is important to take
responsibility for the teaching in such ways. Here are a couple of my own:

> Preparing to enter the shower
> I vow with all beings
> to wash off the last residue
> of thoughts about being pure.

> Preparing to enter the shower
> I vow with all beings
> to cleanse this body of Buddha
> and go naked into the world.[12]

Now for Wu-men's comment about this case, rather extensive this
time: "Old Jui-yen buys and sells himself." Yes, he walks himself and

sleeps himself. He is never astray from that solitary fellow. But don't suppose that he is self-centered. His function was the same as that of Pai-chang and the Buddha: to be in touch with the mind and to convey it.

"He brings forth lots of angel faces and demon masks and plays with them. Why? *Look!* One kind calls, one kind answers, one kind is aware, one kind will not be deceived by others." *"Look!"* is an exclamation or shout like *"kats'!"* It scares away demons and angels.

"If you still cling to understanding, you're in trouble." If you suppose that cautioning and promising form the entire significance of this case, then you are caught simply in its routine and haven't yet glimpsed Jui-yen's joy.

"If you try to imitate Jui-yen, your discernment is altogether that of a fox." Distinguish between following Jui-yen's marvelous model and merely imitating him. Following him, you know the master. Imitating him, you cling to his bushes and grasses.

Instead of composing an original verse for this case, Wu-men quotes a Dharma poem by Ch'ang-sha (Chōsa), who lived more than two hundred years earlier.[13] It is one of the most important cautionary poems in Zen literature, a succinct presentation of Jui-yen's purpose: "Students of the Way do not know truth; / they only know their consciousness up to now." Ch'ang-sha and Wu-men are scolding us: we students of the Tao are only caught up in consciousness, the mind road that runs from the past to the present and is projected by conjecture into the future. We are preoccupied with the mind of "certain certainties," to use T. S. Eliot's expression— bills, taxes, dental appointments, and all the other points on our respective time lines. We are not aware of true nature, which is not born, does not die, and has nothing substantial to be called anything—yet is charged with infinite possibilities.

"This is the source of endless birth and death; / the fool calls it the original self." Yes, the consciousness that is preoccupied only with past, present, and future is the ocean of birth and death itself. Immersed in that ocean, there can only be endless repetition of coming and going. As Hakuin wrote:

> Lost on dark paths of ignorance
> we wander through the Six Worlds,
> from dark path to dark path—
> when shall we be freed from birth and death?[14]

CASE 13

Te-shan: Bowls in Hand

THE CASE

Te-shan one day descended to the dining hall, bowls in hand. Hsüeh-feng asked him, "Where are you going with your bowls in hand, Old Teacher? The bell has not rung, and the drum has not sounded." Te-shan turned and went back to his room.

Hsüeh-feng brought up this matter with Yen-t'ou. Yen-t'ou said, "Te-shan, great as he is, does not yet know the last word."

Hearing about this, Te-shan sent for Yen-t'ou and asked, "Don't you approve of this old monk?" Yen-t'ou whispered his meaning. Te-shan said nothing further.

Next day, when Te-shan took the high seat before his assembly, his presentation was very different from usual. Yen-t'ou came to the front of the hall, rubbing his hands and laughing loudly, saying, "How delightful! Our Old Boss has got hold of the last word. From now on, no one under heaven can outdo him!"

WU-MEN'S COMMENT

As to the last word, neither Yen-t'ou nor Te-shan has yet dreamed of it. When you examine them closely, you find they are just like Punch and Judy in a booth.

WU-MEN'S VERSE

When you realize the first word,
you understand the last;
the first and the last—
as to this, it is not one word.

First the dramatis personae: Te-shan (Tokusan) was an early ninth-century master in the Ch'ing-yüan line who is about eighty years old here. He is renowned for his nonverbal teaching, including his energetic use of a stick. "If you speak, you get thirty blows. If you do not speak, you get thirty blows."[1] This should not be misunderstood simply as roughneck teaching designed to corner students and force them to some kind of realization. Rather it is a presentation of the Middle Way which is neither verbal nor nonverbal. As a younger man, Te-shan was a great scholar of the *Diamond Sutra* who became a Zen teacher through a remarkable series of incidents outlined in Case 28. From a subtly articulate philosopher, he became a master who taught almost without speaking.

Hsüeh-feng (Seppō) is about forty years old in this story, cook of the monastery, a very responsible position. Though he had studied many years under several teachers, he did not yet have much understanding. He worked diligently on his practice, and Yamada Rōshi calls him "a man of effort" to distinguish him from his brother monk, Yen-t'ou, "a man of talent." This is not an invidious comparison, for Hsüeh-feng's great effort brought him profound realization and many creative disciples who went on to become famous teachers. The genius Yen-t'ou, however, was killed at age sixty and left no enduring line.

In one sense Hsüeh-feng was a disciple of Yen-t'ou, though he was older than Yen-t'ou by some six years; nominally, of course, both were students of Te-shan. Hsüeh-feng came to his realization with Yen-t'ou when they were on pilgrimage together:

> The two monks stayed overnight in the village of Ao-shan, where they were snowbound for several days. Yen-t'ou spent much of his time sleeping, but Hsüeh-feng sat up all day and most of each night doing zazen. During one of his waking moments Yen-t'ou said, "What are you doing, sitting there all day long like a mad deity by the road?"

Hsüeh-feng pointed to his chest and said, "I am not yet peaceful here."

Yen-t'ou said, "What kind of experiences have you had in the past? Tell me, and I will examine them for you."

So Hsüeh-feng told him about a realization of emptiness he had with the teacher Yen-kuan [Enkan], and about an awakening he had upon reading the verse Tung-shan Liang-chieh had written on his own enlightenment:

> He is the same as me,
> Yet I am not he.[2]

"On still another occasion," Hsüeh-feng said, "I asked our teacher Te-shan whether or not I could share the same experiences as our ancestors, and he gave me a blow with his stick. "It was," he said, "as though I were a bucket whose bottom suddenly dropped out."

With this Yen-t'ou gave a shout and scolded him, saying, "Don't you know that what enters from the gate cannot be the treasure of the house? If you want to propagate the Great Teaching, it must flow point by point from within your own breast to cover heaven and earth. Only then will it be the action of someone with spiritual power."

At that instant, Hsüeh-feng suddenly had realization and cried loudly, "Today, for the first time, Ao-shan has become enlightened!"[3]

With this profound experience, Hsüeh-feng went on to become one of the most capable Zen teachers of all time, and his many successors in turn have inspired the world. Te-shan's teachings and Yen-t'ou's earnest prompting led Hsüeh-feng, the man of effort, to full realization of his talent. But in today's drama, he is in middle life, not yet at ease with himself.

One day, the old teacher Te-shan descended to the dining hall, bowls in hand, ready for his meal. The term I translate as "bowls in hand" is *t'o-po*, the Chinese derivation of the Sanskrit *pindapāta*, meaning "living on alms." *T'o* means "entrust," *po* is "bowl." In transliterating from the Sanskrit, the old scholars chose ideographs that were closest to the original in pronunciation, which also enriched the original concept. To this day in Japan, monks and nuns take ceremonial trips to nearby communities to collect money or rice. This ceremony is called *takuhatsu*, the Japanese pronunciation of *t'o-po*. Those monks and nuns entrust their bowls to the lay world for their livelihood.

It was with a naive spirit of trust, then, that Te-shan came down to the dining hall. Some versions of this story say the meal was late. Hsüeh-feng challenged him, saying, "Where are you going with your bowls in hand, Old Teacher? The bell has not rung, and the drum has not sounded." Te-shan turned and went back to his room. One might expect him to say, as head of the temple, "The meal is late. You know our schedule is tight. When we have to wait for the meal, that means the time for the monks to rest is shortened, and they need their rest. So it's important that we have our meals on time." But he said no such thing. He just turned and went back to his room. This is the first noteworthy point of the case.

The Zen teacher's room is called the *fang-wen*, or *hōjō* in Japanese, a term derived from the ten-foot-square hut in which Vimalakīrti lived. Vimalakīrti was a lay disciple of the Buddha, it is said, who lived frugally though he was very wealthy. When he was ill, the Buddha sent Mañjuśrī and five hundred disciples, eight thousand bodhisattvas, and hundreds of thousands of gods and goddesses and others to ask after his health. This multitude was easily accommodated in Vimalakīrti's modest cottage, and it is said that each of the dignitaries was seated upon a lion throne that measured ten feet by ten feet.[4] Vimalakīrti was completely at home in his cottage, so he could accommodate everyone. Eventually it became the custom to call the abbot of the monastery by the name Fang-wen or Hōjō, the one who contains multitudes.

Like Vimalakīrti, Te-shan too felt altogether comfortable in his little room. It contained the whole universe in harmony. If you get acquainted with him through kōan study, you will appreciate how consistently at ease he was in his vast dwelling place. Hsüeh-feng's reminder prompted his return there. As he turned around and headed back, he gave a silent teaching. Indeed, there are many stories about Te-shan's silent teaching. Here he is, in the *Book of Serenity*, dealing with his attendant Huo:

> Huo asked Te-shan, "Where have all the Buddhas and Ancestral Teachers gone?"
> Te-shan said, "What did you say?"
> Huo said, "I commanded an exceedingly fine race horse to spring forth, but only a lame tortoise appeared."
> Te-shan said nothing.

The next day, when Te-shan came from his bath, Huo served him tea. Te-shan gave his shoulder a gentle pat. Huo said, "The Old Boss has noticed for the first time." Te-shan again said nothing.[5]

Maybe the Old Boss noticed, but the attendant did not. Hsüeh-feng, too, blinked in his encounter with Te-shan, thinking, "I scored one on my old teacher." He couldn't see Te-shan's turning about for what it was. Reveling in his supposed triumph, Hsüeh-feng told Yen-t'ou about the incident. Yen-t'ou, seeing an opportunity to bring his brother monk to realization, remarked with seeming casualness, "Old Te-shan, great as he is, does not yet know the last word."[6] What is the last word? ..

Te-shan then heard about Yen-t'ou's remark and sent for him. Yen-t'ou secretly whispered his meaning. Te-shan said nothing. You should appreciate Te-shan's calm spirit, and prepare yourself to show that spirit everywhere. And what about Yen-t'ou's whisper? Can you fathom it?

Next day, when Te-shan took the high seat before his assembly, his presentation was very different from usual. Yen-t'ou came to the front of the hall, rubbing his hands and laughing loudly, saying, "How delightful! Our Old Boss has got hold of the last word! From now on, no one under heaven can outdo him!" Suppose you were in the assembly at that time. How would you answer Yen-t'ou's implicit challenge?

Wu-men comments: "As to the last word, neither Yen-t'ou nor Te-shan has yet dreamed of it." That's true. No one can imagine such a thing. When we were children, getting in the last word was very important in an argument. Sometimes adults indulge in this kind of childish compulsion, even by mail, even by depositions. Surely there's always a last word after the last word. What is Yen-t'ou talking about here?

He and Te-shan thought they were doing something important. But as Wu-men comments, "When you examine them closely, you find they are just like Punch and Judy in a booth." Just like Bert and Ernie on TV. In other words, Yen-t'ou and Te-shan were saying: "Let's put on a show and see if we can't get something going here with brother Hsüeh-feng." As Wu-men says in another connection, even in failure it was a wonderful performance.[7]

In his verse, Wu-men continues the theme of the last word, but with a variation: "When you realize the first word, / you understand the last." With the introduction of "first," the dimension changes. The question becomes: "What is the first word?" You must realize it all by itself, and then you will know whether pigs have wings.

"The first and the last—/ as to this, it is not one word." This is a hard couplet to translate, especially the final line; I can't be sure that I have it right. Never mind. The basic question concerns the "this." What is *this*?

Nan-ch'üan Kills the Cat

THE CASE

The priest Nan-ch'üan found monks of the eastern and western halls arguing about a cat. He held up the cat and said, "Everyone! If you can say something, I will spare this cat. If you can't say anything, I will cut off its head." No one could say a word, so Nan-ch'üan cut the cat into two.

That evening, Chao-chou returned from outside and Nan-ch'üan told him what happened. Chao-chou removed a sandal from his foot, put it on his head, and walked out.

Nan-ch'üan said, "If you had been there, the cat would have been spared."

WU-MEN'S COMMENT

Tell me, what is the meaning of Chao-chou putting his straw sandal on his head? If you can give a turning word here, you will see that Nan-ch'üan's challenge was not irresponsible. But if you cannot yet do this—danger!

WU-MEN'S VERSE

If Chao-chou had been there
he would have taken charge;
he would have snatched away the sword
and Nan-ch'üan would have begged for his life.

Nan-ch'üan (Nansen) was also called by his surname, Wang. He was a most resolute and realized teacher who, with Pai-chang, was one of Matsu's two great successors in the late eighth and early ninth centuries. This case is the best known of his anecdotes, but he left many other wonderful dialogues and stories. For example:

> Governor Lu-keng said to Nan-ch'üan, "I have a stone at my house. Sometimes it stands up and sometimes it lies down. Is it possible for me to carve it into a Buddha?"
> Nan-ch'üan said, "Yes, it is."
> Lu-keng said, "Is it impossible for me to carve it into a Buddha?"
> Nan-ch'üan said, "Impossible! Impossible!"[1]

Nan-ch'üan took the governor's questions to their ultimate and reveals to us the teacher's role with students. He joined with the other great teachers of the T'ang period to set forth the configurations of our own Zen work.

Nan-ch'üan and Chao-chou practiced together as teacher and student for forty years, most of them at a monastery at the top of Mount P'u-yüan. In those early days of flourishing Zen study, great teachers had so many disciples that they could not teach everyone individually. They taught through public dialogues at evening meetings and were alert for other less formal chances in the temple and environs. Nan-ch'üan frequently turned to his senior student Chao-chou to recap these encounters. Thus in long seclusion with his great master, Chao-chou established the ground for his own extended career of teaching that inspires us still:

> Passing by the bathroom, Nan-ch'üan saw the monk in charge of heating the bath and asked, "What are you doing?"
> The monk said, "Heating the bath."
> Nan-ch'üan said, "Don't forget to call the cow for its bath."
> That evening the monk came to Nan-ch'üan's room. Nan-ch'üan asked, "What are you doing here?"
> The monk said, "I'm here to tell the cow the bath is ready."
> Nan-ch'üan asked, "Did you bring the reins?" The monk could say nothing.
> Later Nan-ch'üan told Chao-chou about this. Chao-chou said, "I have something to say."
> Nan-ch'üan asked, "Did you bring the reins?" At that Chao-chou grabbed Nan-ch'üan's nose and pulled it.
> Nan-ch'üan said, "All right, all right—but why so rough?"[2]

PLATE 4: *Nan-ch'üan and the Cat*. Courtesy of
The Idemitsu Museum of Arts. (Case 14)

Cut one, cut all—
why just the cat?
The head monks of the two halls;
even Wang, the Old Master.

In the present case, Nan-ch'üan finds monks of the eastern and western halls arguing about a cat. No doubt it was some kind of speculation: maybe one monk was saying that the cat has Buddha nature and another was arguing with him, while the other monks stood around and listened.

Nan-ch'üan happened by with a knife in his hand, perhaps a pruning knife for his work in the garden. Seeing his chance, he grasped the cat and called out, "If you can say something, I will spare this cat. If you can't say anything, I will cut off its head."

Seeing his chance! Nan-ch'üan's mind was at rest in the Buddha Dharma, like a lion under a thorn tree. The argument brought all his senses to their highest focus. "Ha! ha!—here's a chance to feed the cubs!" In daily life, such opportunities to turn the Dharma Wheel appear one after another. With the lion mind of Nan-ch'üan, you can feed everybody, even Nan-ch'üan himself.

But no one could say a word, so Nan-ch'üan cut the cat into two. Why so rough? Teachers have said from the beginning that Nan-ch'üan didn't really kill the cat.[3] In his teishō on this case, Yasutani Rōshi would cleverly mime the act of slicing at the hapless animal while at the same time releasing it. Perhaps that's the way it happened. If so, it takes nothing from the story.

As I have remarked elsewhere, great mimes do not mime.[4] Marcel Marceau *is* that butterfly catcher. He *is* that prisoner with the walls closing in. Pantomimes are events that have been personalized, made intimate, and then presented for all to see. The more intimately the event is realized, the more vivid the presentation. In Plate 4, the Zen artist Sengai depicts Nan-ch'üan holding up the poor cat, knife in hand, with the two monks gaping in amazement. His verse reads:

> Cut one, cut all—
> why just the cat?
> The head monks of the two halls;
> even Wang, the Old Master.

If you cut the skein, then every thread is cut—and this is the act of Nan-ch'üan. Everything drops away—everything is killed. The monks were struck dumb, the precepts were fulfilled. Yet as important as Sengai's comment might be, it does not point to the *central* act in the kōan. The inner vitality does not lie in wielding the knife and slaughtering the cat—as again the older teachers point out when commenting on this case.[5]

I used to suppose that the point of this kōan was that one should always be ready to speak up, to take appropriate action. See, for example, how decisively Nan-ch'üan reacts to the argument of the monks. He was able to respond—he was responsible to the Dharma, to the monks, and to all beings. In the same way, when Nan-ch'üan delivered his ultimatum, the head monks, at least, should have been able to come forth with something appropriate. True enough, but still that is not the central matter. What is the central act of this kōan? What is the intimate event? Establish this fundamental motif, and you will find that the second half of the case opens up as well.

Chao-chou had been outside the monastery on an errand. When he returned and Nan-ch'üan told him what happened, he placed his sandal on his head and stepped serenely out the door. I am told that putting a sandal on the head was a sign of mourning in old China, and this adds a certain poignancy and even logic to the kōan. But don't suppose that Chao-chou is just going through the motions of mourning as he walks out the door. True mourning is more intimate than just expressing regret or saying a prayer. What is true mourning? Touch this dimension, and you can walk out with Chao-chou. He was responding directly to Nan-ch'üan's account of the incident from a mind unfazed by birth and death. Some people say that Chao-chou meant the monastery was topsy-turvy with monks arguing about intellectual matters. If Chao-chou had been there, they say, he would have responded to Nan-ch'üan's challenge and the cat would have been spared. Such interpretations sidestep the case and jump ahead to the verse. Stick with the kōan: how do you see Chao-chou—walking out the door with his sandal on his head? Not only did Chao-chou's tongue have no bone in it, his activity was like lightning, free of words and standards. Speculation palls, metaphysics collapse, and the great mystery is exposed.

Nan-ch'üan said, "If you had been there, the cat would have been spared." The old teacher is not expressing regret. He is pleased with his great disciple, and moreover he is pleased that the cat had not died in vain.

Wu-men clarifies matters further: "Tell me, what is the meaning of Chao-chou putting his straw sandal on his head? If you can give a turning word here, you will see that Nan-ch'üan's challenge was not irresponsible. But if you cannot yet do this—danger!" The word "danger" here is written with the ideograph that means "narrow pass"—the narrow way between birth and death on the one hand and no-birth and no-death on the other.

There is another risk. Let's say you have a bit of insight into Nan-ch'üan's execution and Chao-chou's response, but you hesitate for some reason that is outside the context of the kōan. Then you are placing yourself at risk. You haven't really taken care of that cat yet. Free yourself. Cut one, cut all, and the mind of Nan-ch'üan and the mind of Chao-chou will appear clearly before you.

Wu-men comments further in his verse: "If Chao-chou had been there / he would have taken charge; / he would have snatched away the sword / and Nan-ch'üan would have begged for his life." This echoes Nan-ch'üan's final words to Chao-chou: "If you had been there, the cat would have been spared." Yes, but then there would be no story and no turning words.

What would Chao-chou have done? Remember the old story of the demon who sat beside the road and demanded the magic passwords? If people could say nothing, or if they said the wrong words, they lost their heads. Nobody could kill the demon, but the most modest farmer, pushing his cart to the market, could make him laugh and clap his hands.

This is the way of the Zen dialogue, the *mondō*. Now *my* words and conduct carry the crucial theme, now *you* play a counterpoint. Host and guest, parent and child, we switch roles and have fun, bringing forth the music of the stars:

> When Hsüan-sha came to P'u-t'ien District, he was entertained with a hundred diversions. The next day, he asked the Elder Hsia-t'ang, "Where has yesterday's commotion gone? Hsia-t'ang held up the corner of his robe. Hsüan-sha said, "There is no connection whatsoever."[6]

Hsüan-sha might seem to be correcting Hsia-t'ang here. Not so. They were both giving teishōs for the ages. Now this point, now that. Nan-ch'üan wields the sword that kills. Chao-chou wields the sword that gives life. The central matter of the first part is like going to bed. The central matter of the second part is like arising and going to work. Now Nan-ch'üan, now Chao-chou.

Tung-shan's Sixty Blows

THE CASE

Tung-shan came to see Yün-men. Yün-men asked him, "Where were you most recently?"

Tung-shan said, "At Ch'a-tu."

Yün-men said, "Where were you during the summer?"

Tung-shan said, "At Pao-tzu Monastery in Hu-nan."

Yün-men said, "When did you leave there?"

Tung-shan said, "August 25th."

Yün-men said, "I spare you sixty blows."

Next day, Tung-shan came again and said, "Yesterday you said you spared me sixty blows. I don't know where I was at fault."

Yün-men said, "You rice bag! Do you go about in such a way, now west of the river, now south of the lake!"

With this, Tung-shan had great satori.

WU-MEN'S COMMENT

If Yün-men had provided essential fodder at that time and awakened in Tung-shan the one path of vitality, then Yün-men's house would not have been vacated.

All night, in the ocean of yes-and-no, Tung-shan struggled to the ultimate. As soon as dawn broke, he went again to Yün-men, who explained everything in detail. Even though Tung-shan had realization, he was not yet brilliant.

Now let me ask you: Should Tung-shan have been given sixty blows or not? If you say yes, then grasses, bushes, and trees should all be beaten. If you say no, then you make Yün-men a liar. If you can be clear about this, then you and Tung-shan exhale ch'i with the same mouth.

WU-MEN'S VERSE

The lion rejects her cub;
she kicks it and dodges away;
the second arrow connected beyond causation;
the first was light, the last one deep.

Yün-men (Unmon) is the founder of the Yün-men school and a student of Hsüeh-feng, the teacher we met in Case 13 with Te-shan and Yen-t'ou. He lived from the closing years of the T'ang period into the time of the Five Dynasties; he died about A.D. 949, more than eighty years after Lin-chi.

Yün-men developed a notable style of teaching using metaphors that combine ordinary things in strange ways. One of his kōans in *The Blue Cliff Record* goes like this: "Within heaven and earth, in the midst of the cosmos, there is one treasure hidden in the body. Holding a lantern, it goes toward the Buddha Hall. It brings the great temple gate and puts it on the lantern."[1] The great temple gate is actually three gates: a large one in the middle and a small one on either side. The center part has two stories, and conventionally in the second story there is a single large room that contains life-sized images of the Eighteen Arhats. Yün-men's challenge is mysterious and fanciful, but it could not be more specific.

Though Yün-men was Hsüeh-feng's disciple, he was enlightened by Mu-chou (Bokushu), Lin-chi's elder brother monk, a fierce and exacting teacher who in his mature years lived in a little house by a road that was commonly traversed by Zen monks on pilgrimage. Frequently monks would stop to see him in their quest to deepen their realization. He would listen to their footsteps and sometimes would not even bother to answer their knock. Yün-men was turned away for three days in a row, but at last Mu-chou relented: "Who's there?" Yün-men answered, giving his monk-name, "Wen-yen." So Mu-chou opened the gate a little and Yün-men started to step in, but Mu-chou shut it right on his leg—with a stroke so vigorous it not only brought him to realization but broke his leg as well.[2]

Many consider Yün-men to be the greatest of all Zen masters. He is certainly one of the best documented, and his dialogues show a consistently rigorous and uncompromising adherence to the essentials as well as a compassionate concern for the liberation of his monks from the bondage of their concepts:

> A monk asked, "Why is it that one cannot become a monk if one's parents do not allow it?"
>   Yün-men said, "Shallow."
>   The monk said, "I don't understand."
>   Yün-men said, "Deep."[3]

Always in tune with the student, the topic, and the implications, Yün-men is presenting a teishō to the monk, to the assembly, and to you and me. The monk is obviously not ready to hear, but Yün-men saves his breath for someone who is.

Yün-men's disciple Tung-shan Shou-ch'u (Tōzan Shusho) should not be confused with Tung-shan Liang-chieh, founder of the Ts'ao-tung (Sōtō) school, who lived about one hundred years earlier. The Tung-shan in this case came from northwestern China and walked south to take up Zen study with Yün-men. At last, after staying here and there, he arrived and held the interview that forms the first part of this case.

"Where were you most recently?" Yün-men asks. "At Ch'a-tu," Tung-shan replies. Ch'a-tu, we are told, was a village near Yün-men's monastery. He stayed there overnight before coming to see Yün-men. Thus Tung-shan offers a matter-of-fact reply.

Zen teachers always want to get acquainted before offering instruction—especially Yün-men, who is remembered for his capacity to fit the teaching to the student. But by way of getting acquainted, Yün-men may also be probing for an expression of realization. "Where do you come from?" really means "In this world of coming and going, where do you stand?"

After Tung-shan's straightforward reply, Yün-men asks, "Where were you during the summer?"—referring to the period of intensive training held at Buddhist centers ever since the monsoon retreats in early India.

Again this seems to be a commonplace question, but you can be sure that Yün-men's eyes are fixed on his new student, watching for vital signs.

"At Pao-tzu Monastery in Hu-nan," replies Tung-shan. There were many great temples in Hu-nan, a district renowned for its beautiful scenery. Tung-shan must have offered this answer uneasily, no doubt wondering when Yün-men would bring him up short.

It is not yet the moment. Yün-men gives him a little more leeway: "When did you leave there?"

"August 25th," replies the hapless Tung-shan. Surely he knows that now he is in for it, for the great Yün-men would not just go on making small talk. But what other answers are possible?

Sure enough, Yün-men lowers the boom. "I spare you sixty blows!" The original Chinese is "three-score blows," and while in both Chinese and English the word "score" means twenty, it also means "a great many." In any case, as Yamada Rōshi points out, Yün-men is saying, "I wouldn't dirty my stick on the likes of you." This is a far worse beating than actual blows.[4] Yamada Rōshi inscribed the words of Yün-men's riposte on the monitor's staff at the Koko An Zendō.

Just as Yün-men was not making small talk with his first three questions, so he was not just probing for an expression of insight. After Tung-shan's first reply, "At Ch'a-tu," he probably knew very well that his guest didn't have a glimmer. But he continued to build his *upāya*, his skillful means, with his subsequent questions. It surely would have been premature to say "I spare you sixty blows" right away.

Uneasiness has a role in Zen practice. Just as good actors know they can put their stage fright to good use, so a good student understands that anxiety during an interview with the teacher can be a potent condition. One is out on the edge, so to speak, where inspiration comes more readily. Sometimes people regard this feeling of apprehension as a fear of authority and get themselves into quite a psychological tangle. Labeling emotions can be useful, as Vipassana practice teaches us, but derivative labeling can take one far afield. In the presence of a good teacher, one is open and vulnerable not only to the teacher but to inspiration. Yün-men knew this very well, and thus his line of questioning was profoundly compassionate.

So Tung-shan went to bed that night feeling miserable. As Wu-men comments, "All night, in the ocean of yes-and-no, Tung-shan struggled to the ultimate"—"Where did I go wrong? Why did the teacher say that he spared me sixty blows?" A most promising condition. Promising conditions are one thing to the experienced Zen teacher, and quite another to the student.

In this connection, I think of a story Bernard Phillips used to tell about himself when he was attending sesshin with Yasutani Rōshi. Bernard didn't like being struck with the monitor's staff at all, but there is an understanding in most Zen temples that if you don't want to be whacked, you can request that a sign be placed over your seat saying, in effect, "Don't whack here." At Bernard's request, such a sign was placed over his seat. In those days in Yasutani Rōshi's dōjō we beginning students would take turns timing the zazen during sesshin. Senior people, busy with their lay careers in the daytime, would come during the evening and turn up the pressure. One evening one of these senior people, a very big fellow, came in to help out. Quietly he accepted the staff from the Buddha—and then, without noticing the sign above Bernard's head, he brought the staff down on Bernard's shoulder with a crisp snap. *Wham-o!* Bernard leaped to his feet and gesturing at the sign shouted in English, "What's the matter with you? Don't you see that sign? It says 'Don't hit!' " The monitor, a very conscientious person, was quite taken aback. The next time Bernard had a chance to see Yasutani Rōshi, he shouted at him too. "That fellow hit me. He didn't even look at the sign. What's the matter with him! What's the matter with this dōjō!" Yasutani Rōshi said, "Wonderful! Wonderful! Please keep that enthusiastic spirit in your practice, moment by moment." It was Bernard's turn to be taken aback at Yasutani Rōshi's perception of his condition.

Tung-shan too was unaware that he was in a promising condition. Though he was in great spiritual distress, he was not sulking, not blaming other people, certainly not blaming the teacher, nor was he punishing himself. He was *using* his distress by focusing on the question "Where was I at fault?" rather than falling into the despair of "What a mess I am!" This is the stuff of mastery.

"As soon as dawn broke, he went again to Yün-men"—respectfully yet desperately—asking, "Yesterday you said you spared me sixty blows. I don't know where I was at fault."

Then Yün-men shot his second arrow: "You rice bag! Do you go about in such a way, now west of the river, now south of the lake!" As Wu-men says ironically, "He explained everything in detail." With this, Tung-shan had great realization. The question is: "What did he realize?"

Wu-men comments, "If Yün-men had provided essential fodder at that time and awakened in Tung-shan the one path of vitality, then Yün-men's house would not have been vacated." Maybe Wu-men is saying that Yün-men should actually have delivered the blows. It is true that after about five generations, people in the Yün-men line became Lin-chi teachers. Hsüeh-tou (Setchō), compiler of *The Blue Cliff Record*, was one of the last of the Yün-men tradition.

Yet Yün-men's house was not really vacated. We are all still living there. Chao-chou himself did not establish an enduring line, but here we are, breathing his Mu. When we asked Senzaki Sensei what we should do after he was gone, he would say, "Close down!" That's what we did, but that was not the end of his great influence.

There is something mysterious about the survival of Zen schools. Some of them seem just to roll along on their own momentum, while others with extraordinary inspiration die out as formal entities. The Kuei-yang line disappeared before the Sung period, while the Lin-chi line survives vigorously to this day—yet their founders were cousins in the Dharma. Yamada Rōshi used to say that the Kuei-yang school died out because the teachers were too easy on their students. Maybe so. But when I look around today I see questionable doctrines and practices perpetuated from generation to generation. I don't think any of us have the last word on this mystery.

"Even though Tung-shan had realization, he was not yet brilliant," Wu-men says. That's true—at what point does anyone become brilliant? One of my students exclaimed—"brilliant from the beginning!" Sooner or later he *was* brilliant:

> A monk asked, "What is the sword of Tung-shan?"
> Tung-shan said, "Why?"
> The monk said, "I want to know."
> Tung-shan said, "Blasphemy."[5]

A worthy son of a great father!

Wu-men goes on to discuss the sixty blows. "Now let me ask you: Should Tung-shan have been given sixty blows or not? If you say yes, then grasses, bushes, and trees should all be beaten." If Tung-shan was brilliant from the beginning, then surely he deserved no more beating than trees and flowers. "If you say no, then you make Yün-men a liar." Don't make him a liar; you'll put all of us out of business!

"If you can be clear about this," Wu-men goes on to say, "then you and Tung-shan exhale *ch'i* with the same mouth." *Ch'i*, the moving power of the universe, can be translated as "essence," "energy," or "breath." Take Wu-men's powerful metaphor to heart.

Wu-men's verse refers to Chinese folklore. The first line reads literally: "The education of lion cubs is the art of the lost child." It was said that the mother lion pushes her three-day-old cubs over a cliff and only nurtures those who can scramble back, as Tung-shan scrambled back to Yün-men.

"She kicks it and dodges away"—that is, "I spare you sixty blows!"

"The second arrow connected beyond causation." Yün-men's "Oh, you rice bag!" has no cause and effect, and no compassion, for compassion means "suffering with others" and there is no *with* here. Beyond intimacy! No inside! No outside!

"The first was light, the last one deep." Yes. And unerringly to the point!

CASE 16

Yün-men: The Sound of the Bell

THE CASE

Yün-men said, "See how vast and wide the world is! Why do you put on your seven-piece robe at the sound of the bell?"

WU-MEN'S COMMENT

All you Zen students, training in the Way, don't be victimized by sounds; don't follow up on forms. You may have realization on hearing a sound or enlightenment on seeing a form—that's natural. But don't you know that true Zen students can ride sounds and veil forms? They see all and sundry clearly; they handle each and every thing deftly.

Perhaps you are such a person. But tell me—does the sound come to the ear, or does the ear go to the sound? And if you have transcended sound and silence, what do you say at such a point? If you listen with your ear, it is hard to understand. If you hear with your eye, you are intimate at last.

WU-MEN'S VERSE

With realization, all things are one family;
without realization, all things are disconnected.
Without realization, all things are one family;
with realization, all things are disconnected.

Here we meet Yün-men again. His genius leaves me in awe. He takes the high seat before his assembly and says, "See how vast and wide the world is! Why do you put on your seven-piece robe at the sound of the bell?" The seven-piece robe, the *chia-sha* (*kesa*), is a kind of Buddhist surplice worn by Mahayana monks and nuns on ceremonial occasions.

When the bell sounds, the monk or nun dons the *chia-sha* and goes to the Buddha hall for teishō or to the zendō for zazen. There are two elements to be careful about here. Yün-men is not challenging us at the level of propriety. He is not asking why one should be prompt. He is not even suggesting that one *should* be prompt. The second point is that he is not talking about "samādhi power." He is not referring to the ability to respond promptly that one finds with long Zen training. When the bell rings, without a thought you come in to do zazen. Very commendable, perhaps. But we can be sure that it is not Yün-men's purpose to dwell on such ordinary matters.

In examining a kōan, you must face its essential aspect—and you must face its truth carried to the ultimate. When Yün-men says, "See how vast and wide the world is!" he is not referring, say, to the world bounded by the Koʻolau Mountains and the horizon of the Pacific Ocean, but to countless universes in endless dimensions, seen and unseen. He means your consciousness of countless universes, known and unknown. When you truly appreciate Buddha nature pervading the whole universe, then it has pervaded you too. You are one with the majesty of the universe. Suspicions are gone, grudges are gone, self-punishment is gone—concern about schedule, doubts about motives, all have disappeared in the original garden where the morning stars sing together and all the sons and daughters of God shout for joy. *That* is the world so vast and wide—at least for a moment!

"Why do you put on your seven-piece robe at the sound of the bell?" As Yamada Rōshi says, "But why? Ah, this *why!* It is the wonderful charm, the magic talisman that brings the Zen student to enlightenment."[1] In the context of the wide world, why do you rise and go to work at the sound of your alarm clock? Why do you pick up the phone when it rings? Why? With that "why" the Buddha arose from beneath the Bodhi Tree. With that "why" Bodhidharma came from India to China. With that "why" you stand up and sit down. At that point Samantabhadra, the Bodhisattva of Great Action, herself appears.

In our mealtime sutras we read, "We and this food and our eating are vacant."² The original Chinese reads, "The three wheels are vacant." The "three wheels" are the actor, the action, and the thing acted upon—the subject, the verb, and the object. When there is nothing to be called you, nothing to be called the universe, you and your dreaming and your world are all vacant, empty, void. "All things are empty by nature, not born, not destroyed, not stained, not pure, without increase or decrease."³ Then why do you feed the cat when she cries?

Wu-men comments: "All you Zen students, training in the Way, don't be victimized by sounds; don't follow up on forms." Senzaki Sensei used to ask, "When you hear a dog bark, do you think of your own dog?" That is a very interesting question. For if you do, then very soon—immediately, in fact—you are running through the fields in a totally different place and time. You are following up on the sound and its associations—on and on. Your mind is unsettled, and so you are led around by sounds and forms. You are at the mercy of the bark. When you are at rest in silence, however, that bark is at your mercy—your own bark.

I often suggest using the bark or the sound of the monitor's staff—*clap! clap!*—as a reminder. Time to return to your practice! But be careful about this advice. It is intended as an *upāya*, a skillful means to strengthen your practice. But when Wu-men heard the sound of the drum announcing dinner, he did not simply use it as a signal to go to the dining room or return to Mu. There was just that sound—and Mount Sumeru at the center of paradise leaped up and danced.⁴

These first two lines of Wu-men's cautions have useful implications for daily conduct as well: "Don't be victimized by sounds; don't follow up on forms." If you aren't at peace with yourself, you cannot see what is happening around you. You cannot function because you are preoccupied with yourself.

In this connection, I am reminded of a story about Shidō Munan:

A young woman whose parents owned a food store lived near Munan. Suddenly, without any warning, her parents discovered she was with child. She would not confess who the man was, but after much harassment at last named Munan.

In great anger the parents went to the master with the accusation. "Is that so?" was all he would say.

After the child was born it was brought to Munan. By this time he had lost his reputation, which did not trouble him, but he took very good care of the child. He obtained milk from his neighbors and everything else the little one needed.

A year later the young woman could stand it no longer. She told her parents the truth—that the real father of the child was a young man who worked in the fish market.

The mother and father of the young woman at once went to bring the child home. They apologized profusely to Munan and asked his forgiveness.

Munan only said, "Is that so?"[5]

This story panders to the stereotype of the Wily Woman, a frequent irritant in Asian (and world) literature, but at the same time I am grateful to know Munan. In Japanese "Is that so?" is *Ah, sō des' ka?* It is not actually a question at all but the mildest kind of temporizing. It carries no defensiveness, or projection, and is repeated on every possible occasion. Munan was temporizing. "Let's see how this comes out," he might have been thinking. "Meantime, here is a little mouth to feed." He absorbed the responsibility, and if that involved blame from others, well, that was their problem.

I think again of Senzaki Sensei. Many of his students in Los Angeles in the early 1950s were emerging from a long preoccupation with spiritualism and Theosophy. They were dealing with confused concepts about past lives, guidance from angelic beings, astral walking, and the like. People would corner this kind, clear-eyed man and talk on and on about the mysteries of the pyramids or transmissions from ageless beings in the Himalayas. He would smile gently and say, "Oh, really? I didn't know that." Since he was not preoccupied with himself at all, he was not victimized by sounds and did not follow up on forms. When you just insist on your own point of view, you are only protecting yourself and the galaxies sing to deaf ears. Senzaki taught by encouraging and listening, and I am sure that some of his guests reflected afterward, "You know, I did all the talking. Maybe I should go back and listen to him."

"You may have realization on hearing a sound or enlightenment on seeing a form—that's natural." Maybe the sound of a mango falling on the roof will prompt realization of your true nature, as a stone hitting a bamboo stalk did for Hsiang-yen.[6] Maybe the sight of a distant jacaranda tree in full bloom will enlighten you just as peach flowers did for Ling-yün

(Rei'un).[7] That is natural. For a person who is honed through long, ardent zazen, "Bow-wow!" is just "Bow-wow!"

"But don't you know that true Zen students can ride sounds and veil forms?" The realized person is master of sound and sight. Everything goes smoothly because associations do not appear and create diversions. A consummation devoutly to be wished!

Then Wu-men gets to the heart of it. "Perhaps you are such a person"— perhaps you are master of sounds and sights—"but tell me, does the sound come to the ear, or does the ear go to the sound?" You can relate this to Dō-gen Zenji's couplet in the *Genjō Kōan*:

> That the self advances and confirms the ten thousand things is
>   called delusion;
> That the ten thousand things advance and confirm the self is
>   enlightenment.[8]

Perhaps, Wu-men is saying, you can truly hear: *Gong-g-g!* He remarks, "If you have transcended sound and silence, what do you say at such a point?" It is not enough to be a mute who has had a dream. You must come forth on your own two feet swinging the sword of General Kuan, killing the Buddha when he appears, killing Bodhidharma when he appears. "What do you say?" This is the key question.

It is all very well to contain the vast wide world. It is all very well to cast off body and mind and find Mu everywhere. But can you step from the top of a hundred-foot pole without falling on your face?

For those of you who can't answer, Wu-men cautions: "If you listen with your ear, it is hard to understand. If you hear with your eye, you are intimate at last." Probably Wu-men is recalling the enlightenment of Tung-shan Liang-chieh. Tung-shan's teacher, Yün-yen (Ungan), had given him the kōan "The Discourse of the Nonsentient." When this became clear, he exclaimed:

> How truly wonderful, how truly wonderful!
> The discourse of the nonsentient is marvelous!
> If you listen with your ear, you can't discern it.
> When you hear with your eye, you have it at last.[9]

To hear with the eye is the intimacy of true freedom. This is the freedom of the stone woman who gives birth, of the wooden horse that whinnies, of the golden fox chasing the silver dog.[10]

The Buddha Śākyamuni, solitary and alone, entered into vast universes of endless dimensions. But when he was struck with the thought of his five companions it was like the sound of a great temple bell, and he freely arose and walked the dusty roads of India for the rest of his life, turning the Wheel of the Dharma. The "why" becomes clear at last.

Hakuin disliked Wu-men's comment. It created too much fuss, he said—we should leave it up to the individual whether or not to pursue enlightenment. It seems to me, however, that Wu-men shows us important aspects of the Buddha Way here—ideally perhaps, but very clearly and, as Shibayama Rōshi says, very kindly.[11] Surely we need this sort of light on the path.

Wu-men's verse begins: "With realization, all things are one family." As always, Wu-men's words should be taken to the ultimate. "Realization" means that the fundamental truths set forth by Śākyamuni and his successors are made altogether real for me by experience. "All things" includes huge star systems and infinitely tiny elements, as well as people, animals, plants, and so on. It is not biological or intellectual "oneness" that Wu-men is talking about. How do you realize "All things are one family?"

"Without realization, all things are disconnected." With this disjunction, Kuan-yin weeps. Families fall apart, cities are looted, nations exploit nations, and the earth itself is laid waste.

"Without realization, all things are one family." Indeed, but it takes some realization to appreciate it. Back in the old days of the New Age, I used to hear people say, "It's all God, it's all One." The flowers smile and the animals postulate. Deliver us from such pernicious oneness!

Wu-men had a further point to make with his final line: "With realization, all things are disconnected." This you must get on your own. It is the "why?" of the bell, the "why?" of the sound, the "why?" of putting on your robe, the "why?" of chanting sutras.

Years ago, Yasutani Rōshi wrote a piece for the *Diamond Sangha* entitled "Why Do We Recite Sutras?"[12] It was a very grandmotherly article designed for the beginners we were in those days. I imagine today he would just let his title stand and examine us individually, demanding "Why? Why?"

Kuo-shih's Three Calls

THE CASE

Chung Kuo-shih called his attendant three times, and three times his attendant responded. Kuo-shih said, "I was about to say that I was ungrateful to you. But the fact is that you are ungrateful to me."

WU-MEN'S COMMENT

Kuo-shih called three times and his tongue fell out. His attendant answered three times, and his responses were brilliant. Kuo-shih was old and feeling lonely. He held the cow's head to make it eat grass. The attendant would have none of it. Delicious food does not attract a person who is full. Tell me, at what point was there ingratitude to the other?

> When the nation is at peace,
> talented people are esteemed;
> when the house is prosperous,
> the children are refined.

WU-MEN'S VERSE

You must wear an iron cangue with no hole;
this curse passes to descendants, no trivial matter.
If you want to support the gate and sustain the house,
you must climb a mountain of swords with bare feet.

Kuo-shih (*Kokushi*) means "National Teacher" and usually implies "Teacher of the Emperor"; it is a posthumous title granted by imperial edict. There have been many such *kuo-shih* in Far Eastern Buddhism, but when the title is used alone as a name, it always refers to the protagonist of this case: Nan-yang Hui-chung (Nanyō Echū), or Chung Kuo-shih (Chū Kokushi), the first and most renowned of all the *kuo-shih*. It was his tomb that Hsiang-yen was tending when the *"tock!"* of a stone opened his mind.[1]

The facts of Hui-chung's life are not completely clear, and wherever you turn you find the details a little different. We do know that he was the Dharma successor of Hui-neng (Enō), the Sixth Ancestor, and that Hui-neng died in A.D. 713. Hui-chung himself died sixty-two years after his teacher's death. Allowing for his youth and a solid period of Zen study, you can be sure that he lived a very long time, probably into his nineties.

It is said that after Hui-neng's death, Hui-chung retired to the mountains of what is now Honan province and remained there forty years without ever emerging—living and practicing in a small temple with a single companion named Ching-tso-shan (Seizasan). His reputation, however, spread widely and the Emperor Su-tsung repeatedly invited him to come to Ch'ang-an, the capital. Finally, in 761, he agreed to go. Ching-tso-shan scolded him for this decision, declaring that it was too soon for Hui-chung to become a teacher.[2] A kalpa of practice and realization isn't enough.

Ching-tso-shan remained behind; we hear no more about him. One of my students has suggested that Hui-chung felt free to reenter the city *because* his friend remained behind for solitary practice. The two of them continued to be a pair, and Hui-chung was inspired in his busy life of teaching by the constant zazen of his faraway friend. In any case, Hui-chung took up residence in a monastery in Ch'ang-an and gave lectures at the palace and private instruction to the emperor. After Su-tsung's death, his successor, the Emperor Tai-tsung (Daisō), continued the patronage and conferred upon Hui-chung the title Liang-ti Kuo-shih (Ryōtei Kokushi), "Teacher of the Two Emperors." His dialogues with these emperors are recorded in *The Blue Cliff Record*:

> The Emperor Su-tsung asked Chung Kuo-shih, "What is it that controls the Ten Bodies [of the Buddha]?"
> Kuo-shih said, "Your Majesty should walk on Vairocana's head."
> The Emperor said, "I don't understand."
> Kuo-shih said, "Never consider yourself to be the pure and clear Law body."[3]

The "Ten Bodies of the Buddha" are ten important figures in the Buddhist pantheon, beginning with Vairocana, the Buddha of the Dharmakāya, the pure and clear body of the Law. Chung Kuo-shih is pointing directly to the emperor's own nature, which cannot be seen in terms of metaphysics or idealized human qualities.

The second episode was equally important:

> The Emperor [Tai-tsung] asked, "What should I do after you are gone?"
> Kuo-shih said, "Build a seamless tomb for this old monk."
> The Emperor asked, "Please tell me what kind of design you wish for your tomb."
> Kuo-shih sat quietly for a while, and then asked, "Do you understand?"
> The Emperor said, "I do not understand."
> Kuo-shih said, "After I am gone, my attendant Tan-yüan will know about it."
> After Kuo-shih's death, the Emperor summoned Tan-yüan and questioned him about the conversation he had held with the National Teacher. Tan-yüan sat quietly for a while, and then asked, "Do you understand?"
> The Emperor said, "I do not understand."[4]

Tan-yüan (Tangen) then responds with a wonderful verse, but the main kōan point is the seamless tomb. Everything else is just explication.

Chung Kuo-shih and his disciple handled their delicate teaching roles with equanimity, resolution, and incisiveness. Emperors Su-tsung and

Tai-tsung were matter of fact in their understanding, however, and could not see into the world of metaphor—they could not see that the world *is* metaphor. Kuo-shih graciously suggests to Su-tsung that he melt his archetypes, and gently he brings Tai-tsung to the seamless pagoda. It is too bad that his two imperial students could not understand. But they were Sons of Heaven, after all, and had a lot to release.

In connection with the present case, I recall my own teacher, Senzaki Sensei, dramatizing Chung Kuo-shih's calls and the responses of his attendant, thought to have been his disciple Tan-yüan. (Senzaki used the Japanese pronunciation of Tan-yüan's monk-name, Ying-chen.) The story went like this:

> "Ōshin!"
>
> Ōshin comes up to the teacher's quarters from the monastery below, bows, and says, "Yes, Master?"
>
> "Oh, there you are. Thank you for coming, but I don't need you right now." Then a little later,
>
> "Ōshin!"
>
> Ōshin drops what he is doing and comes again, "Yes, Master?"
>
> "Oh, thank you. You may return now." Ōshin bows and returns below, and again there is the call,
>
> "Ōshin!"
>
> Again he comes up and responds, "Yes, Master?"[5]

Since the attendant was a veteran monk, the second call was fresh and new and so was the third call. He never became dulled by repetition because he was no longer oriented to sequence. Every impulse from the vernal universe was of interest to him.[6]

> Yün-men called to his attendant daily for eighteen years, and when he would appear, Yün-men would say "What is it?" Finally, after all those years, the attendant awakened. Yün-men said, "From now on, I won't call you any more."[7]

In dealing with the National Teacher and his attendant, however, the kōan point lies in the final exchange: "I was about to say that I was ungrateful to you. But the fact is that you are ungrateful to me." At last the old teacher was convinced.

This passage is translated in a number of different ways by various scholars and teachers. My rendition follows Shibayama Rōshi's explication and is quite literal.[8] What do you make of these vivid, ironic words? Rightly realized, they lay bare the living nature of calling and answering.

Don't try this out in a restaurant. If you call the waiter over and then say, "Oh, that's all right, I don't need you right now"—well, the game ends very soon. It gets old in the family, too, though not for the one calling:

> "Mommy!"
> "Yes!"
> "Mommy!"
> "Yes!"
> "Mommy!"
> "Yes!"

When you are freshly receptive, then perhaps you can understand Chung Kuo-shih's final words about ingratitude. Be careful not to get snared by the ordinary meanings here. Chung Kuo-shih's "ungrateful" is an altogether positive term that is best carried to the ultimate—*absolutely* ungrateful.

I'd say the most ungrateful person in history is the Buddha Śākyamuni himself. But Chung Kuo-shih and Tan-yüan give the Old Founder pretty good competition. You might suppose that such ingratitude is a denial of love. If so, you have not yet seen these two intimate friends clearly.

During Chung Kuo-shih's time, it was said that no monk had completed his training until he had had at least one interview with the old master. In *The Blue Cliff Record* we find Nan-chüan, two generations younger, traveling with fellow monks to see him:

> Nan-ch'üan, Kuei-tsung, and Ma-ku went together to pay respects to Chung Kuo-shih. When they were halfway there, Nan-ch'üan drew a circle on the ground and said, "If you can say something, then let's go on."
>
> Kuei-tsung seated himself within the circle, and Ma-ku made a woman's bow before him. Nan-ch'üan said, "Well then, let's not go on."
>
> Kuei-tsung said, "What do you mean?"[9]

Nan-ch'üan's meaning was quite in line with the point Kuo-shih made with his three calls. Let's be ungrateful together!

Wu-men comments, "Kuo-shih called three times and his tongue fell out." It was used up completely for the sake of Tan-yüan and us all! "His attendant answered three times, and his responses were brilliant." He was confirmed by that call each time, just as Yün-men invites you to be confirmed by the sound of the bell. The waiter, unfortunately, will not be confirmed by your call, unless he happens to be a true server. The true server is the one who hears the sounds of the world—Kuan-yin with her thousand arms piled high with entrées and desserts.

"Kuo-shih was old and feeling lonely." After all, being ungrateful is a lonesome condition. One is cut off completely. But don't be taken in by appearances! Can you see how Tan-yüan was ungrateful too? And lonesome too?

"He held the cow's head to make it eat grass." Kuo-shih was being too grandmotherly. Surely one call is enough!

"Delicious food does not attract a person who is full." Full to the eyes! Full to the spiral nebulae!

"Tell me, at what point was there ingratitude to the other?" If you can make a clear response to Wu-men here, your own ingratitude will be completely vivid.

Wu-men then quotes an aphoristic poem by Ta-kung-wang:[10] "When the nation is at peace, / talented people are esteemed." That one call—"Ying-chen!"—was a thunderclap and the response was rain falling in torrents. In all this commotion, the nation was completely at peace. The silence was unbroken. "When the house is prosperous, / the children are refined." The National Teacher esteemed his talented student and gave him the highest praise. He cultivated the wealth of realization, and his child showed every promise of maintaining the family brilliance.

In his own verse, Wu-men continues the theme of parents and children most vividly. One must wear "an iron cangue with no hole." A cangue is a wooden yoke like the stocks used by our American ancestors to pillory criminals. But this is an iron device with *no* hole—like the "iron flute with no holes played upside down."[11] Truly upholding the Dharma is a heavy responsibility, and in fact there's no way to do it. Anything one does is off by a thousand miles.

"This curse passes to descendants, no trivial matter." Tan-yüan wore that impossible cangue when he dealt with his imperial pupil. He left the same curse, and on it goes. I pass this curse to my successors and they take it gladly. We know it's crucial, and we know it's ridiculous.

"If you want to support the gate and sustain the house, / you must climb a mountain of swords with bare feet." You sustain the Dharma by walking hand in hand with your sisters and brothers of the Buddha Sangha, completely open to their human anguish, feeling that anguish intimately as your own.

Tung-shan's Three Pounds of Flax

THE CASE

A monk asked Tung-shan, "What is Buddha?"
Tung-shan said, "Three pounds of flax."

WU-MEN'S COMMENT

Old Man Tung-shan attained something of clam-Zen. He opened the two halves of
his shell a bit and exposed his liver and intestines. Be that as it may, tell me: where
do you see Tung-shan?

WU-MEN'S VERSE

Thrusting forth "three pounds of flax!"
The words are intimate, mind is more so;
if you argue right and wrong,
you are a person of right and wrong.

The name "Tung-shan" simply means "East Mountain." Zen teachers are
commonly named for their locations, and there are many "East Mountains" in China. Fourteen "Tung-shans" are listed in my directory of ancient Chinese Zen masters.[1] Best known is Tung-shan Liang-chieh, revered as founder of the Ts'ao-tung or Sōtō school. In this case, however, we

again meet Tung-shan Shou-ch'u, who in Case 15 showed Yün-men that he had a good grip on his rice bag. Here he shows the brilliance that was not yet evident then.

In those halcyon days of Zen training, a good teacher had more students than could be seen individually in private interviews. Everyone, however, had a chance for interaction during the evening meetings. The teacher would step to the high seat and deliver a few well-chosen words. Monks would then come forward, one by one, and each would ask a question or make a presentation and thus set up an exchange. It seems that most of the dialogues recorded in Zen literature come from this setting, and the ceremony survives in the so-called Dharma Combat (*hōsen* or *shōsan*) meetings in modern centers, including our Diamond Sangha.

Tung-shan's preliminary words are not recorded. A monk stepped forward, made his bows, and asked, "What is Buddha?" This question appears four times in the forty-eight cases of *The Gateless Barrier* and countless times throughout Zen literature. The Buddha is the first of the Three Treasures of Buddhism—the other two being Dharma and Sangha. The name refers first to Śākyamuni, the founder of our Way, the Enlightened One. It also refers to many other figures in the Buddhist pantheon. We recite the so-called "Ten Names of the Buddha" during our mealtime service:

> Vairocana, pure and clear, Dharmakāya Buddha;
> Locana, full and complete, Sambhogakāya Buddha;
> Śākyamuni, infinitely varied, Nirmānakāya Buddha;
> Maitreya, Buddha still to be born;
> All Buddhas everywhere, past, present, future;
> Mahayana Lotus of the Subtle Law Sutra;
> Mañjuśrī, great wisdom Bodhisattva;
> Samantabhadra, Mahayana Bodhisattva;
> Avalokiteśvara, great compassion Bodhisattva;
> All venerated Bodhisattvas, Mahāsattvas;
> The great Prajñā Pāramitā.[2]

The first three entries on this list are the archetypal Three Bodies of the Buddha, standing for the three fundamental aspects of reality: Dharmakāya, the void that is charged with infinite possibilities; Sambhogakāya, the fullness and harmony of the universe and its beings; and Nirmānakāya, the unique individuality of each being and the infinite variety of the universe. Maitreya is the Future Buddha, potent in each of us and in the world; "All Buddhas" are at once the unknown enlightened ones and also all beings—every one enlightened; the *Lotus Sutra*, an allegorical, devotional text, is included, a mark of its widespread veneration in Mahayana Buddhism, even in relatively austere Zen practice; Mañjuśrī is the Bodhisattva of Wisdom, holding both a book of learning and a sword for cutting off delusion; Samantabhadra is the Bodhisattva of Great Action, turning the Dharma Wheel with all beings; and Avalokiteśvara is Kuan-yin (Kannon or Kanzeon), the Bodhisattva of Mercy, the one who hears sounds of the world—enlightened by these sounds, she includes them all as she enters into the world's work. Finally, all bodhisattvas are included, and all mahāsattvas (noble beings) as well, together with Prajñā Pāramitā, Perfected Wisdom.

There are a great many more Buddhas, each with his or her particular quality of enlightenment and verity, found in *The Sutra of Names of the Buddha*, an early Chinese work in twelve fascicles.[3] Patriarchs and matriarchs in our lineage are Buddhas as well, great spirits who enlightened themselves by their own efforts. The name is also given to the myriad monks, nuns, and lay people who followed their examples—and it is given to you and me and to all people who realize Buddha nature after long practice who are nonetheless Buddhas from the beginning. No library could hold all their names—all our names. And finally, "Buddha" refers to the spiritually instructive nature of the universe itself—totally void, every being reflecting and indeed including all other beings.

There are likewise an almost infinite number of bodhisattvas, each of them bearing a name indicating a particular quality of realization and potency, like these listed in the *Avatamsaka (Hua-yen) Sutra*: "Great Light, Eternal Light, Understanding the Seed of Buddhahood, Mind King, One Practice, Always Manifesting Spiritual Powers, Sprouts of Wisdom, Abode of Wisdom, Lamp of Truth, Illumining the World, Sustaining the World."[4] As bodhisattvas they are Buddhas too, as the "Ten Names of the Buddha" indicates, together with Prajñā Pāramitā—their wisdom and their teachings.

The question "What is Buddha?" might be paraphrased: "What is the essential aspect of life in this world? What is the substance of life and death? Can you show it to me concretely?" However often the question is asked, it never fails to be a challenge.

Regarding Tung-shan's response, Yüan-wu remarks that some students suppose that Tung-shan was in the temple storeroom at the time, weighing out flax for the market.[5] Thus they render Tung-shan's reply to mean "This flax weighs three pounds." Indeed, flax was important for monks as it was made into linen for their robes. But the words "this" and "weigh" do not appear in the original, which is simply *Ma san-ching* (*Masangin*—"Flax three pounds"). Senzaki Sensei's poem is to the point:

> What is Buddha?
> Masangin.
> What is Buddha?
> Masangin.
> What is Buddha?
> The third stick of incense has just burned off.[6]

That's all, folks! As Wu-men says in another context, "Because it's so very clear, / it takes so long to realize."[7] Tung-shan's response is like that of the child who hears a siren and cries out "Fire engine!" No mistake, crystal clear! Altogether convincing!

To be convincing is to communicate beyond the shadow of a doubt. If your manner conveys one message and your words another, you are not communicating. I recall going to Yamada Rōshi with what I was sure was the point of a kōan. He disapproved and sent me back to my cushions for more work. I explored the matter as deeply as I could, but did not find any other point. So I returned and made what I thought was the same presentation as before. This time he approved. I said, "That is exactly the response I gave last time." The rōshi said, "I wasn't convinced." It seems that with my additional work I had grown more intimate with the kōan—and with the universe. And thus on the second try my manner was more in keeping with the fact. I was able to communicate at last.

One reason we appreciate young children is that the pale cast of thought is absent from their responses—and they appreciate *us* when we can play their game. Many haiku, especially those of Bashō, are splendid examples of the directness of the child:

> You light the fire
> and I'll show you something nice—
> a huge ball of snow![8]

Yün-men is closer to Tung-shan than Bashō and just as straightforward, as I quoted earlier:

> A monk asked Yün-men, "What is the discourse that transcends Buddhas and Ancestral Teachers?"
> Yün-men said, "Rice cake."[9]

The fact and its rich presentation are one in Yün-men and in Tung-shan. With their "Rice cake" and "Three pounds of flax," they evoke the unswerving candor they retained from the beginning. Thus they enter the Kingdom of Heaven, and without their spirit we cannot follow.

Wu-men comments: "Old Man Tung-shan attained something of clam-Zen." What is clam-Zen? Very simple. Open up and show everything! Close up and show nothing! "He opened the two halves of his shell a bit and exposed his liver and intestines." Just a bit, just three words in the original—just three syllables: *Ma san-ching*. As Yamada Rōshi says, "Actually just *Ma!* would be enough. Just *Mmmm!* would be enough."[10] "Be that as it may," Wu-men continues, "tell me: where do you see Tung-shan?" Trot him out!

Wu-men exclaims in his verse, "Thrusting forth 'three pounds of flax!'" What is this thrusting forth? *Crack!*[11] "Three pounds of flax!" Don't say, "Tung-shan was explaining in effect that by weighing out three pounds of flax he was Buddha in action." Blasphemy!

Here the greatness of Tung-shan becomes apparent. There is a noetic flavor, an insightful taste, to his "Three pounds of flax." The flavor of knowledge, of wisdom, of understanding, infuses "Three pounds of flax!"—"Rice cake!"—"Oak tree in the garden!"—even "*Kaaats'!*"

When someone begins a kōan presentation by saying, "Well, I think the teacher is saying . . . ," I want to interrupt: "Mistaken already!" "Well, I think he is saying . . . " begins a discourse that takes the subject back to its place in history a thousand or more years ago. The intimacy set forth by Wu-men—"the hair of your eyebrows entangled with theirs, seeing with the same eyes, hearing with the same ears"—is nowhere to be seen, heard, or felt. "Well, I think he is saying . . . " shows nothing of your liver and intestines, not even your skin.

Showing and being shown is kenshō. Kenshō, however, is only the initial inspiration. It opens the way, and practice follows on cushions and in everyday life. Work in the interview room is one such practice—to tangle eyebrows with me and with Tung-shan. Only in tangling is there life. Discursive explanation is too often the way of death.

"Words are intimate, mind is more so." Intimacy is what we are about as Zen students. Standing off is misery. Notice your emotions. When you are standing off, for whatever reason, you are miserable. Some people decide that they are miserable, as a delinquent child might decide that he or she is bad. "That's bad!" then confirms a mistaken self-image.

I learned when I worked in a juvenile hall many years ago that if I said to a boy, "You seem to be straightening out pretty well these days," he would immediately mess up in some way. Perhaps this was because I objectified him and distanced myself. But if I took him to task and gave him hell for something, he would come around a little later and ask, "Want to play a game of ping-pong?" This is hopeful, but a long way from true intimacy.

Wu-men understood this human tendency very well. "If you argue right and wrong / you are a person of right and wrong." It is very simple: when you hold yourself aloof from Tung-shan, then that's the kind of person you will be. If you want to interpret, then you will be an interpretive person. If you decide you want to be right, then you will be a righteous person, self-righteous, in fact. If you decide to be intimate, then you and Tung-shan can squat on the same zafu—you and your protagonist in the family or on the job or in the Buddha Sangha can hold hands and work together. This is Zen on your cushions and in your daily life. This is Buddha if anything is.

Wu-men and Freud tangle here. You do everything on purpose. What is your purpose? If you wish to present "Three pounds of flax," then you can be a presentational person. You will have clam-Zen down cold. Open up and show!

Nan-ch'üan: "Ordinary Mind Is the Tao"

THE CASE

Chao-chou asked Nan-ch'üan, "What is the Tao?"

Nan-ch'üan said, "Ordinary mind is the Tao."

Chao-chou asked, "Should I try to direct myself toward it?"

Nan-ch'üan said, "If you try to direct yourself you betray your own practice."

Chao-chou asked, "How can I know the Tao if I don't direct myself?"

Nan-ch'üan said, "The Tao is not subject to knowing or not knowing. Knowing is delusion; not knowing is blankness. If you truly reach the genuine Tao, you will find it as vast and boundless as outer space. How can this be discussed at the level of affirmation and negation?"

With these words, Chao-chou had sudden realization.

WU-MEN'S COMMENT

Questioned by Chao-chou, Nan-ch'üan lost no time in showing the smashed tile and the melted ice, where no explanation is possible. Though Chao-chou had realization, he could confirm it only after another thirty years of practice.

WU-MEN'S VERSE

Spring comes with flowers, autumn with the moon,
summer with breeze, winter with snow.
When idle concerns don't hang in your mind,
that is your best season.

Chao-chou came to Nan-ch'üan when he was eighteen years old, and this dialogue probably took place not long thereafter.[1] He was deep-minded, but not yet mature, caught up in the travail of Zen students and of students of all religions who have done with building and collecting for permanence and aren't sure what comes next.

"How should I practice?" he is asking. Some Zen teachers try to intensify this natural anxiety in their students by deliberately frustrating them, hoping they will finally be cornered and somehow break through to a realization of their true nature.[2] There is a fine line between this kind of treatment and Nan-ch'üan's method of bringing Chao-chou's inherent doubt into focus and then into resolution. While it is true that his responses to Chao-chou's questions could be called frustrating, actually they just frustrate Chao-chou's mistaken tendencies and allow his profoundly human longing to bear fruit.

"What is the Tao?" The word "Tao" has become English, and its meaning, "Way," resonates with our nomadic heritage—hunting and gathering, always on the move. This life of travel was a difficult existence, and Bruce Chatwin relates it to "travail."[3] The Buddha Tao is the travail of spiritual longing; it is also the broad avenue of fulfilled spiritual purpose.

In the Chinese language, "Tao" is an ancient word so central to Chinese culture that it designates one of China's primary religions, Taoism. Its use in Buddhism reflects the early translators' practice of replacing Sanskrit terms with indigenous Chinese words.[4] They used it both for *bodhi* (enlightenment) and for Dharma, the Second Treasure of Buddhism, which itself has many implications: the teaching, the practice, the void, the nature of things, the Law of Karma, and things themselves. Thus "Buddha Dharma" becomes "Buddha Tao"—Fu-tao, or Butsudō in Japanese, the Dharma or Way of the Buddha.

When Buddhism appeared in Japan in the sixth century, priests of the indigenous religion codified their own practice and called it Shintō, the

Tao of the Gods. As various Japanese arts developed—tea ceremony, flower arrangement, archery, and so on—these too were Tao: Chadō, the Way of Tea; Kadō, the Way of Flowers; Kyūdō, the Way of Archery; also Judō, Kendō, Aikidō—a long list. I should also note that the Tao of Taoism played a most important role in the acculturation of Dhyāna Buddhism, the meditative practice brought to China by Bodhidharma. My teacher Senzaki Sensei used to say, "Taoism is the mother of Zen, and Dhyāna Buddhism is the father."[5]

So for the student of Zen Buddhism, "Tao" is a word that echoes and re-echoes. When Chao-chou asks Nan-ch'üan, "What is the Tao?"—he is asking a most fundamental question. Yet Nan-ch'üan finds it not fundamental enough. Notice that in the course of their dialogue, Nan-ch'üan does not answer Chao-chou's questions in the way that Chao-Chou seems to anticipate. Rather, he picks out the most profound implication and responds *there*. He stands on his own two feet and is not drawn into Chao-chou's concerns about how to practice.

"Ordinary mind is the Tao." The Chinese compound I translate as "ordinary" also means "usual" or "normal." The etymology is "constant" or "eternal." The everyday is the eternal, and this is reminiscent of Yün-men's declaration that every day is a good day.[6]

C. Y. Chang quotes an old Zen poem in connection with this case:

> What our eyes see is "ordinary":
> it does not frighten people,
> but it always remains
> like the moonlight on the chilled window;
> even at midnight it shines on thatched cottages.[7]

This constant "ordinary" is not the commonplace mind of self-centered preoccupation. Selfish conduct, speech, and thought obscure the vast, moonlit mind of Nan-ch'üan.

Nan-ch'üan is pointing to transformation here. Standing up before realization is the same as standing up after, yet they are not the same. Once you find intimacy with vast emptiness—the genuine Tao—your act of standing will be the act of the entire universe standing. And in the same act you will be standing alone.

In asking, "Shall I direct myself toward it?" Chao-Chou doesn't grasp Nan-ch'üan's "ordinary mind." He presses on with his real concern: "How should I practice?"

All Zen students can resonate with this question. I resonate with it. In late 1961 and early 1962, Anne Aitken and I lived on the outskirts of Tokyo and practiced with Yasutani Rōshi. We communicated with him surprisingly well, though he spoke no English, I spoke only broken Japanese, and Anne spoke no Japanese at all. Still, some of our subtle questions went unanswered. When Nakagawa Sōen Rōshi wrote us that he would be coming to Tokyo from his temple in Mishima, both of us looked forward to the chance to ask about our practice in detail. But I was sick when the day came, so Anne went by herself and asked my question: "Should I use effort or not?" This question preoccupies many students and is essentially what Chao-Chou asks: "Should I direct myself toward it or not?" Anne came back late in the day, exhilarated as one always was after being with Sōen Rōshi, full of stories of her encounter. Finally, I was able to ask about my question. She laughed and replied: "He said, 'That is a very difficult question.' " Perhaps he was suggesting, like Nan-ch'üan, that I was caught up with purpose and method.

When Chao-chou asked, "Should I direct myself toward it?" Nan-ch'üan responded, "If you direct yourself, you betray your own practice." Nan-ch'üan is saying, in effect: "You are setting up a division here, one seeking the other. Zen practice is not a matter of grasping at something." Of course he is not denying the importance of practice. But Kuan-yin has not directed herself toward or away from the Tao. Kuan-yin in her diligent practice is all right just as she is.

But this wasn't enough for Chao-chou and he pressed on with admirable spirit: "How can I know the Tao if I don't direct myself?" He probably sensed the separation implied in his question, but he didn't know the alternative middle way of neither directing nor not-directing.

Nan-ch'üan patiently brings Chao-chou back—brings us all back—to the point with his ensuing response. I used to think this kōan was very discursive. How could it enlighten anyone? Surely, Zen words should be sharp—like "Three pounds of flax!" I still feel that Nan-ch'üan is being very grandmotherly. But that is the nature of the true teacher, patient beyond reason, repeating the same message over and over: "Sink into Mu, settle into Mu, let everything else go." The ash from that incense fills several pots.

"The Tao is not subject to knowing or not knowing." Nan-ch'üan is saying that the Tao is not to be found simply in your relative world of trying and not trying, knowing and not knowing, attaining and not attaining.

To direct yourself toward something is to postulate attainment. Postulation thus replaces attainment—and true attainment is out the window. You are left clinging to something conjectural.

"Knowing is delusion." This reminds me of the condolence story in *The Blue Cliff Record*:

> Tao-wu and Chien-yüan went to a house to pay condolences. Chien-yüan rapped on the coffin and asked, "Living or dead?"
> Tao-wu said, "I won't say living; I won't say dead."
> Chien-yüan asked, "Why won't you say?"
> Tao-wu said, "I won't say! I won't say!"[8]

Like Nan-ch'üan, Tao-wu knew the grave risks of knowing. Yet he also knew that "not knowing is blankness." Tao-wu, like Bodhidharma, "did not know," but there is more than one kind of not-knowing. Yasutani Rōshi used to say there were three kinds of silence in the interview room. One is: "My silence is my presentation." The second is temporizing: "Let's see what the Old Boss will do." The third is blankness: "Duuuh!"

"If you truly reach the genuine Tao, you will find it as vast and boundless as outer space." This is like Bodhidharma's response to Emperor Wu's question, "What is the first principle of the holy teaching?"—"Vast emptiness, nothing holy."[9] Can this be discussed at the level of affirmation and negation? No Way.

Wu-men comments: "Questioned by Chao-chou, Nan-ch'üan lost no time in showing the smashed tile and the melted ice, where no explanation is possible." Nan-ch'üan was long-winded, but he didn't explain anything. He just showed the charred remains after the firestorm.

"Though Chao-chou had realization, he could confirm it only after another thirty years of practice." As I commented in the preceding case, kenshō is just the initial inspiration. Some people suppose that it will somehow do their work for them. This is like expecting the honeymoon to sustain the marriage. Nonsense. The honeymoon does not guarantee you a happy marriage any more than admission to graduate school guarantees you tenure somewhere. Move on from your milestones. Practice! Practice!

Wu-men's verse reads:

> Spring comes with flowers, autumn with the moon,
> summer with breeze, winter with snow.
> When idle concerns don't hang in your mind,
> that is your best season.

A lovely poem, but what are "idle concerns?" "Oh," some people say, "concepts, thoughts, ruminations, fantasies." That's a bit general—and not, I think, what Wu-men intended specifically. The entire verse is about seasons and how to enjoy your own season—how to enjoy your own ordinary mind. What is your best season?

Sung-yüan's Person of Great Strength

THE CASE

*The priest Sung-yüan asked, "Why can't the person of great strength lift up a leg?"
Again he said, "It is not with the tongue that you speak."*

WU-MEN'S COMMENT

*Sung-yüan certainly emptied his stomach and turned out his guts. However, there
is no one who can acknowledge him. Yet even if someone could immediately acknowledge him, I would give him a painful blow with my stick if he came to me. Why?
Look! If you want to know true gold, you must perceive it in the midst of fire.*

WU-MEN'S VERSE

*Lifting my leg, I kick the Scented Ocean upside down;
inclining my head, I look down on the Four Dhyāna Heavens;
there is no place to put my complete body—
please add the final line here.*

Sung-yüan (Shōgen) was a master of the Lin-chi line who died in 1202 at
the age of seventy-one. The teaching was generally in decline during his
time, but Sung-yüan stood out as a master vigorous in realization. We ven-
erate him particularly as the great-grandfather in the Dharma of Dai-ō

Kokushi, who established an enduring stream of Rinzai Zen in Japan. Thus he is in the direct line of our own heritage.

Yamada Rōshi tells us that when Sung-yüan was nearing the end of his life, he posed three questions as turning words to his disciples. The first two form this case. The third question was: "Why is it that someone of great satori does not cut off the vermilion thread?"[1] I understand the vermilion thread to be the line of blood itself—the line of menstruation, sexuality, and birth. We take up this question elsewhere, in the introductory phase of our kōan study, not to mention our daily lives.

Sung-yüan had received a robe as symbol of transmission from his own teacher, Mi-an (Mittan). He wanted very much to transmit this robe in turn to a worthy successor, but no one could answer his questions and he put the robe away. Later, after his death, Yün-an (Un'an) was declared his successor—and all of us become his successors when we personalize his intention.

"Why can't the person of great strength lift up a leg?" This is an echo of a case in the *Book of Serenity*:

> Lo-p'u addressed his assembly and said, "I have one matter to ask you about. If you say, 'Yes, that's right,' you are putting another head above your own. If you say, 'No, that's not right,' you are looking for life by cutting off your head."
> A monk stepped forward and said, "Green Mountain always lifts up its legs."[2]

Why can't the person of great strength lift up a leg? How is it that Green Mountain is always lifting its legs? It is possible to explain away these paradoxes by saying the person of great strength symbolizes one thing and Green Mountain another, but with such an explanation we terminate Sung-yüan's succession.

Kōans should be approached essentially—which is to say, personally. You yourself are the agent of all this paradox. It is deep in your own realization of Mu, deep in the universal realization of Mu, that Sung-yüan's mind becomes clear. Then Green Mountain, Sung-yüan, the person of great strength, and you yourself all fit on a single cushion.

"The person of great strength" is strong in realization and in integrating realization into daily life. Athletes provide an analogy, and their writings can be very interesting for the Zen student. When an athlete is "up," it is as though he or she were floating, as well as driving hard. Hands rise spontaneously to catch the ball, legs work naturally to run. It is as though the player is in a dream.

When I was ten years old, we lived at the corner of 14th and Harding avenues in the suburb of Kaimuki in Honolulu. One Sunday afternoon we heard the sound of a car accident two blocks away. My father jumped from his chair, ran the two blocks, and found a small crowd of people watching a man trying vainly to lift a car off his wife. Apparently she had been thrown from the vehicle and was then run over. Brushing through the on-lookers, Dad stepped to the car, lifted it up, and the man was able to drag his wife from beneath the wheel.

In those days, of course, cars were lighter than they are today, but lifting the vehicle unaided was a great feat nevertheless. Dad had at that time about the same build that I have now, tall and thin, with no more than average strength. Afterward he marveled that he had achieved such a thing, remarking that nothing seemed to be in his mind from the time he arose from his chair to the time he released the weight of the car from his friend and then helped to look after her. Perhaps the fact that the couple were close family friends lent him some power.

Most people have such peak experiences to one degree or another—in nature, in athletics, in sex, and so forth. Though they can be related by analogy to Sung-yüan's metaphor, they are not the same. His person of great strength steps *beyond* the peak experience into lifetime transformation. Thoughts were gone temporarily from my father's head and he was in an altered state of consciousness, but I don't think he was particularly changed by his experience. With the Great Death of realization—death to a life of abstraction and birth to intimacy with things as they are—the root of conceptual thinking is plucked out. Maintain the garden of your Zen study and don't let it grow back!

A man of great strength once stood up after zazen at the Koko An Zendō. With that standing up, the universe stood up. His *idea* of standing up was erased. Like the patient of a skillful dentist, he felt only relief. He has enjoyed his loss ever since, deepening and clarifying it.

What is great strength? I'm not sure I can put it in words. It rings like a fine bell, however, and there is no mistaking it. What is great weakness? It is a return to categorical thinking, to summarizing, to generalizing, to abstracting.

Sung-yüan's next question is in the form of a statement: "It is not with the tongue that you speak." There are many kōans similar to this—in fact, there are three in a row in *The Blue Cliff Record*, where Pai-chang asks his disciples, "How would you say something with your lips and throat closed?" The ensuing dialogues make it clear that a casual response won't do.[3]

Shibayama Rōshi rewords Sung-yüan's command to run parallel with Sung-yüan's first question: "Why is it that a person of great strength does not use the tongue in speaking?"—pointing out that "why?" is the key word to both kōans.[4] "Why do you put on your seven-piece robe at the sound of the bell?"

Frequently people ask about the inquiring spirit that is so often mentioned as a requisite of Zen practice. They worry about whether or not they have enough of it. To inquire about inquiry may be all right in the beginning, but sooner or later one must just sink in to that "why?" Being stuck in the anxiety of "why?" is the same as being stuck in Mu. After your Great Death, your successor will come along.

Wu-men comments: "Sung-yüan certainly emptied his stomach and turned out his guts." He showed everything. Wu-men is unqualified in his approval. "However, there is no one who can acknowledge him." No one in Sung-yüan's assembly could acknowledge him, and Wu-men scolds us for our failure too. "If someone could immediately acknowledge him, I would give him a painful blow with my stick if he came to me. Why?" There's that "why" again.

"*Look!* If you want to know true gold, you must perceive it in the midst of fire." It is only in the furnace that pure gold is smelted. It is only in the furnace of the Great Death that the most brilliant realization emerges. Sung-yüan's spirit and the spirit of his Lin-chi tradition, which includes Wu-men, is there in the challenge of your practice: "Not yet!" "Not enough!" "Not enough yet!"

Wu-men's verse reads: "Lifting my leg, I kick the Scented Ocean upside down." This is a reference to the Hua-yen cosmology which, in the words of Thomas Cleary, "represents the world system resting on an ocean of fragrant water, symbolizing the 'repository consciousness' wherein are stored all experiential impressions."[5]

"Inclining my head, I look down on the Four Dhyāna Heavens." The Four Dhyāna Heavens are progressively lofty realms of unimaginable liberation, purity, harmony, and wisdom. The person of great strength who does not lift up a leg is identical with the one who turns everything over in the vastness of space—identical with the one who views the expansive universe and the accomplishments of all its beings from the loftiest vantage.

"There is no place to put my complete body." The whole universe is full already. Well, be careful. Wu-men can't sustain such a pretentious stance for long.

"Please add the final line here." The original just says, "Please continue one line." This is not a test of your prosody. It's a test of your whole life!

CASE 21

Yün-men's Dried Shitstick

THE CASE

A monk asked Yün-men, "What is Buddha?"
  Yün-men said, "Dried shitstick."

WU-MEN'S COMMENT

It must be said of Yün-men that he was too poor to prepare even the plainest food and too busy to make a careful draft. Probably people will bring forth this dried shitstick to shore up the gate and prop up the door. The Buddha Dharma is thus sure to decay.

WU-MEN'S VERSE

  A flash of lightning,
    sparks from flint;
  if you blink your eyes,
    it's already gone.

Yün-men was a tenth-century teacher, a student of Hsüeh-feng, who went on to become one of the truly great luminaries of the classical period of Chinese Zen. He was renowned for his succinct presentations. Here's an example from C. Y. Chang's *Original Teachings of Ch'an Buddhism:*[1]

> What is the true Dharma eye?
> Universal!

That's a single word of a single syllable in Chinese. The meaning has no bounds, and there is only one way to present it. As D. T. Suzuki used to say, "When you raise one corner of a table, the whole table comes up." Now here's another:

> What is the sword of Yün-men?
> Ancestral!

Don't suppose that Yün-men is saying that he's wielding the sword of his ancestors. He would cut you down!

> What is the straight path to Yün-men?
> Intimate!

As I remarked in my comment to Case 18, such presentations as "Intimate!" have a noetic flavor. They are insightful, that is, yet they are not logical discourses. Yüan-wu summed up the traditional analysis of Yünmen's teaching method as:

> Containing the whole world,
> cutting off the myriad streams,
> following the waves.[2]

This can be interpreted as (1) including the lucid reality of phenomena—mountains, rivers, towers, highways, people, animals, plants, stones, clouds—living and yet fundamentally empty, (2) cutting off myriad speculations and interpretations, and (3) allowing the presence of others, understanding them, and responding to them accordingly—a large order filled by Yün-men each time he took the high seat.

Sometimes Yün-men did speak a little more at length, often with simple words of encouragement, but inevitably he would end up with a vital presentation:

When Yün-men arrived to take up duties as the new master of a monastery, he was honored with a tea ceremony. After the ceremony, he was asked to give a talk, so he took the high seat and said, "Since you have all gathered here, it is incumbent on me to make some remarks. May I point out the way of truth which was transmitted by our ancestors? Be careful!"[3]

Be careful! That's it! That is the way of truth transmitted by our ancestors. Thus Yün-men brings forth the precise thunderbolt that shatters everything.

It is said that Yün-men would not permit his students to take notes. "What good is recording my words and tying up your tongues?" However, one of his senior disciples wore paper robes to meetings and secretly made extensive notes on his sleeves. Thanks to his disobedience, we have a comprehensive record of this marvelous teacher and across space, time, and culture we can enjoy Dharma Combat with him.[4]

Now about the dried shitstick. It seems that it was a soft stick that was used the way our ancestors used a corncob in their outhouses. I am old enough to remember seeing a withered corncob on a string in my grandparents' outhouse in Upper Lake, California. Hanging beside it was an old Sears-Roebuck catalog with pages torn out. And beside that was a packet of toilet paper. It was a time of transition in rural American hygiene.

Apparently the term was used as an epithet—as in "You shithead!" We find Lin-chi using it in this way elsewhere in our kōan study:

> Lin-chi took the high seat and said, "On your lump of red flesh, there is a person of no rank going in and out of your faces. If you beginners have not yet proved that one—look! Look!"
>
> A monk stepped forward and asked, "What is the true person of no rank?"
>
> Lin-chi descended from the high seat and seized him. The monk hesitated. Lin-chi pushed him away and said, "The true person of no rank—what a dried shitstick!"[5]

Nakakawa Sōen Rōshi had a great teishō on this case which I recount elsewhere.[6] That was back in the 1960s, when people were not so used to hearing the word "shit" in polite society. On and on he would ramble, telling story after story about shit. We laughed in shocked delight and at the same time felt a fine sense of liberation. My own shit story prompted a poem. In the Japanese internment camp where I was held during World War II, I was awed by the vitality of our sump of night soil, ripening for use in the garden:

> In fermenting night soil
> fat white maggots
> steam with Buddhahood.[7]

Like Sōen Rōshi's stories, this is a digression. Yün-men is not merely challenging you to put aside your ideals of purity—that goes without saying. It has nothing to do with "Shitstick!" Nor does the usual scholarly commentary: "Yün-men was not making disparaging remarks about [the Buddha] here. Rather he was making a dramatic attempt to nullify all religious dogma, which is only a hindrance to the total realization of one's own Buddha-nature"[8] This is okay as far as it goes. But, regrettably, it is not at all to the point.

Please don't try to work on this kōan—or any kōan—by logic. If you say, "Everything is Buddha, shit is one thing, therefore shit is Buddha"— then you are off the mark. You miss it completely. Nor does the point lie merely in the succinctness of Yün-men's presentation. Don't suppose because Zen responses are often brief that brevity is the essence of their significance. Polonius said, "Brevity is the soul of wit"—but actually it is not. Brevity is often the form of wit, but what is its soul?

Wu-men comments: "It must be said of Yün-men that he was too poor to prepare even the plainest food and too busy to make a careful draft." Yes, Yün-men was voluntarily poor at explaining. He wasted no time in cooking up food for thought, no time in formulating a tidy summary. Even the shit was dried up on his stick. Yet it looms up and takes over, reaching to the Tusita Heaven where Maitreya Buddha stirs in his deep samādhi. It won't be long now!

"Probably people will bring forth the dried shitstick to shore up the gate and prop up the door." Probably, Wu-men is saying, in the future people will shout "Dried shitstick!" in an effort to dazzle students and keep the Dharma going. But what can come of such fakery? "The Buddha Dharma is thus sure to decay."

I take this caution seriously. Charisma is an amber light, maybe even a red light. If people are inexperienced, they might be dazzled and then waste a lot of time with teachers who shout and wave their arms. Ultimately you will see through the fakery, but with your disappointment your deep motive to realize the Dharma might disappear. Be careful. What appears to be creative might just be trumped up. Give your intuition a chance to bring a teacher to the test. Worthy teaching will reveal the nameless that is vast and fathomless, it will cut off speculation, and it will be faithful to the one who is taught.

Wu-men's verse reads: "A flash of lightning, / sparks from flint." Yün-men's light plays brilliantly about our ancient house.

"If you blink your eyes, / it's already gone." Or, as Yün-men urged his new students, "Be careful!" Pay attention, as Dōgen says, as though your head were on fire![9]

CASE 22

Mahākāśyapa's Flagpole

THE CASE

Ānanda asked Mahākāśyapa, "The World-Honored One transmitted the robe of gold brocade to you. What else did he transmit to you?"

Kāśyapa said, "Ānanda!"

Ānanda answered, "Yes!"

Kāśyapa said, "Knock down the flagpole at the gate."

WU-MEN'S COMMENT

If you can give a turning word that is intimate to this case, then you will see that the meeting at Mount Grdhrakūta is still vigorously in session. If you cannot, then Vipaśyin Buddha, who has been striving from earliest times, has not yet attained true subtlety.

WU-MEN'S VERSE

"The call is good, the answer is intimate"—
how many discuss this with glaring eyes!
Elder brother calls, younger brother answers—the family disgrace;
there is a spring that does not belong to Yin and Yang.

Mahākāśyapa was a Brahman of India in the fifth century B.C. who succeeded the Buddha Śākyamuni as the first Ancestral Teacher of our lineage. His name in its abbreviated form is the same as that of the Buddha Kāśyapa—a mythological personage, the sixth of the Ancient Seven Buddhas, preceding Śākyamuni in the great dream lineage.

During Śākyamuni's life, Mahākāśyapa was one of his most prominent disciples, renowned especially for his grasp of the Vinaya, the moral teachings. After the Buddha's death, Mahākāśyapa convened a great council of five hundred elders to codify their master's teaching. He was elected chairman of the council and served as interlocutor in discussions of the Vinaya and the Dharma. Thus he is in large measure responsible for the establishment of classical Buddhism.

Ānanda was a younger cousin, possibly nephew, of Śākyamuni Buddha. It is said that he was born on the very night that Śākyamuni experienced his great realization. He served the Buddha as his attendant for the last twenty years of the Buddha's life. Later at the great council of elders, he was selected to recite the Buddha's teishōs as he remembered them, for he had perfect recall. He could even set forth those which were given when he was a child too young to attend them. This was truly perfect recall! So every sutra begins with Ānanda's words, "Thus I have heard."[1]

Perfect recall is not necessarily a talent that affords ready kenshō. Like other geniuses among our ancestors in the Dharma, Ānanda had a hard time initially in the practice. In fact, he was unable to realize his essential nature during the Buddha's lifetime. Ultimately, however, he found his intelligence to be an asset in his teaching.

In this case, Ānanda shows himself to be preoccupied with transmission. He says to Mahākāśyapa, "The World-Honored One transmitted to you the robe of gold brocade. What else did he transmit?" Was it something tangible? Something mystical? Many cases in our kōan study examine the subject of transmission. *The Gateless Barrier* includes two in addition to this story: Case 6, the account of Mahākāśyapa's own transmission, and Case 23, "Neither Good Nor Evil," in which the head monk Ming seeks to rectify what he and his brothers suppose to be an error in transmission. Thus we are impressed with the weighty nature of this subject. But at one point Wu-men comments, "If you say the eye treasury can be transmitted, that would be as if the gold-faced old fellow were swindling people in a loud voice at the town gate. If you say the eye treasury cannot be transmitted, then why did the Buddha say he transmitted it to Mahākāśyapa?"[2]

In the T'ang and Sung periods of China it was the custom for a teacher to present his own portrait to his student as a sign of transmission. From the Kamakura period in Japan onward, the teacher's calligraphy conveying the disciple's new teacher-name has been the token. But again, like the robe of the Buddha, such things are only symbols, bits of paper, fingers pointing to something.

Mahākāśyapa responds to Ānanda's question directly. He does not say, "Don't preoccupy yourself with transmission." Rather, he calls out, "Ānanda!" Nothing gets one's attention more keenly than hearing one's name.

Ānanda says, "Yes!" In Case 10, Ch'ing-shui replies in the same way to Ts'ao-shan with the same consummation. But the subsequent responses of the two teachers differ, at least in expression.

In *Zen in English Literature*, R. H. Blyth tells about his first experience of listening to a teishō on *The Gateless Barrier*—perhaps it was on this very case. The rōshi kept saying, "When someone calls 'Hello!' you should respond 'Yes!' " He repeated "Hello!" and "Yes!" so often that Blyth began to watch for them as a kind of joke.[3] It *is* a kind of joke—roosters and dogs and children know all about it. When the son of one of our Koko An Zendō members was four years old, he would say to his mother, "Guess what?" She would respond "What?" He would then shout "That's what!"—and go off into gales of laughter. This joke took a year or so to get used up. Zen students know about such jokes, too, I hope. Lin-chi and his people certainly did, or so it seems by the way they were always shouting at one another.[4] Everybody laughs, and every leaf of every tree is shaken.

When the telephone rings: *Ring!* That is the only sound anywhere! When your child cries out "Telephone!" in response, that is the only sound anywhere! The whole universe rings! The whole universe cries "Telephone!" It's the call we've been waiting for.

When you have thrown everything away—all thoughts of yourself, all thoughts of transmission to yourself—then the whole universe shouts "*Hello!*" Just "*Hello!*" And the whole universe shouts "*Yes!*" Just "*Yes!*" This is the fact of transmission.

Mahākāśyapa then says, "Knock down the flagpole at the gate." The flag is a banner run up to announce that the rōshi is giving a teishō today. Some students say, "Mahākāśyapa means, 'Pull down the flag, there is no need for a teishō.' " Of course, in one sense no teishō is needed. Is that the meaning here? He doesn't just say, "Pull down the flag." He cries out, "Knock down the pole, flag and all!" This is the denouement.

Wu-men comments: "If you can give a turning word that is intimate to this case, then you will see that the meeting at Mount Grdhrakūta is still vigorously in session." It was at Mount Grdhrakūta, the legend of Case 6 says, that the Buddha twirled a flower and Mahākāśyapa smiled—and the Dharma was transmitted for the first time.

Twirling the flower was a calling out. Smiling was a response. Mahākāśyapa and Ānanda continue the meeting, as we do in our own dialogues. What is Mu? When you respond, you are wearing the Buddha's robe of gold brocade.

Take another look at Wu-men's comment, "If you can give a turning word that is intimate to this case . . ." Intimate! Over and over we find this word stressed in Zen study. When you are intimate you are one with. When you are not intimate, you are in your head, separated, lost in your thoughts, unable to hear.

To be intimate with Mahākāśyapa and Ānanda is to realize the treasure of calling and answering. This realization is transformational—in the family, in the Buddha Sangha, in the workplace, one is warmhearted, kind, and generous. The person who understands Zen as something limited to his or her own samādhi cannot be truly intimate. "Tough-guy" Zen is a *travesty* of Zen. This is a most important point.

And if you cannot be intimate, then "Vipaśyin Buddha, who has been striving from earliest times, has not yet attained true subtlety." Vipaśyin Buddha was the very first of the Ancient Seven Buddhas. He appeared in earliest mythological times—earlier than Adam, one might say. From the very beginning Vipaśyin Buddha—you yourself—has been struggling to realize essential nature and still he can't readily answer "Yes!"

Wu-men's verse reads: "The call is good, the answer is intimate—/ how many discuss this with glaring eyes!" Many people argue whether the call "Ānanda!" or the response "Yes!" was closer to the point. T'ang period monks liked to argue the Dharma among themselves, even as Zen students today fall into disputes about crucial points. Nan-ch'üan stepped in on one such occasion, in Case 14, and we get the sense that other teachers strongly disapproved of such arguments. I myself find them to be quite natural, even helpful, in moderation. Like reading Zen books, discussing points found in the old texts can be a kind of teishō or personal interview. Some of my colleagues would not approve, but I think it is better to trust people to exhaust their speculative proclivities naturally. For if they are ardent students of zazen, they will learn to discriminate truth from error in the disputative process and eventually their speculation will be supplanted by expositions of the Buddha Way.

"Elder brother calls, younger brother answers—the family disgrace." Wu-men is referring to the family he cherished most of all. What is the disgrace? See into Wu-men's irony here.[5]

Finally we come to the "spring that does not belong to Yin and Yang." This is the only reference to Yin and Yang in our kōan study, despite all the stress given to them in some practices that take the name of Zen. According to Taoist philosophy, they are the polarities of life: action and passivity, light and dark, male and female, acid and alkaline. These are useful points of reference, but they do not touch the essential matter. What is the season that does not belong to Yin and Yang?

Interpret this final line in the context of the kōan, and also in terms of everyday life. What is the spring that does not belong to Yin and Yang in relation to Mahākāśyapa and Ānanda? How would you realize it, say as you look out the window in the early morning?

Hui-neng: "Neither Good Nor Evil"

The Sixth Ancestor was pursued by Ming the head monk as far as Ta-yü Peak. The teacher, seeing Ming coming, laid the robe and bowl on a rock and said, "This robe represents the Dharma. There should be no fighting over it. You may take it back with you."

Ming tried to lift it up, but it was as immovable as a mountain. Shivering and trembling, he said, "I came for the Dharma, not for the robe. I beg you, lay brother, please open the Way for me."

The teacher said, "Don't think good; don't think evil. At this very moment, what is the original face of Ming the head monk?"

In that instant Ming had great satori. Sweat ran from his entire body. In tears he made his bows saying, "Beside these secret words and secret meanings, is there anything of further significance?"

The teacher said, "What I have just conveyed to you is not secret. If you reflect on your own face, whatever is secret will be right there with you."

Ming said, "Though I practiced at Huang-mei with the assembly, I could not truly realize my original face. Now, thanks to your pointed instruction, I am like someone who drinks water and knows personally whether it is cold or warm. Lay brother, you are now my teacher."

The teacher said, "If you can say that, then let us both call Huang-mei our teacher. Maintain your realization carefully."

PLATE 5: *Hung-jen and Hui-neng.* Courtesy of the Idemitsu
Museum of Arts. (Cases 23 and 29)

Paintings by proper artists follow laws;
Sengai's paintings follow none.
Buddha said the essential nature of the law is no law;
the no-law law is also the law.

> *Trans. by Norman Waddell* (See Notes, Case 23, n.3)

WU-MEN'S COMMENT

It must be said that the Sixth Ancestor forgets himself completely in taking action here. He is like a kindly grandmother who peels a fresh lychee, removes the seed, and puts it into your mouth. Then you only need to swallow it down.

WU-MEN'S VERSE

It can't be described; it can't be pictured.
It can't be praised enough; stop groping for it.
The Original Face has nowhere to hide.
When the world is destroyed, it is not destroyed.

Hui-neng was called the Sixth Ancestor because he was sixth in succession from Bodhidharma, who brought the seeds of Zen Buddhism to China. Hui-neng was born in 638, the son of a civil servant who lost his position and then died young, leaving his family penniless. It is said that Hui-neng had no schooling and that as a youth he peddled firewood to support himself and his mother. One day, while delivering wood to a customer, he heard a monk reciting the *Diamond Sutra*; his mind opened and he experienced deep realization. One tradition states that this moment occurred at the lines: "Dwell nowhere, and bring forth that mind."[1]

The young Hui-neng approached the monk and asked who his teacher might be. The monk said his teacher was the Fifth Ancestor, Hung-jen (Gunin), who lived a thousand or more miles away at the temple of Huang-mei (Ōbai) in North China. Hui-neng resolved to go there and study. A neighbor kindly agreed to support his mother, and Hui-neng set out like the young Śākyamuni to seek his spiritual fortune. Arriving finally at Huang-mei, so the story goes, he was shown into Hung-jen's presence. Hung-jen asked him:

> "Where are you from, that you come to this mountain making obeisance to me? What is it that you seek here?"
>
> Hui-neng said, "I come from Ling-nan in the South. I have come this long distance seeking no particular thing, only the Buddha Dharma."
>
> Hung-jen said, "If you are from Ling-nan, then you are a barbarian. How can you become a Buddha?"
>
> Hui-neng said, "Though people from the North and the South

are different, there is no north or south in the Dharma, or in Buddha Nature. Though my barbarian's body and your body are not the same, what difference is there in our Buddha Nature?"[2]

Hung-jen recognized the worth of his new student but assigned him to the harvesting shed to husk rice, no doubt awaiting developments.

A few months passed and Hung-jen felt the need to name a successor. He announced a contest for this purpose, saying, "Whoever believes he is worthy of transmission should submit a poem showing his understanding of the Way, and I will acknowledge the writer of the most cogent poem as next master in our line." All the monks felt that the leader of the assembly, Shen-hsiu (Jinshū), had the clearest insight of all, so none of them wrote anything. Shen-hsiu, however, wasn't sure of his own attainment. Instead of turning in a poem, he inscribed one anonymously on a wall that was being prepared for a mural. If it were approved, he could step forward and announce his authorship. If it were disapproved, he could just keep quiet. So he wrote:

> The body is the Bodhi Tree;
> the mind is like a clear mirror;
> moment by moment, wipe the mirror carefully;
> let there be no dust upon it.

Hung-jen praised this poem and had all his monks commit it to memory. He said nothing, however, about making its author his successor.

When Hui-neng heard a monk reciting the poem, he recognized immediately the limitation of its author's realization. Learning of the contest for the first time, he dictated his own poem to the monk, who wrote it on the wall beneath that of Shen-hsiu:

> Bodhi really has no tree;
> the mirror too has no stand;
> from the beginning there's nothing at all;
> where can any dust alight?

Although everyone was impressed with this second poem, there was quite a disturbance when it was rumored that the nondescript layman in the harvest shed had dictated it. Hung-jen recognized the worth of the poem, but he prudently rubbed it out with his slipper, saying it was of no value. That night, however, he summoned Hui-neng to his room and preached to him on the *Diamond Sutra*. Hui-neng grasped the inner sense of the sutra at once, and immediately Hung-jen conveyed the robe and bowl of Bodhidharma to him as symbols of transmission. Warning him that jealous monks would seek to do him harm if he remained at the monastery, the teacher personally rowed Hui-neng across the river and advised him to polish his realization secretly for some time before emerging as a teacher.[3] Next day, Hung-jen told his monks what had happened and they became agitated. Certain that their old teacher had made a mistake in choosing a young layman as his successor, they set out in pursuit of Hui-neng in order to bring back the precious symbols of transmission. Ming (Myō), the head monk, a former general who was powerful in body and will, soon outdistanced the others in the pursuit.[4] The story in the present case picks up here.

Is it a true story? From very early times, Buddhist history has been retold to present archetypal themes clearly. On examining the internal evidence, most scholars believe that Hui-neng could not have been illiterate. In fact, the historical validity of the entire *Sutra of Hui-neng* is doubtful.[5] Never mind. Scholars seek historical facts, Zen students seek religious themes. My own view is that where scholarship helps to clarify the themes, it can be very useful. The rest can distract the student of religion from resolving life-and-death questions.

Such chronicles as this should be read for their value as folk stories. And from that perspective, what a fine story it is! It is especially important for us to see the mythic import of Hui-neng's illiteracy, his lay status, and the defeat of Shen-hsiu. These elements teach us that the Tao is not established on words, that it is transmitted outside tradition, and that it is not concerned only with wiping away dusty thoughts. Other points of interest include Hung-jen's act of rowing his successor to the "other shore," a metaphor common to all world religions, the dangers of the kind of gossip and malice that distracted the monks at Huang-mei, and the importance of allowing one's realization to mature and not seeking to teach too soon. The whole case is an adult fairy story that orients our deepest consciousness to the Way.

As head monk, Ming must have had some understanding of the Dharma. Yet he allowed himself to be carried away by group perceptions.

This is all too human. With the drop of a hat, incautious Zen students including you and me will get drawn into group emotions and neglect the Buddha Way.

It seems, however, that with his exertions Ming's anger drained away and there was nothing left in his mind—just running after Hui-neng. The Sixth Ancestor, seeing him coming, laid the robe and bowl on a rock and said, "This robe represents the Dharma. There should be no fighting over it. You may take it back with you." These words must have been startling to Ming. He tried to lift up the robe, but it was immovable as a mountain. Ah! There you see the state of his mind! Suddenly he was in touch with the profound and subtle law of the Tathāgata: the Dharma cannot be transmitted by outward symbols, and it is vain to chase after them.

I am reminded of Frederick Franck's story of his conversion to vegetarianism. As a small child during World War I, he lived with his family in Holland, then a neutral country, less than a mile from the Belgian border, and so witnessed "the incomprehensible horror of seeing living human flesh in the tatters of German, Belgian, and French uniforms coming across the border on pushcarts and other improvised ambulances. It sensitized me against all forms of physical violence." During those childhood years, Franck was forced against his will to eat fish and meat and became preoccupied with a home-grown kōan: Is it more evil to eat whole sardines than a slice of cod? Finally, one day his doubts were resolved: "It happened in a restaurant when a fragrant *fillet de sole amandine* was put in front of me. I took my fork, but it refused to touch the fish; I ate the *pommes duchesse* and never knowingly ate animal flesh again."[6] The fork would not touch the fish, just as the robe would not budge for the head monk Ming. Now Ming had to take another step. Shivering and trembling, he said, "I come for the Dharma, not for the robe." He wasn't just making a defensive excuse; he had suddenly realized his own true intention. "I beg you, lay brother, open the Way for me." Thus he opens himself sincerely.

Hui-neng said, "Don't think good; don't think evil." This is an essential preamble to true realization. In the *Hsin-hsin ming* (*Shinjinmei*; "Precepts of the Faith") we read: "To set up what you like against what you dislike—this is the disease of the mind."[7] Comparisons are odious. I hear grown-up people say, "I don't like so-and-so." Such prejudice limits one's understanding of the Buddha nature of the world and its beings.

Rather than setting up "good and evil" in the mind, set up right views—the first step of the Eightfold Path. These are the views that are in keeping with the interdependence of things and their essential emptiness. "Don't think good; don't think evil" means really, "Find the silent place of essential harmony in your mind, and be ready for what might come."

Hui-neng goes on to say, "At this very moment, what is the original face of Ming the head monk?" This challenge is the source of the kōan "What is your original face before your parents were born?" For Ming it was a fresh, new, existential question, and he had great realization. Sweat ran from his entire body. In tears he asked, "Besides these secret words and secret meanings, is there anything of futher significance?"

Hui-neng answered, "What I have just conveyed to you is not secret. If you reflect on your own face, whatever is secret will be right there with you."

Ming said, "Though I practiced at Huang-mei with the assembly, I could not truly realize my original face." Ming's pursuit and Hui-neng's words give him a perspective that is altogether changed.

"Now, thanks to your pointed instruction, I am like one who drinks water and knows personally whether it is cold or warm." At last it is intimate. "Lay brother, you are now my teacher." Ming was ready to follow his new guide.

Hui-neng said, "If you can say that, then let us both call Huang-mei our teacher." Hui-neng had Hung-jen's caution in mind and was saying, in effect, "I must deepen my realization for a while." I cannot be your teacher at this time. You had best return to Huang-mei and bring peace to the monastery there."

This is not a kōan point, but it is important. Hung-jen's monastery was apparently a center of jealousy and distrust. The monks were upset that a mere layman had written a fine poem—and then that he had been selected as Hung-jen's successor. If there is no harmony in the Buddha's temple, how can its residents bring harmony to the world and fulfill their vows?

Finally, Hui-neng cautions the head monk Ming: "Maintain your realization carefully." This is advice for us all. Practice certainly does not end with realization.

Wu-men comments: "It must be said that the Sixth Ancestor forgets himself completely in taking action here." His body and mind fall away, in fact—and the needs of the head monk Ming stand paramount.

"He is like a kindly grandmother who peels a fresh lychee, removes the seed, and puts it into your mouth. Then you only need to swallow it down." Wu-men is not saying that Hui-neng explains everything discursively, but that his teaching is so effective that you only need to be present to understand it.

Wu-men's verse reads: "It can't be described; it can't be pictured; / it can't be praised enough; stop groping for it." *It* is your original face. *It* can be presented, but it's beyond praise and cannot be described. One can't generalize about it. It most assuredly is not something confined in a robe or a bowl, as Hui-neng understood very well. He wisely hid them away, and the practice of numbering ancestors stopped with him.

"The Original Face has nowhere to hide." It is not secret at all. There are no boundaries at all.

"When the world is destroyed, *it* is not destroyed." Why not?

Feng-hsüeh: Equality and Differentiation

THE CASE

A monk asked the priest Feng-hsüeh, "Speech and silence are concerned with equality and differentiation. How can I transcend equality and differentiation?"
Feng-hsüeh said,

> *I always think of Chiang-nan in March;*
> *partridges chirp among the many fragrant flowers.*

WU-MEN'S COMMENT

Feng-hsüeh functions like lightning, creating an appropriate way to practice. But why does he get involved with the tongue of a predecessor and not free himself? If you can see intimately into this point, the Way will open for you naturally. Now set aside the samādhi of words—just give me one phrase!

WU-MEN'S VERSE

> *It was not a verse of elegant tone!*
> *Before speaking, it's already expressed;*
> *if you go on chattering glibly,*
> *you'll find yourself at a loss.*

Feng-hsüeh (Fuketsu) was a tenth-century master in the Lin-chi line. Like Hakuin in Japan eight hundred years later, he was a key figure in the destiny of Lin-chi Zen, for in his generation he alone carried the burden of transmission, while the lines of his peers died out.

In this case an obviously philosophical monk asks him, "Speech and silence are concerned with equality and differentiation. How can I transcend equality and differentiation?" The Chinese terms here, *li* and *wei*, are set forth in a treatise on Buddhist philosophy attributed to the talented priest Seng-chao (Sōjō), who lived in the early fifth century. The two terms refer to two ways of perceiving: *li* is the "fundamentally equal"; *wei* is the "subtly differentiated."[1] The "fundamentally equal" is expressed in such lines as "Buddha nature pervades the whole universe."[2] It is the mystery of the Dharmakāya: quiet, void, yet richly potent. What, then, is the "subtly differentiated"?

> Yun-men addressed his assembly and said, "Each of you has your own light. If you try to see it, you cannot. It is dark, dark. Now, what is your light?"
>
> Answering for the group he said, "The kitchen pantry, the front gate."
>
> And he added, "It is better to have nothing than something good."[3]

Yun-men says it is better to have nothing than to have even such good things as Buddha nature and a sense of brilliant uniqueness. Well, I would say that slipping into a nice hot bath is even better than nothing.

The priest Seng-chao articulated *li* and *wei*, but he knew very well that ultimately they are not different. It is said that at age thirty-one Seng-chao got into political trouble and was sentenced to be executed. By his request, his sentence was stayed for a week, and during that time he composed the *Pao-tsang lun* (*Hōzōron*; *Jewel Treasury Treatise*), of which one chapter is taken up with *li* and *wei*.[4] His death poem reads:

> The four elements essentially have no master,
> the five shadows are fundamentally empty;
> the naked sword will sever my head
> as though cutting the spring breeze.[5]

The four elements that have no master (no self) are earth, water, fire, and air. The five shadows are the five skandhas, the bundles of elements that make up "personality": form, sensation, thought, conceptual power, and consciousness. All of these are empty, as the *Heart Sutra* says. Seng-chao internalized this fact to the ultimate point where the loss of his head would be no more than the sharp blade whistling through the breeze.

The philosophical monk who questioned Feng-hsüeh wanted to cut *li* and *wei* just as cleanly, but he didn't know how to go about it. In Zen Buddhism, dualistic teachings of form and emptiness, universal and particular, enlightenment and ignorance, can be very useful. But if they are reified as concepts, they take on a life of their own and are hard to shake off.

In response to the monk's earnest question, Feng-hsüeh replies, "I always think of Chiang-nan in March; / partridges chirp among the many fragrant flowers." Chiang-nan is a broad area south of the Yangtze River that in T'ang times had beautiful scenery and many great temples. These two lines are from a poem usually (probably falsely) attributed to Tu-fu, a well-loved poet of T'ang China and later popular in Korea and Japan.[6]

Feng-hsüeh's quotation is his direct response to the monk's request to transcend *li* and *wei*. There are many similar requests and responses in Zen literature:

> A monk asked Tung-shan Liang-chieh, "Among the three Bodies of the Buddha, which one does not fall into a category?"
> Tung-shan said, "I am always intimate with it."
> Later a monk asked Ts'ao-shan, "What did our late master mean when he said, 'I am always intimate with it'?"
> Ts'ao-shan said, "If you want my head, cut it off and take it."[7]

How do you transcend the Three Bodies of the Buddha? Or equality and differentiation? Heads are not always so useful.

Wu-men's comment clarifies the matter to some degree: "Feng-hsüeh functions like lightning, creating an appropriate way to practice." That's right—just like the sharp sword swinging through the wind. Not any old sword, but precisely the right one in the hand of an adept. Next time he might use an axe. Lightning will do when working with a storekeeper, thunder for a poet, rain for a child, and a bright day for an old woman.

"But why does he get involved with the tongue of a predecessor?" Why does he resort to quoting some old poem? It behooves us to treat this matter of quoting others with close attention. In *The Blue Cliff Record* there are four cases devoted to Chao-chou quoting from the *Hsin-hsin mei*:

> The Supreme Way has no difficulties;
> it is simply a matter of not choosing.[8]

Chao-chou was certainly intimate with the quotation—it was, in fact, no longer a quotation but the ground beneath the Bodhi Tree from which his students and the rest of us can clearly perceive the morning star. The same is true of Feng-hsüeh's quotation.

"If you can see intimately into this point, the Way will open for you naturally." If you are truly intimate with Feng-hsüeh and his response here, then you will emerge from the dōjō of oneness and turn the Dharma Wheel with Feng-hsüeh's own hand and walk the streets of your city with his own feet.

"Now set aside the samādhi of words—just give me one phrase!" There are all kinds of samādhi: listening to a teishō is one kind. Samādhi simply means "one with." There are jokes in Japan about the "samādhi of academia" and the "samādhi of wealth." Wu-men is really saying, "Don't be so fascinated by your flow of logic. Let's hear one phrase." What kind of phrase? One appropriate phrase that is *charged* with your realization.

Wu-men's verse reads: "It is not a verse of elegant tone!" Tu-fu or whoever wrote the lines was not as elegant a poet as, say, Li-po was. Scholarly exploration aside, what is all this about not being elegant?

"Before speaking, it's already expressed." If Feng-hsüeh had stood mute, the kōan would be different—and would be a very good one at that. All is revealed!

"If you go on chattering glibly, / you'll find yourself at a loss." This seems an ordinary caution directed toward good Zen practice. Too much chatter is distracting and gossip is destructive; you should avoid such impediments to the practice. There is more. "At a loss" means being unable to relate to the fact that appears. Just that flower; just that question—completely unique, out of the nowhere into the here. When there is a lot of chatter, the uniqueness of the thing and the uniqueness of the moment are lost. The silence itself is inaccessible. Only the drone of the voice can be heard, "Yakity yakity yakity"—very monotonous.

The true Zen student is grounded in the fundamental place that is no other than subject-and-object. That is the place of transformation in the presence of flowers and birds, where a single verse wells up from unknown depths:

> I always think of Chiang-nan in March;
> partridges chirp among the many fragrant flowers.

CASE 25

Yang-shan's Sermon from the Third Seat

THE CASE

Yang-shan dreamed he went to Maitreya's realm and was led to the third seat. A senior monk struck the stand with a gavel and announced, "Today, the one in the third seat will preach."

Yang-shan arose, struck the stand with the gavel, and said, "The truth of the Mahayana is beyond the Four Propositions and transcends the Hundred Negations. Listen, listen."

WU-MEN'S COMMENT

Tell me, did he preach or not? If you open your mouth, you are lost. If you cannot speak, then it seems you are stumped. If you neither open your mouth nor keep it closed, you are one hundred and eight thousand miles off.

WU-MEN'S VERSE

In broad daylight, under the blue sky,
he preached a dream in a dream.
Absurd! Absurd!
He deceived the entire assembly.

Yang-shan (Kyōzan) was an early T'ang master, a cousin of Lin-chi in the Dharma. He lived in the ninth century and is revered as the founder, with his master Kuei-shan, of the Kuei-yang school of T'ang Zen. This is the school remembered for harmony rather than for confrontation in its dialogues:

> Yang-shan went with Kuei-shan to the fields to help him with plowing. He said, "How is it that this side is so low and the other side is so high?"
>
> Kuei-shan said, "Water can level all things; let the water be the leveler."
>
> Yang-shan said, "Water is not reliable. It is just that the high places are high and the low places are low."
>
> Kuei-shan said, "Oh, that's true."[1]

Student and teacher are in perfect accord. Equality and variety are in perfect harmony.

Yang-shan was known to his contemporaries as Little Śākya, a name we might render as "Śākyamuni Junior," and he certainly was a true son of the Buddha himself. He acquired this name through a fabulous story:

> A magician flew in from India one day. Yang-shan asked him, "When did you leave India?"
>
> The magician said, "This morning."
>
> Yang-shan said, "What took you so long?"
>
> The magician said, "Oh, I went sight-seeing here and there on the way."
>
> Yang-shan said, "You obviously have occult power, but you haven't yet dreamed of the great occult power of the Buddha Dharma."
>
> The magician returned to India and told his followers, "I went to China to find Mañjuśrī, and instead I found Little Śākyamuni."[2]

It's interesting that a teacher who scorned ordinary occult accomplishments such as flying through the air would be remembered for his dream of going to Maitreya's mythological realm. Maitreya is the Buddha still to be born. Due to appear a very long time from now, he is waiting in the Tusita Heaven in deep samādhi, gradually evolving with all beings toward his ultimate role as world teacher.

Yang-shan's dream that he went to Maitreya's realm, the Tusita Heaven, seems to have the quality of *makyō*, "uncanny realm," the vision or other sense distortion that is experienced during zazen. Pronounced *mo-*

ching in Chinese, this term is related to the name of Māra, the Evil One. The Chinese *Śūraṅgama Sūtra* sets forth fifty kinds of *makyō*, some of which are clearly milestones on the path, but it warns that preoccupation with these positive symptoms can lead one astray. Here is one example:

> Suddenly you will see Vairocana seated on a radiant throne surrounded by thousands of Buddhas, with hundreds of *lacs* of countries and of lotus flowers. . . . This is the effect of being awakened by your mind's spirituality, the light of which penetrates and shines on all the worlds. This temporary achievement does not mean you are a saint. If you do not regard it as such, you are in an excellent progressive stage, but if you do, you will succumb to demons.[3]

I am reminded of a story that John Wu told in his class on Christian mysticism at the University of Hawaii many years ago. Apparently a priest who had a vision of the Virgin Mary at a young age then spent the rest of his life painting, rubbing out, and repainting his vision on the wall of his cell. He treated a sign of promise as its fulfillment, and there he remained. A cautionary tale.

Zen teachers tend to be scrupulous in their concern that *makyō* can be delusive. Yet they will acknowledge that a *makyō* commonly precedes deep realization and may even confirm that realization.[4] In any case, a *makyō* shows where a Zen student stands both in practice and in life. You may find yourself appearing as the central figure in a ritual that confirms you on the path, much as Yang-shan was confirmed as a teacher. No bluff is possible here. Some of my students have found themselves to be Buddhist figures, covered with gold leaf or gold light. It is an experience that transcends sexual identity—women might find themselves to be Śākyamuni, men to be Kuan-yin. There is a sense of the very old, or timeless, and a strong feeling of encouragement.

Distinguish such a *makyō* from the ordinary sensory distortion that appears commonly in zazen. Colored lights, a feeling of transparency, bells when there are no bells—these are symptoms that you have reached a place that is deeper than ordinary thinking. You can take heart: your practice is going well. There is no drama, however. You have not yet reached the ancient place that can promise realization before long. Likewise the ordinary dream may have some significance, but if it does not include a strong sense of very old times, it is not true *makyō*.

Although it is not identified as such, Case 35 of *The Blue Cliff Record* is surely a *makyō*. Wu-chu (Mujaku) visits Mount Wu-t'ai, believed to be the abode of Mañjuśrī, the mythological incarnation of wisdom. In wild and rough terrain, Mañjuśrī conjures up a temple where Wu-chu could spend the night. They have quite a remarkable dialogue, and next day when it is time for Wu-chu to go, Mañjuśrī orders his servant boy to see him to the gate. Wu-chu asks the boy, "What temple is this?" and when the boy points, he turns his head. The temple and the boy too have vanished completely. A dream—and the dialogue of that dream is one of the toughest kōans we face:

> Wu-chu asked Mañjuśrī, "How is the Buddha Dharma being maintained here?"
> Mañjuśrī said, "Sages and ordinary people are living together. Dragons and snakes are mixed."
> Wu-chu asked, "How many are there?"
> Mañjuśrī said, "Front three three, back three three."[5]

That's the kind of wild nonsense that appears with complete coherence in a *makyō* or in a deep dream.

When Yang-shan told his teacher Kuei-shan about his dream, Kuei-shan remarked, "You have reached the level of sage."[6] What do you suppose he meant by that? Yamada Rōshi once remarked to me, "It is possible to be enlightened without being a sage"—using "enlightened" in the rather technical sense of having had a glimpse of essential nature. And, of course, it is possible to be a sage without being enlightened in that narrow sense. Kuei-shan is saying, however, "You are an enlightened sage." High praise indeed.

What is a sage? A mature human being, I would say. Yang-shan could dream that he went to the Tusita Heaven and was led in to sit at the third seat because that was his seat, just below Maitreya and Śākyamuni. He had matured to that level. He really was Little Śākya. The seating arrangement in Yang-shan's dream should be seen in the context of Asian society. We don't pay much attention to the hierarchy of seating in Western culture, but in the Far East the most honored guest sits nearest the altar—or, in Japan, nearest the *tokonoma*, the alcove which is the center of the household. The next most honored seat is the next one, and so on down. I have seen a number of polite arguments about who should sit in the high seat—surely *you*, not I, should occupy the high place. Sometimes tempers become ruffled, faces flush, voices rise, and even brief wrestling matches may erupt. These confrontations commonly occur when two individuals are fairly equal in status. If the pecking order is clearly established, there may be polite murmurs of protest but that is all. Yang-shan's place was clear to everyone present, and to himself.

Although I have never read that Yang-shan's dream was a *makyō*, I think the old teachers must have recognized it as such—a *makyō* that goes beyond promise and presents the essential world itself. There, in the presence of the Buddhas, Yang-shan confidently arose, struck the stand with a gavel, and said: "The truth of the Mahayana is beyond the Four Propositions and transcends the Hundred Negations. Listen, listen."

The Four Propositions are the one, the many, being, and nonbeing. The Hundred Negations are made up with four negatives for each of the propositions—not, not not, neither not nor not not, and both not and not not—making sixteen. Then each of these sixteen is found in the past, present, and future. That makes forty-eight. These have either appeared or have not yet appeared, so that makes ninety-six. Negate the original four and you get the Hundred Negations. "Out! Out!" cries Kuei-shan. "Erase! Erase!" The truth of the Mahayana has nothing whatever to do with such intellection. It is found, as the Buddha pointed out in the beginning, beyond the realm of words. Yet even with the word "beyond" perhaps some kind of image appears.

> The Emperor Wu of Liang invited the Mahāsattva Fu to speak on the *Diamond Sutra*. Fu took the high seat, shook the lectern once, and descended. The Emperor was astonished.
> Chih-kung asked, "Your Majesty, do you understand?"
> The Emperor said, "I don't understand."
> Chih-kung said, "The Mahāsattva Fu has expounded the Sutra."[7]

The Mahāsattva Fu was a contemporary of Bodhidharma, though perhaps they never met. He is not part of our lineage, formally speaking, but is one of the great personages who appeared from the potent matrix of Chinese Buddhist culture in those early, pre-T'ang times.

Yang-shan rapped the gavel—just like Fu shaking the lectern. He then added words of explication, ending with a cautionary "Listen! Listen!" Pay attention! Who is hearing that sound?[8] Don't neglect this point.

Wu-men comments: "Tell me, did he preach or not? If you open your mouth, you are lost. If you cannot speak, then it seems you are stumped. If you neither open your mouth nor keep it closed, you are one hundred and eight thousand miles off." You will have to wait around for Maitreya, as Wu-men remarks in his comment to Case 5, and ask him about it. Wu-men is simply echoing Yang-shan. Cut through the miasma and listen.

"Did Yang-shan preach or not?" It is popularly said in Zen that the Buddha Śākyamuni did not preach a word throughout his life. The Zen Buddhist sermon, the teishō, is a "presentation of the shout," and the shout is that of the peacock or coyote or the mallet striking the wooden drum. At its best, the teishō has no trace of meaning. And, like the other shouts, it is the very quality of wisdom. Listen! Listen!

Wu-men's verse reads: "In broad daylight, under the blue sky, / he preached a dream in a dream." That's how it is. Like Shakespeare's play within the play of Hamlet, which is all play, the dream is within the dream of broad daylight and blue sky, where the Buddha Dharma and the Dharma of trees and birds are completely clear. All life is a dream, as the *Diamond Sutra* says. When he was ninety-four, Yamamoto Gempō Rōshi inscribed the ideograph "dream" which the artist Shin Segawa incised in a wooden plaque that hangs in our temple in Honolulu. I get the sense that "dream" is the way the rōshi summed up his life. Out of a misty dream our life appears and into a dream it returns.

"Absurd! Absurd!" Wu-men's verse continues, "he deceived the entire assembly." Shibayama Rōshi points out that another version of the story ends with the words "The monks dispersed," presumably with joy at Yang-shan's teaching.[9] But maybe they were fooled into their delight. Maybe they thought that the truth of the Mahayana is simply a matter of transcending the Four Propositions and the Hundred Negations. If so, they didn't really listen.

Fa-yen: Two Monks Roll Up the Blinds

THE CASE

The great Fa-yen of Ch'ing-liang took the high seat before the midday meal to preach to his assembly. Raising his hand he pointed to the bamboo blinds. Two monks went and rolled them up in the same manner. Fa-yen said, "One gains; one loses."

WU-MEN'S COMMENT

Tell me, which one gained? Which one lost? If you have the single eye regarding this, you will see where the National Teacher Ch'ing-liang failed. But I must warn you strictly against arguing gain and loss.

WU-MEN'S VERSE

When they are rolled up the great sky is bright and clear,
but the great sky still does not match our Way.
Why don't you throw away that sky completely?
Then not a breath of wind will come through.

Fa-yen (Hōgen) is revered as the last great founder of T'ang Buddhism, for his Fa-yen school was the fifth of the five principal Zen traditions. His dates are 885 to 958, so his time extended beyond the end of the T'ang period and through the Five Dynasties. His original teacher was Ch'ang-ch'ing (Chōkei), a brother monk of Yün-men, but he changed teachers in a memorable episode:

> Ti-tsang asked Fa-yen, "What is your journey?"
> Fa-yen said, "Going around on pilgrimage."
> Ti-tsang said, "What do you expect from pilgrimage?"
> Fa-yen said, "I don't know."
> Ti-tsang said, "Not knowing is most intimate."[1]

Ti-tsang (Jizō) was Fa-yen's cousin in the Dharma but became his teacher forthwith. "Not knowing is most intimate" brought Fa-yen directly to the Bodhi Tree, though not, it seems, to the Buddha's own experience:

> Next day Fa-yen prepared to set off again on his pilgrimage. Ti-tsang walked with him to the gate, and as they passed through the garden Ti-tsang pointed to a boulder and said, "Most monks say that the Three Worlds exist because of the mind and all phenomena arise from recognition. Tell me, does that stone exist in the mind or outside?"
>
> Fa-yen said, "In the mind."
>
> Ti-tsang said, "That stone will be very heavy for you to carry about in your mind."[2]

With this Fa-yen realized that he was not as enlightened as he thought, so he remained with Ti-tsang for further training and ultimately became his Dharma successor.

Quite a lot can be said about these two Dharma exchanges. First of all, it is clear that Fa-yen was on pilgrimage before he had very much understanding. Most modern teachers discourage their students from drifting from teacher to teacher in early phases of their practice. They reason that such beginners might get confused by the different teachings, and this is probably true. Yet a new setting and a new method can sometimes be stimulating, as it was for Fa-yen, and I have even suggested on occasion that a student might do better working with somebody else. This kind of careful exploration is very different from casual hopping around, of course.

Second, note that Ti-tsang did not hesitate to engage in a Dharma dialogue with someone else's student. Today teachers in Japan, at least, will not usually do this, out of respect for the process the student has begun with the original teacher. But there is a certain lack of trust implicit in this modern protocol. We're all in it together—teachers and students. Let's turn the Dharma Wheel, carefully, together!

Third, and most important, this dialogue touches the depths of insight. "Not knowing is most intimate!" Here Ti-tsang is echoing Fa-yen's "I don't know," from the deepest dimensions of his own intimacy, showing Fa-yen the very source of everything—the source Bodhidharma revealed in his audience with Emperor Wu when he said, "I don't know."[3] Fa-yen had a glimpse of that mysterious source and was ready to move on with new confidence. But Ti-tsang was not convinced and showed him that he was not yet free.

Zen practice is like this. Preliminary experiences, even if they are profound revelations, must be seasoned and clarified. Be careful on this point. Don't be hasty. Allow yourself to ripen and to actualize your harmony with Buddha, Dharma, and Sangha.

Certainly Fa-yen had become a true master by the time he made the presentation recounted in this case. Thanks to his sound foundation of practice with Ch'ang-ch'ing and his rigorous work with Ti-tsang, he had become an enlightened sage.

The first point is Fa-yen's act of lifting his hand and pointing. Yamada Rōshi stresses its importance. "The pointing finger should not be mixed up with the blinds," he says in effect.[4] Here it is! "Its own pageant!" Fa-yen has expounded the sutra!

Be that as it may, we still must deal with Fa-yen's remark about the two monks: "One gains; one loses." The *Heart Sutra* says there is essentially no loss and no gain.[5] Of course Fa-yen knew about this as a fact of life, his and ours. Thus his use of "gain and loss" seems bizarre. Here trust comes into play. This is the great Fa-yen—his words merit our respectful attention, even when they seem inappropriate or incorrect. What is he pointing to here?

Surely Fa-yen was not speaking comparatively. For if he were, he would not only be omitted from Wu-men's anthology but would have disappeared from memory along with his anonymous monks. Comparisons are odious. It is our obligation as Zen students to avoid invidious thinking and invidious talk. Setting what we like against what we do not like can distort the harmony and equality of our varied world. The students in Fa-yen's assembly knew this very well, and students in our own Sangha know it too.

It might seem that Fa-yen is judging: this one raises the blinds mindfully; that one with a loss of concentration. Not so. Remember Chao-chou in Case 11. To the first monk who raised his fist he said, "The water is too shallow for a ship to anchor." To the second who raised his fist he said, "Freely you give, freely you take away, freely you kill, freely you give life." Chao-chou was not judging, and neither was Fa-yen. Both teachers were giving teishōs—Chao-chou in the huts of his friends, Fa-yen from the high seat in his monastery.

Ultimately Fa-yen is not saying merely that gain is gain, loss is loss, high places are high, and low places are low—though this is certainly an overtone of his words. To see into his meaning, you must take gain and loss as the fundamental configuration of the universe, beyond evolution and entropy.

Wu-men's comment: "Tell me, which one gained? Which one lost?" That's easy. The first one gained; the second one lost. By now maybe you can smile with Fa-yen.

"If you have the single eye," Wu-men continues, the eye of nonduality, "you will see where the National Teacher Ch'ing-liang failed." Ch'ing-liang (Seiryō) was Fa-yen's posthumous title. Wu-men sets 'em up, and he knocks 'em down.

Well, all teachers fail. The Buddha himself was swept away. "One gains; one loses" doesn't convince anybody. And neither does "no loss, no gain." Trees fall when they are old, and countless beings make their homes in the rotting logs. "Gain and loss" defines the universe and yet fails to define it.

Wu-men emphasizes this point: "But I must warn you strictly against arguing gain and loss"—and not only gain and loss but also sage and ordinary person, tall and short, birth and death. As he says elsewhere, "When you argue right and wrong, you are a person of right and wrong."[6]

When you look deeply into Fa-yen's comment about the two monks, you find yourself—and you find the old master having fun with you. When he said, "One gains; one loses," the outcome is a draw. What can you gain from zazen? Not much, I would say. What can you lose? Quite a lot, really.

Wu-men's poem reads: "When they are rolled up the great sky is bright and clear." "They," of course, are the bamboo blinds. From one perspective, our practice is a matter of rolling them up. Yasutani Rōshi's calligraphy for "sky" hangs beside me in the interview room. "Sky" is the word

Kumarajiva and his colleagues chose to translate the Sanskrit term *śunya-tā*—the void that is potent with all things. In human terms, "great sky" is the "I don't know" of Ti-tsang and Bodhidharma. When all concepts of sage and ordinary person, tall and short, birth and death, are rolled up, there is the vacant, cloudless realm of no time and no space where there is nothing holy or mundane.

"But the great sky still does not match our Way." As Yamada Rōshi says, "Even the sky must be beaten. Not enough! Not yet! Not enough yet!" Emptiness is the Cave of Māra, a trap for the fiercest tiger in the Dharma world.

"Why don't you throw away that sky completely?" Step from the top of that hundred-foot pole, jump from the empty sky, and "then never a breath of wind will come through." One of my students remarked, "This is the seamless tomb of the Great Death." I would say it is the cardinal singing on the telephone wire—everything else drops away.

Nan-ch'üan: "Not Mind, Not Buddha, Not Beings"

THE CASE

A monk asked Nan-ch'üan, "Is there a fundamental truth that has never been expounded for people?"

Nan-ch'üan said, "There is."

The monk said, "What is the fundamental truth that has never been expounded for people?"

Nan-ch'üan said, "It is not mind; it is not Buddha; it is not beings."

WU-MEN'S COMMENT

At the question, Nan-ch'üan used up all his personal treasure immediately and became quite debilitated.

WU-MEN'S VERSE

Scrupulous care dissipates your virtue;
no-words truly have an effect;
though the great ocean becomes a field,
it cannot be communicated to you.

Here we meet Nan-ch'üan again, the great ninth-century master best remembered as the central figure in the story of his killing a cat (Case 14). He was a student of Ma-tsu and the teacher of Chao-chou, who presented us with the kōan Mu. This dialogue about the teaching that has never been taught is an abbreviation of a story that appears as Case 28 in *The Blue Cliff Record*:

> Nan-ch'üan came to the Honored Priest Pai-chang Nieh-p'an. Pai-chang asked, "Is there a secret and supreme Dharma which has not been expounded for people by any of the holy ones in the past?"
>
> Nan-ch'üan said, "Yes, there is."
>
> Pai-chang asked, "What is this secret and supreme Dharma which has not been expounded for people?"
>
> Nan-ch'üan said, "It is not mind; it is not Buddha; it is not beings."
>
> Pai-chang said, "You have expounded like that!"
>
> Nan-ch'üan said, "Just that is my exposition. How about you, Honored Priest?"
>
> Pai-chang said, "I am not a great Zen master. How can I know whether or not there is a Dharma that has never been expounded for people?"
>
> Nan-ch'üan said, "I don't understand."
>
> Pai-chang said, "I already explained it fully to you."[1]

This Pai-chang was the Dharma successor of the Pai-chang we met earlier in Case 2. He was thus a brother in the Dharma of Nan-ch'üan but a good deal older, both in years and in experience, as this story from *The Blue Cliff Record* shows.[2]

By shortening the story for *The Gateless Barrier*, Wu-men changed the roles of the participants. In the original *Blue Cliff Record* account Nan-ch'üan is the guest and Pai-chang Nieh-p'an is the host. In *The Gateless Barrier* abbreviation, Nan-ch'üan is the host and Pai-chang becomes a nameless monk. Wu-men puts Nan-ch'üan in control in his short version as though to say: "Wait a moment! Nan-ch'üan is making an important point with his first response. Take that up before you work on Pai-chang's words."

So we should have a look at the three things—mind, Buddha, and beings—which *it* is not. First, the mind is conscious thought, but that is not its limit. As Dōgen says: "Mountains, rivers, earth, the sun, the

moon, and the stars are mind. . . . Just wholeheartedly accept and trust
that to study the Way with mind is this mountains-rivers-and-earth-itself
thoroughly engaged in studying the Way."³

Next, the Buddha is many things: Śākyamuni, of course, the founder
of our Way, and also his enlightenment. The Buddha is the illuminative
nature of the universe and the various qualities of enlightenment. There
are many Buddhas in the Buddhist pantheon. The Buddha is also your own
nature and mine, which we seek to actualize in many dimensions, including that of moral conduct. Dōgen says: "There is a simple way to become
a Buddha. When you refrain from unwholesome actions, are not attached
to birth and death, and are compassionate toward all . . . beings, respectful to elders and kind to juniors, not excluding or desiring anything, with
no designing thoughts or worries, you will be called a Buddha."⁴

Finally, beings include everyone and everything: human and nonhu-
man, sentient and nonsentient, existent and nonexistent. A gargoyle is a
being, even an uncarved gargoyle. The usual term, *chung-sheng* (*shujō*), is
literally "all" or "the many beings," and though it is usually limited in
context to human beings or sentient beings, the essential meaning is
much broader. Here again is Dōgen in explanation: "Grasses, trees, and
the earth are mind. They are beings by virtue of being mind, and the Buddha nature of existence on account of being [the many] beings. The sun,
the moon, and the stars—all are mind. They are the many beings by reason
of being mind, and are the Buddha nature of existence because of being
the many beings."⁵ Mind, Buddha, and beings have been linked in Buddhist thought since early times. The Zen proverb "Mind, Buddha, and
beings—these three are not different" comes from the *Avatamsaka (Hua-
yen) Sūtra.*⁶

But, Nan-ch'üan says, that's not *it!* Tell me, what is the antecedent of
it? "Well," you might respond, "*it* is the teaching that has never been expounded." Not incorrect, but that doesn't advance world understanding
at all.

The question is not about one truth among many which has or has not
been expounded for people. It is about the fundamental matter itself. This
fundamental matter is under constant scrutiny in our practice, and we
have excellent precedents: Mañjuśrī asked Vimalakirti, "What is the Bodhisattva gate to the Dharma of not-two?"⁷

Have a look at the portrait of Vimalakirti by Hakuin Zenji in D. T. Suzuki's *Manual of Zen Buddhism*, which illustrates his response. His mouth is firmly shut in a silent exposition which, Zen people like to say, was like thunder.[8] Here's another:

> Yang-shan asked a monk, "Where have you come from?"
> The monk said, "Lu Mountain."
> Yang-shan asked, "Did you go to Five Elders Peak?"
> The monk said, "I didn't visit there."
> Yang-shan said, "Then you didn't go to the mountain at all."[9]

Yang-shan wants to hear the monk's description of the view from the mountain—whatever the peak. There is a sword in the questions of true Zen masters. "What is *it*?" The monk didn't notice he was in danger, so he blithely responded to the surface meaning. Really, who cares what the monk did on his vacation! Certainly Yang-shan didn't. But he let the monk off easy. "You didn't go to the mountain at all." You have no idea what *it* might be! As Yün-men comments on this case: "Yang-shan's words were spoken out of benevolence, but the conversation fell into grasses"—into confusion.[10]

Nan-ch'üan spoke out of benevolence, too, though his expression "not mind, not Buddha, not beings" was framed negatively. Like Yang-shan, Nan-ch'üan is shouting "Erase! Erase!" *It* is not mind, not Buddha, not beings, for all the expansive meanings of such notions. Maybe even *it* will get stale and have to be erased someday. Can you express his point positively? At least in terms of Western philosophy, Buddhism is the *via negativa*, but not to the degree of Hinduism with its *neti neti*, "not this, not this." Really Nan-ch'üan is affirming *it*.

In the same way, the *Diamond Sutra* says: "The Buddha does not have the thirty-two marks of the Buddha. Therefore, he is called Buddha."[11] The Buddha does not have a bump in the middle of his forehead as Buddhas do; he doesn't have the long earlobes as Buddhas do; he doesn't have any of the attributes of a Buddha. Therefore he is called Buddha. Coming forth and affirming Buddha is the point of all this negation! Nan-ch'üan is preaching the affirmation of *it* in the same way. And not only Nan-ch'üan—the fly buzzes it; the candle flickers it; the train whistles it.

Wu-men comments: "At the question, Nan-ch'üan used up all his personal treasure immediately and became quite debilitated." He had nothing left. I used to understand this to mean that by presenting everything,

Nan-ch'üan was left with nothing for himself—that he disappears in his presentation. This may be part of Wu-men's meaning, but I think he is being rather critical as well.

As Wu-men points out in his verse, "Scrupulous care dissipates your virtue; / no-words truly have an effect." We can equate virtue with the "personal treasure" in Wu-men's comment. The Chinese term used here is a compound that means "noble virtue," but virtue is the key element. Pronounced *te* in Chinese and *toku* in Japanese, this is one of the keys to Asian culture, and indeed to human culture. It is the *te* of the *Tao-te ching*, the central text of Taoism. This title was translated *The Way and Its Power* by Arthur Waley and as *The Canon of Reason and Virtue* by Paul Carus.[12] Take "power" and "virtue" together and you have an approximation of the meaning of *te*. It is related to the "bright virtue" of Confucian texts that puzzled the young Bankei and brought him to Zen.[13]

In Buddhism, *te* or *toku* stands for the authority that accumulates with thorough practice and clarity of insight. You feel it, and others feel it. It is like the respect for oneself and from others that is experienced in traditional societies with age, experience, and wise decisions. In the Buddha Sangha, it appears with bodhisattva work that fulfills the first vow: to save the many beings. It accumulates like the ash which builds bit by tiny bit in the incense pot.

Incense ash as a simile for virtue brings my first teacher, Senzaki Nyogen Sensei, to mind. He lived in the United States from 1905 until he died in 1957. He did zazen by himself for twenty years while working in San Francisco and studying English and Western culture. Then he began teaching in the apartments of friends—his "floating zendō," as he called it. In 1927 he was able to establish his own zendō in his apartment and from then on until his death he taught a small Sangha of students in San Francisco and later in Los Angeles. During those fifty years he kept all the ash from the incense he burned during his own zazen and that of his Sangha. Ultimately he had a great bronze pot full of ash. That ash was his *toku*—and not merely as a figure of speech. When he became old, two students offered to take him to Japan for a visit. Thus he was able to return to his home temple, Enkakuji, for the first time in fifty years, and he called on other temples, too, where he had connections. Senzaki Sensei insisted upon taking that enormous, incredibly heavy, bronze pot full of incense ash with him on the airplane and then on trains and busses to each of the temples he visited. His two friends had quite a struggle carrying it for him. At each temple he would set it on the altar, light incense, and then recite sutras. I think of my old teacher when I offer incense at the Koko An Zendō before Bodhidharma. We are accumulating quite a little pot of virtue there.[14]

All such virtue, as Wu-men says, your own and indeed everybody else's, can be dissipated if you stoop to explain everything. Once when I was little and having dinner with my family, I asked, "Why are babies born in hospitals?" The topic was neatly diverted to a time when my father had my brother and me alone. He reminded me of my question (which I had by then forgotten) and proceeded to lay out the reproductive process in clinical detail. It took me quite a while to recover from the shock. A natural response when the topic was first raised would have been best, I think. On other occasions, silence itself can be a full presentation. I frequently suggest to students that if they talk about their practice, they will feel a loss, a diminishing of their experiences by trying to put them into words. Their listeners will be reduced, as well, as my brother and I were reduced, and my father too, by his well-meaning exposition of sperm and egg.

Wu-men seems to suggest that Nan-ch'üan expounded at a rather intellectual level and tried to sum everything up in a discursive way. Certainly Pai-chang didn't care for Nan-ch'üan's presentation. Though it is important for us to get at the crux of *it*, and to show Nan-ch'üan's mind as our own, still, we can, with Wu-men, reserve judgment on the young Nan-ch'üan and be thankful that he went on to deepen his realization.

"No-words truly have an effect"—like Vimalakirti's thunderous silence. Wu-men is gently admonishing Nan-ch'üan here. "Though the great ocean becomes a field, / it cannot be communicated to you." Even if the sun becomes cold and the moon grows hot, there certainly is a secret and supreme doctrine that has never been communicated by any of the holy ones of the past. Even Śākyamuni Buddha did not reveal it to the world, or to you. Don't skip over this point.

CASE 28

Lung-t'an:
Renowned Far and Wide

THE CASE

Te-shan visited Lung-t'an and questioned him sincerely far into the night. It grew late and Lung-t'an said, "Why don't you retire?" Te-shan made his bows and lifted the blinds to withdraw, but was met by darkness. Turning back he said, "It is dark outside."

Lung-t'an lit a paper candle and handed it to Te-shan. Te-shan was about to take it when Lung-t'an blew it out. At this, Te-shan had sudden realization and made bows.

Lung-t'an said, "What truth did you discern?"

Te-shan said, "From now on I will not doubt the words of an old priest who is renowned everywhere under the sun."

The next day Lung-t'an took the high seat before his assembly and said, "I see a brave fellow among you monks. His fangs are like a sword-tree. His mouth is like a blood-bowl. Give him a blow and he won't turn his head. Someday he will climb the highest peak and establish our Way there."

Te-shan brought his notes on the Diamond Sutra *before the Dharma Hall and held up a torch, saying, "Even though you have exhausted the abstruse doctrines, it*

PLATE 6: *Lung-t'an and Te-shan*. Courtesy of The Idemitsu Museum of Arts. (Case 28)

Punctuate what mind?
Past? Present? Future?
The candle is blown out
and the *Diamond* is ashes.

is like placing a hair in vast space. Even though you have learned all the secrets of the world, it is like letting a single drop of water fall into an enormous valley." And he burned up all his notes. Then, making his bows, he took leave of his teacher.

WU-MEN'S COMMENT

Before Te-shan crossed the barrier from his native province, his mind burned and his mouth sputtered. Full of arrogance, he went south to exterminate the doctrine of a special transmission outside the sutras. When he reached the road to Li-chou, he sought to buy refreshments from an old woman.

The old woman said, "Your Reverence, what sort of literature do you have there in your cart?"

Te-shan said, "Notes and commentaries on the Diamond Sutra.*"*

The old woman said, "I hear the Diamond Sutra *says, 'Past mind cannot be grasped, present mind cannot be grasped, future mind cannot be grasped.' Which mind does Your Reverence intend to refresh?"*

Te-shan was dumbfounded and unable to answer. He did not expire completely under her words, however, but asked, "Is there a teacher of Zen Buddhism in this neighborhood?"

The old woman said, "The priest Lung-t'an is about half a mile from here."

Arriving at Lung-t'an's place, Te-shan was utterly defeated. His earlier words certainly did not match his later ones. Lung-t'an disgraced himself in his compassion for his son. Finding a bit of a live coal in the other, he took up muddy water and drenched him, destroying everything at once. Viewing the matter dispassionately, you can see it was all a farce.

WU-MEN'S VERSE

Seeing the face is better than hearing the name;
hearing the name is better than seeing the face.
He saved his nose,
but alas he lost his eyes.

One of the delights of Zen study is getting acquainted with the old teachers and coming to know them as persons. With this case, we further our acquaintance with Te-shan, a contemporary of Lin-chi in the ninth century.[1]

Case 13, "Te-shan: Bowls in Hand," one of the best known of all Zen kōans, presents him in full maturity. Here with Lung-t'an we see him in his younger years, perhaps in his late thirties. By then he was already a well-established scholar of the *Diamond Sutra*, lecturing frequently on this important Mahayana text.

Evidently he felt threatened by the Zen teaching of realization that is not established on words and was wary of transmission that is outside tradition. So he traveled several hundred miles south with the avowed purpose of stamping out such heresy. This is the old story of coming to scorn and staying to pray. Whether he knew it or not, something was at work in his psyche as he made his journey.

On the road to Li-chou with its many Zen monasteries, he stopped at a wayside refreshment stand. Here he met a great teacher of Zen who, like others of her sex, the Chinese recorders sadly fail to identify by name. Te-shan didn't pay any particular attention to her, but she discerned the potential of her new customer as he asked for *tien-hsin* (*tenjin*). This Buddhist term means "refreshment," but the old woman played with its etymology: "punctuate the mind."

"Your Reverence," this wise old woman politely asked, "what sort of literature do you have there in your cart?" This was her opening wedge in their Dharma dialogue.

"Notes and commentaries on the *Diamond Sutra*," he replied shortly. He had no idea that he was setting himself up. Most commentators say here that the old woman then suggested a game: "I want to ask you a question. If you can answer, I will serve you without charge. If you cannot answer, then I won't serve you at all." Te-shan agreed, and she lowered the boom: "I hear the *Diamond Sutra* says, 'Past mind cannot be grasped, present mind cannot be grasped, future mind cannot be grasped.'[2] Which mind does Your Reverence intend to punctuate?"

Duh! For all his wisdom, Te-shan was confounded by the old woman. What would you reply in such a case? If you can't reply, you are in good company. But, as Wu-men says, Te-shan was not completely crushed. He deduced that the old woman must be a well-trained student of religion. So he asked, in effect, "Who is your teacher?"

We can admire Te-shan's character here. Instead of giving way to anger or despair at his defeat, he recognized in a moment that he had been mistaken—not only in overlooking the virtue of the tea seller, but also in all of his "knowledge" of the sutra. Like Chao-chou when he set out on his twenty-year pilgrimage, he was ready to be taught.

This is an important lesson. If your defenses are impervious, no one can get in—and you can't get out. There is no fissure through which your vine of life can find its way to the sunshine. You have no way to grow. One of the hallmarks of the mature Zen student is the capacity to acknowledge and accept correction. Looking back at Case 13, we can see how Te-shan's early willingness to accept suggestions evolved into a way of teaching. When Hsüeh-feng remonstrated with him for appearing too soon, he simply turned and went back to his room. No self-justification. Beautiful!

He was still feeling a bit defensive, however, when he showed up to see Lung-t'an (Ryūtan), a teacher in the line of Ch'ing-yüan, who was contemporary with Huang-po and Pai-chang. His name means "Dragon Pond," and according to another text Te-shan played on this name in making his initial presentation:

> When Te-shan arrived at Lung-t'an [master and temple have the same name], he called out, "I have heard of the renowned Lung-t'an, but here I see neither dragon nor pond."
> Lung-t'an called back, "You yourself have arrived at Lung-t'an."[3]

Te-shan challenges Lung-t'an from the standpoint of emptiness, learned through his study of the *Diamond Sutra*. Lung-t'an responds from a step beyond emptiness. That must have shattered Te-shan's defensiveness at last—and encouraged him to inquire and to listen.

Lung-t'an kindly answered Te-shan's many earnest questions until late at night. Then abruptly he showed him true darkness, and Te-shan could light his Dharma candle at last. Te-shan said, "From now on I will not doubt the words of an old priest who is renowned everywhere under the sun." How do you see this? What are the words of renowned Lung-t'an?

Next day, Lung-t'an took the high seat before his assembly and said, "I see a brave fellow among you monks. His fangs are like a sword-tree. His mouth is like a blood-bowl. Give him a blow and he won't turn his head." An extraordinary pronouncement! During sesshin, the monitor wields his stick upon request and we bow in thanks. Ordinarily, however, wouldn't you turn your head if you were suddenly hit with a stick? I would.

"Someday he will climb the highest peak and establish our Way there." Our Way, the Buddha Tao, is surely not a matter of isolation. The last of the Ten Oxherding Pictures, intended to show steps on the Buddha Tao, shows Pu-tai (Hotei) entering the marketplace with "bliss-bestowing hands"—mingling with butchers and prostitutes, not off on a peak some-where.[4]

Lung-t'an is making a difficult point here: Te-shan's basic character, which appeared to be antisocial and preoccupied with emptiness when he was young, permitted him to evolve a teaching that can only be called tren-chant silence. Character development is like this. The passive young person becomes a tolerant parent. The angry young person stands up for jus-tice as an adult. The bundle of affinities we call the self is patterned uniquely at birth, and it evolves with inspiration—and we evolve it—for better or for worse. Herakleitos said, "Character is fate."[5] Given my orig-inal bundle, I could never have become a doctor or a physicist. The pattern of Te-shan's character was evident from the beginning: aloof and fervent. Given his bundle, he evolved to be teacher of Hsüeh-feng and Yen-t'ou, and out of his line emerged the Yün-men and Fa-yen schools.

Earlier I told about Te-shan's encounter with his attendant Huo as an example of his silent teaching style.[6] I also quoted his remark, "If you speak, you get thirty blows. If you do not speak, you get thirty blows." He could certainly be formidable:

> One evening Te-shan took the high seat before his assembly and said, "I shall not allow any questioning tonight. Questioners will get thirty blows."
>
> A monk came forward, and when he was about to make bows, Te-shan gave him a blow.
>
> The monk said, "I wasn't intending to ask a question. Why should I get a blow?"
>
> Te-shan asked, "What is your native place?"
>
> The monk said, "I am from Korea."
>
> Te-shan said, "You deserved thirty blows before you got in the boat."[7]

Even Lung-t'an should be beaten! Wu-men says: "Finding a bit of a live coal in the other, he took up muddy water and drenched him, destroying everything at once. Viewing the matter dispassionately, you can see it was all a farce." Yamada Rōshi was critical of Lung-t'an, as well, and remarked that if he had not been so generous, Te-shan might have become a better teacher.[8] An even better teacher!

Wu-men's verse begins: "Seeing the face is better than hearing the name; / hearing the name is better than seeing the face." These two lines form kōan points and relate to Lung-t'an's original message to Te-shan: "You have arrived here in person!" From this personal view, when in your practice is seeing the face better? When is hearing the name better?

"He saved his nose." Asian people point to their nose by way of indicating themselves, as Western people point to their chest. He saved that point of identity.

"But alas he lost his eyes." This might mean that Te-shan was too hasty when he burned his notes. Well, he probably was—but was this Wumen's meaning? I think not. He became altogether blind at last!

Hui-neng:
"Not the Wind; Not the Flag"

THE CASE

Two monks were arguing about the temple flag waving in the wind. One said, "The flag moves." The other said, "The wind moves." They argued back and forth but could not agree.

The Sixth Ancestor said, "Gentlemen! It is not the wind that moves; it is not the flag that moves; it is your mind that moves." The two monks were struck with awe.

WU-MEN'S COMMENT

It is not the wind that moves. It is not the flag that moves. It is not the mind that moves. How do you see the Ancestral Teacher here? If you can view this matter intimately, you will find that the two monks received gold when they were buying iron. The Ancestral Teacher could not repress his compassion and overspent himself.

WU-MEN'S VERSE

Wind, flag, mind move—
all the same fallacy;
only knowing how to open their mouths;
not knowing they had fallen into chatter.

As I mentioned in discussing Case 23, Hui-neng became the sixth Ancestral Teacher in Bodhidharma's line. The greatest figure of Chinese Zen before the time of Ma-tsu and Yüeh-shan, he was born in 638, perhaps a century after the death of Bodhidharma, and died in 713. His story is a romantic folktale taken from the *Sutra of Hui-neng*, the only Buddhist book in the standard collection of Chinese classics.[1]

According to that story, after Hui-neng eluded the jealous monks at Huang-mei he joined a party of hunters and moved around the forest with them for fifteen years, setting animals free from their traps and sticking vegetables in their stew for his own meals. He must have been like a jester for those hunters—a strange but endearing figure who sometimes said interesting things.

Hui-neng was not wandering idly those fifteen years, but was polishing his already profound realization and broad compassion. What does it mean to polish one's wisdom? You hear this expression often in the teishōs of Zen teachers, but how does one go about it? I think it is first of all a matter of keeping one's days steady and clear with zazen. It is also a matter of following up on the Dharma—kōan points, poetical points, biological points, sociological points, psychological points. There are a couple of kōans that still are not completely clear to me. I muse on them frequently. One day recently, working with a student on one of those kōans, I suddenly saw its basic configurations:

> A monk asked Yün-men, "When it's not the present intellect, and it's not the present phenomena, what is it?"
> Yün-men said, "An upside-down statement."[2]

Upside-down indeed. I had understood this case pretty well all along and was teaching it from that pretty good vantage. I don't teach it much differently now, but it is far more enjoyable.

I gladly give my time to students who sit hard and read Buddhist books and then corner me to talk about this or that point. They are the promising ones—the ones who hold Dharma questions in mind and test themselves against the understanding of others.[3] My first Zen friend, Dr. R. H. Blyth, once said to me, "I am always thinking about the Dharma and how I can try to express it." That is part of polishing wisdom.

Polishing compassion goes hand in hand with polishing wisdom. "What is the application of my understanding? How do I conduct myself to actualize the harmony of all beings and to encourage fulfillment of their marvelous uniqueness?" Such questions must have preoccupied Hui-neng during his fifteen years in the forest.

Finally it seemed to him that he was ready to return to the world of temples and teachers again. Inquiring discreetly he learned that the Dharma Master Yin-tsung (Inshū) was giving talks on the *Mahāparinirvāna Sūtra* at a certain temple. Hui-neng appeared at the gate as our story begins.[4]

To announce that a talk would be given that day, the temple flag had been raised and was waving in the wind. Two monks were arguing about it. One said, "The flag moves. " That is: "The self-evident concrete fact is the movement of the flag. There is just that waving. You can say that the wind is causing the flag to move, but that is secondary to the main fact." The other monk said, "The wind moves." That is: "No, it is the wind that's moving, causing the flag to move. The flag is the secondary factor. Brother, don't you see that?"

They thought they had hit upon an important point of contention in the Buddha Dharma. They had no idea their words were superficial—duckweed floating on the void. This was Hui-neng's great chance: "Gentlemen! It is not the wind that moves; it is not the flag that moves; it is your mind that moves." It is *your* mind that moves. Personal pronouns are usually omitted in Chinese, and one is generally left to guess them from the context. Hui-neng leaves nothing to guesswork, however. He says it is the mind of you monks that is moving. I understand him to mean: "Your mental function is precisely the mind which is neither mine nor yours that is moving around so exuberantly yet does not move."

When I was a much younger Zen student, I supposed that Hui-neng intended to show the two monks that they were being very intellectual. "It is not the flag that moves; it is not the wind that moves—what is moving is the endless stream of thoughts in your heads as you argue back and forth." Partly true, perhaps, but very ordinary. More duckweed. Hui-neng was not wandering idly those fifteen years. I am sure he would not emerge after all that practice simply to preach quietism to the two monks. Some people might suppose that Hui-neng is saying that phenomena find their home in perception and that apart from one's own perception—one's own mind—there is no reality. Thus: "It is your mind that moves."

No, I don't think so. Hui-neng tossed something into the depths beneath such a view. The two monks then felt the profound echo of his words:

"It is your mind that moves"—it is the mind of yourself that moves. You must see into the mind of that self. What is that mind?

Sitting there, show me your reincarnation of Hui-neng, the Sixth Ancestor. Revive the old mummy (and indeed his body is still intact today in the People's Republic of China), and show me his sparkle! Then the Buddha Śākyamuni can consider his work finished—well done!

The two monks apparently could not rise fully to the occasion, but at least they were struck with awe. They reported to their teacher, Yin-tsung, that there was a remarkable personage outside. Yin-tsung had an intuition. He came out immediately and said, "You must be Hui-neng, who long ago received transmission from the Fifth Ancestor." When Hui-neng acknowledged that Yin-tsung was correct, the Dharma Master invited him within, and he remained there for a while. Ultimately Yin-tsung ordained him, and his career of formal teaching began.

Wu-men comments: "It is not the wind that moves. It is not the flag that moves. It is not the mind that moves"—going Hui-neng one better!

"If you can view this matter intimately," he says, "you will find that the two monks received gold when buying iron." Dealing in abstractions, they were given the touchstone of all experience.

"The Ancestral Teacher could not repress his compassion and overspent himself." It is popularly said in Zen circles that Hui-neng was too explanatory in his response to the two monks. Wu-men does pander to this stereotype in making his point. But basically I think that he is acknowledging the Sixth Ancestor here. Hui-neng was fulfilling his vows as the avatar of the Buddha. Having given himself completely, only his words remain—like the smile of the Cheshire Cat.

How does that flag move during the twenty-four hours of the day? Give me the details, beginning at 6:30 A.M. Are Sundays any different? And when the wind is completely still—what is that like? This is a case for the ages, not just for late seventh-century China.

Wu-men's verse reads: "Wind, flag, mind move—/ all the same fallacy." He seems to be saying that the two monks, and Hui-neng as well, were mistaken. That's possible. Remember Case 27: "It is not mind; it is not Buddha; it is not beings." The *it* of that case haunts this couplet: "Wind, flag, mind move—/ all the same fallacy."

The verse continues: "Only knowing how to open their mouths; / not knowing they had fallen into chatter." Wu-men seems to be continuing the stereotype about Hui-neng. But really he is cautioning us all. Only knowing how to open *your* mouth; not realizing that *you* have fallen into chatter. How many of us realize that it is just chatter? "Notice yourself sometime," I say to myself and to you, "Notice the chatter chatter chatter chatter."

Ma-tsu: "This Very Mind Is Buddha"

THE CASE

Ta-mei asked Ma-tsu, "What is Buddha?"
Ma-tsu said, "This very mind is Buddha."

WU-MEN'S COMMENT

If you can grasp the point directly, you wear Buddha's robes, eat Buddha's food, speak Buddha's words, take Buddha's role. That is, you yourself are Buddha. Ta-mei, however, misled quite a few people into trusting a broken scale. Don't you know you should rinse out your mouth for three days when you utter the name Buddha? If you are genuine, you'll run away holding your ears upon just hearing the words, "This very mind is Buddha."

WU-MEN'S VERSE

The blue sky and bright day—
no more searching around.
"What is Buddha?" you ask.
Hiding loot, you declare your innocence.

Ma-tsu (Baso) is known affectionately as Ma Ta-shih (Ba Daishi): Great Master Ma. Ma was his surname; the *tsu* or *so* portion of his name simply means "ancestor" or "patriarch." Great Master Ma, together with Yüeh-shan (Yakusan), was responsible for the golden age of T'ang Zen, for (according to some traditional accounts) he had one hundred and thirty-nine Dharma successors, including Nan-ch'üan and Pai-chang. He lived during the eighth century, about seventy years after Hui-neng, the Sixth Ancestor. As a young monk, Ma-tsu trained at the monastery of Nan-yüeh (Nangaku), Dharma successor of Hui-neng. He was one of several hundred monks at the monastery, lost in the crowd, unknown to his teacher. A senior monk noticed his diligence, however, and mentioned him to Nan-yüeh. The old teacher sought him out and found him in the zendō doing zazen by himself.

> Nan-yüeh asked, "Reverend Sir, what is your purpose in doing zazen?"
> Ma-tsu answered, "I seek to become a Buddha." Nan-yüeh thereupon took a piece of roofing tile and began rubbing it with a stone. Ma-tsu asked, "What are you doing, Venerable Teacher?"
> Nan-yüeh said, "I want to polish this roofing tile and make a mirror."
> Ma-tsu asked, "Can a piece of roofing tile be made into a mirror?"
> Nan-yüeh asked in return, "Can a Buddha be created by doing zazen?" Ma-tsu was dumbfounded and could not reply. Nangaku then went on, "It is like hitching an ox to a cart. When the cart does not move, do you beat the ox or the cart?" Ma-tsu still could not reply.
> Nan-yüeh explained further, "Are you doing zazen or are you sitting as Buddha? Zazen is not just a matter of sitting or lying down. 'Sitting as Buddha' reveals that 'Buddha' has no fixed form. In the midst of transitory things, don't grasp or reject. If you keep the Buddha seated, this is murdering the Buddha. If you cling to the form of sitting, you do not adhere to its inner principle."

Ma-tsu heard these words as though he were drinking ambrosia. He questioned Nan-yüeh:

> "How shall I do zazen in order to merge with the formless?"
> Nan-yüeh said, "Your study of the teaching of the mind-ground is like planting seeds. My expounding the essence of reality is like moisture from the sky. Circumstances have come together for you, so you shall see the Way."
> Ma-tsu asked, "If the Way is not color or form, how can I see it?"

Nan-yüeh said, "The reality-eye of the mind-ground can see the Way. Formless absorption is also like this."

Ma-tsu asked, "Is there becoming and decay, or not?"

Nan-yüeh said, "If one sees the Way as becoming and decaying, compounding and scattering, that is not really seeing the Way. Listen to my verse:

> Mind-ground contains various seeds;
> when there is moisture, all of them sprout.
> The flower of absorption has no form;
> what decays and what becomes?

With this, Ma-tsu suddenly realized the mind-ground. The traditional account continues: "His heart and mind were transcendent. He served his master for ten years, day by day going deeper into the inner sanctum."[1]

Nan-yüeh's descendants founded a Dharma line that includes the Lin-chi and Kuei-yang schools. There is not much more than this story recorded about him, but it is certainly sufficient to show the rich quality of his enlightenment and his magnificent power of teaching. In the early days of Zen Buddhism in the West, however, the story about zazen and the roofing tile was widely misunderstood. Alan Watts used it to justify his thesis that the great Chinese masters condemned zazen as a quietistic practice.[2] I once asked D. T. Suzuki about Watts's interpretation, and he answered in his sweet way, "Mr. Watts misunderstands that story." Too timid to ask about the correct interpretation, for a long time I was filled with doubts about all those metaphors: the tile, the ox, the Buddha, the mirror, the cart, the beating. I felt in my bones that zazen must be the heart of Zen practice, but Mr. Watts was very persuasive.

Quietism is indeed exclusive and aloof. Nan-yüeh is certainly warning against it. Some of my friends do zazen simply as a way of shutting out troublesome things of the world. This is the Zen that Yasutani Rōshi used to call *buji Zen*—safe and uneventful Zen. But Nan-yüeh's purpose was to open the human heart to the sweet rain of the Buddha. If your purpose is just to protect yourself, then you deny yourself that sweet rain, the most refreshing event possible. Let it wet you to the skin, to the marrow, to this very mind.

Zazen is certainly important in that process of absorbing—for us as it was for the Buddha Śākyamuni himself under the Bodhi Tree. Let it be inclusive: "All beings," Śākyamuni exclaimed at the moment of his realization, "have at this moment attained the Way!"[3] As Whitman said in a far different context, "I am large, I contain multitudes."

When Ma-tsu pointed out the ox of this very mind to Ta-mei, he was passing along the lesson he had learned from his old teacher Nan-yüeh. "I wish to become a Buddha," the young Ma-tsu had said. "You are not giving yourself to your own Buddha," his teacher had replied. "What is Buddha?" Ta-mei asked. "This very mind is Buddha," Ma-tsu replied in turn. This is the hot coal that burns in the hearts of true Zen students to the present day.

Be careful not to slip into an antinomian position. I sometimes ask a student, "How about this very mind that tells you to take up a pistol and shoot somebody? Is that the Buddha?" Buji Zen people might say, "Yes, of course." They wander in the limbo of pernicious oneness, where there is no purpose, no meaning, and certainly no Dharma Wheel. The Buddha which is this very mind and body is completely disregarded.

Ta-mei, however, was on track. He first studied philosophy, then, like Hsiang-yen and Te-shan, he took up zazen in middle life. When he heard Ma-tsu's response to his fundamental question, circumstances came together for him and he saw the Way. He settled in a little hut in the forest some distance from Ma-tsu's temple to polish his wisdom and compassion. One day he was discovered:

> A monk hiking in the forest came across a priest doing zazen in a little hut. He told his teacher Ma-tsu about this. Ma-tsu said, "Ah, that must be Ta-mei." He sent the monk back for a dialogue with him.
>
> "Where do you come from?" asked Ta-mei.
> "From Ma-tsu," replied the monk.
> "What is Ma-tsu saying these days?" asked Ta-mei.
> "Not mind, not Buddha," replied the monk.
> "Great Master Ma is confusing people," said Ta-mei. "I still say this very mind is Buddha." The monk reported back to Ma-tsu.
> "The Great Plum [Ta-mei] is ripening," commented Ma-tsu.[4]

Later Ta-mei went on to a career of teaching, and his disciples included T'ien-lung who in turn held up a finger to Chü-chih and started a train of karma that is not yet used up.[5]

Wu-men comments, "If you can grasp the point directly, you wear Buddha's robes, eat Buddha's food, speak Buddha's words, take Buddha's role. That is, you yourself are Buddha." You have taken the Buddhist sacrament. In Christian ceremony you absorb Christ's flesh and blood as you eat the bread and drink the wine. You take up his cross and devote yourself to the salvation of others as Jesus did. You wear Jesus' robes, eat Jesus' food, speak Jesus' words, take Jesus' role. That is, you yourself are Jesus. When you absorb the Buddha's metaphors like moisture from the empty sky, you find the moisture, the empty sky, the wind, the clouds, the birds, are the Buddha's metaphors—your metaphors—and you yourself walk the dusty roads of the Ganges Valley in your daily life.

"Ta-mei, however," Wu-men continues, "misled quite a few people into trusting a broken scale." Wu-men is surely waxing ironical here. I don't think Ta-mei is stuck; he isn't a bit confused by the apparent reversal in Ma-tsu's teaching.

"Don't you know you should rinse out your mouth for three days when you utter the name Buddha? If you are genuine, you'll run away holding your ears upon just hearing the words, 'This very mind is Buddha.'" Indeed. Don't you know that the very word "Buddha," the very words "Jesus," "enlightenment," "salvation," "heaven," "Lotus Land," and the rest of them, all self-destruct? There are three phases in the lives of such concepts. First, they are meaningful; next they become brittle; and finally they break into pieces and disappear. That is because from the beginning they have been without essence. Use them, but don't be used by them.

Wu-men's verse begins: "The blue sky and bright day—/ no more searching around." Everything is clear for the enlightened person and for the unenlightened too. Just as you see, just as you hear. The cushion is black, the candles flicker in the wind. The rooster crows in the distance.

"No more searching around." No more seeking to become a Buddha. No more doubts about Buddha.

"'What is Buddha?' you ask. / Hiding loot, you declare your innocence." Like Ch'ing-shui in Case 10, you have drunk three cups of the finest wine in China and still you say you haven't moistened your lips.

If you've read *The Three Pillars of Zen*, you know the story of Yajñadatta (Enyadata), who appears in the Chinese *Śūrangama Sūtra*. Yajñadatta woke up one morning and looked at the wrong side of his mirror—there wasn't any head there. So he rushed around crying out, "I haven't any head! I haven't any head!" His friends tried to assure him, but he wouldn't listen. Finally they tied him to a pillar to help him calm down. When this didn't work, one of them hit him over the head: *"Katonk!"* He cried out in pain, put his hand to his head, and realized what had been there from the start. He then rushed around shouting, "I have a head! I have a head!"[6]

Ridiculous!

Chao-chou Investigates
the Old Woman

THE CASE

A monk asked an old woman, "What is the way to Mount T'ai?"

The old woman said, "Go straight ahead."

When the monk had proceeded a few steps, she said, "A good respectable monk, but he too goes off like that."

When Chao-chou heard about this, he said, "Hold on! I'll go and investigate that old woman thoroughly for you."

Next day, Chao-chou went and asked her the same question, and she replied in the same way. He returned and announced to his assembly, "I have investigated and seen through that old woman of Mount T'ai for you."

WU-MEN'S COMMENT

The old woman knew how to sit in her tent and plan strategy, but she didn't recognize the notorious bandit. Old Chao-chou could steal skillfully into camp and threaten the fortress at the frontier. Still, he didn't have the aspect of a great person. When you examine them closely, you find they are both at fault. Now tell me, what did Chao-chou determine when he investigated the old woman?

WU-MEN'S VERSE

The question was the same—
the answer was the same as well;
sand in the rice,
thorns in the mud.

Chao-chou, after starting to teach at age eighty, lived into his hundred and twentieth year. Thus he was very old for his entire teaching career, but he didn't repose in his sanctum sanctorum growling "Mu." Despite his advanced age, he got out and mingled with people in the community at large. You'll recall how he visited two hermits in Case 11 and gave them a piece of his mind.

The old woman in this case was a tea seller—as was the woman who gave Te-shan his comeuppance in Case 28 when he asked for refreshment. In their wayside stands, such women were, like gas station attendants in modern Japan, in a position to give directions to travelers. The wise ones used their counters like high seats in the monasteries and expounded the Dharma in terms of light refreshment.

Mount T'ai is Wu-t'ai-shan—a sacred mountain that was believed to be the abode of the Bodhisattva Mañjuśrī, the incarnation of wisdom, commonly found on the zendō altar of a monastery. He is our archetype of insight into the void. The old woman probably said "Go straight ahead" each time she was asked directions to Wu-t'ai-shan. This response reminds me of a story that Nakagawa Sōen Rōshi used to tell about himself. After the war, in the fall of 1948, he visited Senzaki Nyogen Sensei in downtown Los Angeles, in what is now the center of Japan Town. In those days the neighborhood was rougher than it is now. Although he was warned not to walk around after dark, it was like telling a cat not to catch birds. At his first chance he went out alone to see the sights. He walked around the block, crossed the street, and walked around that block. Then he walked around two blocks, crossed the street, and walked around another two blocks. In this way he did not get lost.

At one point he met a drunken sailor who asked him, "Say, can you tell me where I can find a woman?"

Sōen Rōshi said, "What?" His English was rather fragile, and the sailor's enunciation probably wasn't very good by that time of the night.

"Can you tell me where I can find a woman?" asked the sailor again.
Sōen Rōshi finally understood. "Go straight," he said.

"Straight down this street?" asked the sailor.

"Straight down this street," said the rōshi.

There might be moral implications in this story, but fundamentally the rōshi's message was the same as that of the old woman. You can find what you really seek, what all of us really seek, just in that walking. "Go straight" is the Tathāgata's true meaning.

The old woman's response is reminiscent of Lin-chi, as well, who remarked to his assembly: "There are monks who look for Mañjuśrī at Wu-t'ai-shan. Wrong from the start! There is no Mañjuśrī on Wu-t'ai-shan. Do you want to know Mañjuśrī? There is something at this moment at work in you, never doubting, never faltering—this is your living Mañjuśrī."[1] When the old woman said "Go straight ahead," she was expressing Lin-chi's meaning precisely. Sometimes, however, a Zen student will hit upon a cogent presentation while still standing on shaky ground. Sōen Rōshi, though he was walking around and around, knew very well where he was. Where does the old woman stand? This is the question that intrigued Chao-chou when he heard about her. Is this a person with just an inkling or is she deeply realized? He felt moved to learn for himself.

When Anne Aitken and I were studying with Yamada Rōshi in Kamakura in the 1970s, the rōshi heard about a layman in a nearby town who was teaching as a Zen master. His curiosity was aroused and he went to see him for an interview. He told us afterward that he sat before the would-be teacher and said, "Now I will examine you!" His verdict: "That fellow is quite a roughneck!"

Chao-chou and Yamada Rōshi were not just trying to expose a charlatan. For the Zen master, nothing is more interesting than an encounter with someone who has creative insight. Certainly Chao-chou was intrigued, so the next day he set out. When he found the tea seller at her refreshment stand, he asked, "What is the way to Mount T'ai?"

"Go straight ahead," the old woman replied. Chao-chou probably turned (like Te-shan in Case 13, when he was reprimanded for coming too early to his meal) and went off in the direction she pointed. After he had gone a few steps, she called out, as she always did, "A good respectable monk, but he too goes off like that." This was a follow-up intended to prompt the monk to the deeper implications of her imperative, "Go straight ahead." "You are a very earnest monk with a noble bearing, but you too are unable to grasp the Tathāgata's true meaning."

That night, when Chao-chou took the high seat for a Dharma dialogue with his monks, he said, "I have investigated and seen through the old woman of Mount T'ai for you." The case ends here. As in many Zen stories, the ending is not neatly wrapped up and tied in a bow. What happened next? Did the assembly just sit there? I doubt it. Probably someone came forward, made bows, and asked, "What did you find out about that old woman?" What would Chao-chou reply? That is the point of this case as a kōan.

Whether conducting interviews or just conversing informally, the Zen teacher is not merely checking the other but presenting the Great Matter. The traditional title for Case 11 is "Chao-chou Checks Two Hermits," but you can be sure that the hermits felt edified rather than corrected or complimented.

Wu-men comments: "The old woman knew how to sit in her tent and plan strategy, but she didn't recognize the notorious bandit. Old Chao-chou could steal skillfully into camp and threaten the fortress at the frontier." That old robber Chao-chou cuts his way into your precious skin and steals all your delusions and preoccupations, and you don't know what's happening. He "threatened the fortress at the frontier"—he threatened her impregnable defenses and she had no idea that he was anywhere about. "Still," Wu-men says, "he did not have the aspect of a great person." He did not look like a bandit. He does not look at all distinguished. Yamada Rōshi used to say, "Nothing distinguishes the enlightened person."

In his comment on Chao-chou's encounter with the old woman, Shibayama Rōshi quotes a popular writer on Zen who says, "Master Chao-chou and the old woman are good friends with equal ability and their encounter ended in a tie." He scolds the writer and says in effect: "He missed the essence of the kōan; in fact, he doesn't even understand what a kōan is!"[2] With these words, the rōshi lets us peek into his inner room.

Wu-men's verse begins: "The question was the same—/ the answer was the same as well; / sand in the rice, / thorns in the mud." You can break a tooth on an unseen piece of sand. You can cripple yourself on thorns in the mud if you're wearing straw sandals. See into Wu-men's metaphors here, and take care!

The Buddha Responds to an Outsider

THE CASE

An outsider asked the World-Honored One, "I do not ask for the spoken; I do not ask for the unspoken." The World-Honored One just sat still.

The outsider praised him, saying, "The World-Honored One with his great compassion and mercy has opened the clouds of my delusion and enabled me to enter the Way." He then made bows and took his leave.

Ānanda asked, "What did that outsider realize to make him praise you?"

The World-Honored One said, "He is like the fine horse who runs even at the shadow of the whip."

WU-MEN'S COMMENT

Ānanda is the Buddha's disciple, but his realization is less than the outsider's. Now tell me, how do they differ—the disciple and the outsider?

WU-MEN'S VERSE

Walking along the edge of a sword,
running along the ridge of an iceberg,
no steps, no ladders,
jumping from the cliff with hands open.

The World-Honored One is the Buddha Śākyamuni, of course. The "outsider"—literally "one outside the Way"—probably followed one of the many dozen religious paths, such as Jainism, found in India during the Buddha's time. The outsider's question, "I do not ask for the spoken; I do not ask for the unspoken," is framed in a philosophical way. But it does not, I think, have essentially a philosophical purpose. In response to a similar question in Case 24, Feng-hsüeh replied in verse:

> I always think of Chiang-nan in March;
> partridges chirp among the many fragrant flowers.

The intention of both questioners is the same. What transcends the spoken and unspoken? What transcends subject and object? What transcends life and death? Feng-hsüeh replied by quoting somebody's poem. How do you see the World-Honored One here? If the Buddha were to utter some words as he sat there, what would he say?

Yüan-wu remarks that some people say the point here is in being silent, some say it is in being seated, some say it is in not answering. "Fortunately," he goes on to comment, "none of this has anything to do with it." He then quotes an earlier teacher: "Though the fine sword is in its scabbard, its light is sharp and cold."[1] When Mañjuśrī asked Vimalakirti about the Dharma gate of not-two, Vimalakirti responded without drawing his sword.[2] "No-words truly have an effect," as Wu-men points out elsewhere.[3] But if, as Yüan-wu says, the point is not just being quiet, what is it that cleared the clouds of delusion from the outsider's mind? As Ānanda asks, "What did that outsider see to make him praise you?"

Well, he saw the Buddha at rest. It is this rest that we miss in philosophy and in philosophers. At the 1949 East-West Philosophers' Conference at the University of Hawaii, Dr. D. T. Suzuki fascinated his Western colleagues not by *what* he said, because they didn't understand it, but by *how* he said it. He was at ease, at rest. I think Dr. Suzuki's colleagues sensed in him the rest that clears the clouds, the rest that levels mountains to the plains, the rest that grows oats, peas, beans, and barley. Buddhism is called the religion of peace, and Śākyamuni presents that peace here. It is not *buji* peace—safe and uneventful. It is the radical casting away of body and mind. It is the experience of the vast and fathomless void that is potent with all things and all possibilities.[4]

The outsider praised the Buddha, saying, "The World-Honored One with his great compassion and mercy has opened the clouds of my delusion and enabled me to enter the Way." He then made bows and took his leave. "What did the outsider see?" asked Ānanda, the Buddha's attendant and cousin. Not yet a realized person, Ānanda had a fine mind and sought instruction innocently. It is important to ask questions from that naive vantage, your mind like a white sheet of paper. Questions asked from an ideological platform are not really questions. They are not intended to elicit true instruction. Ānanda sensed that something was somehow expressed to the outsider, but his circumstances were not yet ripe.

The Buddha replied, "He is like the fine horse who runs even at the shadow of the whip." The Buddha employs this metaphor more fully in the *Anguttara Nikāya*:

> The one who learns that someone in another village is about to die, and reflects on the transient nature of all life, is like a horse who runs when it sees the shadow of the whip. The one who learns that someone in his own village is about to die, and reflects on the transient nature of all life, is like a horse who runs when it is whipped to the hair. The one who learns that someone in his family is about to die, and reflects on the transient nature of all life, is like a horse who runs when it is whipped to the flesh. And finally, the one who learns that he himself is about to die, and reflects on the transient nature of all life, is like a horse who runs when it is whipped to the bone.[5]

In his commentary on the *Prajñā Pāramitā Sūtra* Nāgārjuna says, "Moral teaching is the skin, meditation is the flesh, higher understanding is the bone, and the mind subtle and good is the marrow." Another echo is Bodhidharma's judgment of four disciples in turn: "You have my skin"; "You have my flesh"; "You have my bones"; and finally, to Hui-k'o, "You have my marrow."[6]

Beginning with the Buddha's pronouncement, all of these metaphors can be read comparatively and progressively. They can also be understood as aspects of the Dharma—now this, now this, now this, now this. I think they are like the Ten Perfections: the Perfection of Relinquishment or Charity (Dāna), Morality (Śila), Patience (Ksānti), Diligence (Vīrya), and so on, are really not a progression.[7] Like the Ten Oxherding Pictures, each phase contains all the other phases.

In the same way, there is no invidious comparison in the Buddha's metaphor of the horse. He was not implying that Ānanda, slow in coming to realization, was in any way inferior to the outsider. The Buddha knew very well that Ānanda would be a fine teacher one day. In fact Ānanda maintained his practice until the Buddha died, and continued with Mahākāśyapa until he could finally understand the essence of transmission and knock down the flagpole once and for all.[8]

In the confines of a Zen center, where people know each other well and have long been friends and colleagues, it is clear who is moving along through the study and who is not. During teishōs some people see the rōshi's points and some do not. Not yet. This can be painful for the slow ones. But really—fast is simply fast, and slow is simply slow. Tall is tall, short is short. If comparisons must be made, then I would suggest that slow and steady wins the race, as the hare learned to his sorrow.

I remember an occasion at the Kamakura Zazenkai, the group that later organized at the Sanun Zendō, when a college student appeared whom we had not seen before. At his second interview with Yasutani Rōshi he had his realization confirmed. As was the practice in that Sangha, this fact was announced to the group and everybody marveled. Later I told Nakagawa Sōen Rōshi about the incident and remarked, "Wasn't he lucky!" At that time, I hadn't a glimmer of what realization might be. Sōen Rōshi responded, "Well, lucky or unlucky, I don't know." The fact is that we never saw that college student again. I am sure that to this day he values that occasion as a milestone in his life. But he didn't have the experience of zazen and work with a good teacher to give him any indication of what might lie beyond that first glimpse. I practiced intermittently for twelve years and diligently for another twelve before I was confirmed as ready for study beyond Mu. Although I was often discouraged when I saw others moving along, I am glad now I had such a solid apprenticeship.

Wu-men comments: "Ānanda is the Buddha's disciple, but his realization is less than the outsider's." That's true. Very troublesome for Ānanda, very troublesome for anyone in that situation. The Perfection of Patience fulfills the practice, however.

"Now tell me," says Wu-men, comparing the disciple and the outsider, "how do they differ?" You can see the trap Wu-men is laying for all his tigers. But don't say Ānanda and the outsider are the same. That would be what Yamada Rōshi called "pernicious oneness." When child and parent are the same, teacher and student are the same, supervisor and worker are the same, then everything is mayonnaise. Nothing moves. "Everything the same; everything distinct," as the Zen proverb says. Form is emptiness, all right, but form is also form and emptiness is emptiness. The ironwood tree is tall; the guava bush is short. The outsider is quick; Ānanda is slow.

Wu-men's verse begins: "Walking along the edge of a sword, / running along the ridge of an iceberg." Precisely following all the rules of balance and gravity, highly trained, highly disciplined, yet completely free. Total circumspection, total emancipation. There cannot be one without the other. Such is the nature of truly asking and truly receiving.

"No steps, no ladders, / jumping from the cliff with hands open." Until I worked on this kōan with Yamada Rōshi, our Diamond Sangha translation of that last line was "climbing the cliff without using the hands." Much different, you will agree. Climbing the cliff without using the hands puts emphasis on the training side of Zen. Some kind of mysterious process up and up the steep cliff just using the feet. But Zen practice is not like this. Zen practice is like training on the low board and then one day diving off the high board. Just jump into the abyss yawning below you. Let everything go!

In this connection, R. H. Blyth quotes the passage in which Don Quixote faces the abyss:

> a vast lake of boiling pitch, in which a great number of snakes, serpents and crocodiles and many other ferocious and fearful creatures are wallowing about: a voice wails from the middle of the lake, "Whosoever thou art, O Knight, who surveyest this horrible sea, if thou wishest to obtain the blessing that lies beneath these gloomy waters, show the might of thy valorous breast, and throw thyself into these black, burning waves; dost thou not so, thou art not worthy to see the great wonders of the castles of the seven fairies, that lie beneath these lugubrious surges." No sooner have these awful words ceased than without a moment's consideration, without a thought of the danger he runs, without even taking off his massive arms, commending himself to God and to his mistress, he dashes into the middle of the boiling lake. And just when he does not know what will happen to him, he finds himself among flowery fields, beautiful beyond Elysium.[9]

"Readiness is all!" Ready? Jump!

CASE 33

Ma-tsu: "Not Mind, Not Buddha"

THE CASE

A monk asked Ma-tsu, "What is Buddha?"
Ma-tsu said, "Not mind, not Buddha."

WU-MEN'S COMMENT

If you can see through this clearly, your Zen training is complete.

WU-MEN'S VERSE

Present a sword if you meet a swordsman;
don't offer a poem unless you meet a poet.
When speaking say one-third of it;
don't give the whole thing at once.

A short case with a short comment—and a verse inhibiting chatter. Here is Ma-tsu again, picking up where he left off in Case 30. The two cases should be taken together. In Case 30 Ma-tsu told Ta-mei, "This very mind is Buddha." Ta-mei went off and then heard that Ma-tsu was contradicting himself by saying, "Not mind, not Buddha." Ta-mei said he didn't care what Ma-tsu was now saying—he still affirmed that "this very mind is Buddha."

The words "This very mind is Buddha" point to the starry sky—in fact they are the starry sky. "Not mind, not Buddha" is the empty sky. Fullness, emptiness—are these valid distinctions? They are and they aren't. The *Heart Sutra* says:

> Form is no other than emptiness, emptiness no other than form;
> form is exactly emptiness, emptiness exactly form.[1]

There is a lot of confusion about the words "emptiness," "vacancy," and "void" in Buddhist literature. They earn Buddhism a bad name among many inquirers. Nonbeing is perhaps the deepest human fear. Facing this fear is the "dark night" experienced by many students of religion. Realizing emptiness is, however, a most liberating experience. "It doesn't matter," one exclaims. "What a relief!" But at the same time it does matter.

Physicists early in this century used the word "complementarity" to describe the fact that two seemingly paradoxical descriptions of light as wave and as particle are both valid. It is only in description, however, that light is paradoxical. In a similar way, matter and no-matter are a complementarity when put into words. Ma-tsu set up a complementarity when he said "This very mind is Buddha" and then "Not mind, not Buddha." But it is only in presentation that he contradicted himself. The fact itself shines brilliantly.

This fact is evident first of all in the forms of things, the original mystery of beings that fascinates every child and every artist. Even commonplace things can fill one with awe and gratitude. When I practiced at the Zen monastery Ryūtakuji many years ago, I noticed that every stone image in the garden had a mended tea bowl before it, serving as an incense pot. Tea bowls were not broken every day at that temple, or even every year. So many broken bowls, all carefully mended, were the product of long decades of religious concern. At the Maui Zendō we had a sign in the kitchen that read: "Pots and pans are Buddha's body." Books too are Buddha's body, and our pens, paper, clothes, food, and drink. As Tōrei says, all of them are the "warm flesh and blood, the merciful incarnation of Buddha. . . . Who can be ungrateful, or not respectful!"[2]

The Buddha is many things, including my body and yours, including the earth with its awesome vitality. But after a while you will use up the term Buddha, just as you use up any object or concept, just as you use up yourself. In about half a day of cooking with Buddha and worrying as Buddha, you will have had enough. I wonder that Ma-tsu could say "This very mind is Buddha" more than once without getting disgusted with himself. As Wu-men says, "As a true Zen student you will run away, holding your ears, just hearing the name 'Buddha.' " If you don't, you can fall into superstition and structural thinking. The entire *Diamond Sutra* is dedicated simply to showing the vacancy of all concepts.[3] Tan-hsia sums it up:

> Tan-hsia took an image from the altar and burned it on a cold day to keep himself warm. When the caretaker of the temple protested, Tan-hsia said, "I wanted to collect the relics [said to remain after the cremation of a holy person]."
> The caretaker said, "How absurd to try to find relics by burning a wooden statue!"
> Tan-hsia said, "If so, may I have another statue to burn?"[4]

The artist Sengai has a great picture of Tan-hsia, robes hoisted to his waist, warming his backside on the flames consuming the holy statue.[5]

Once a Zen student who was also Christian came to me in tears saying, "I realize that God is only a concept!" But when she understood that she was disillusioned only about a word, her commitment to Christianity was strengthened. The truth of the *Heart Sutra*—"All things are essentially empty"—is not mere Buddhist truth; it is not mere "perennial" truth. It's how things are, pure and simple. Realizing this, you are empowered to take charge of concepts and use them appropriately.

What marvelous concepts! Kingdom of God, Israel, Lotus Land, Dharmakāya, Enlightenment, Salvation—one could make a whole sutra, a whole library of sutras, just with such names. But turning the Dharma Wheel is not a matter of dwelling on names. Play with them, yes, but don't let them play with you.

In that playful realm (the universe itself), the infinite void charges all things with wisdom. These wise things advance and confirm us as the drum announcing the noonday meal confirmed Wu-men[6] or the morning star confirmed the Buddha.[7] Wu-men did not say that the drum was mind or Buddha, or even that the drum was his morning star. Out of the clear void came a thunderous sound. The vast plenum came forth: Boom! Boom! Boom! *Boom-boom-boom-boom!*

Wu-men comments: "If you can see through this clearly, your Zen training is complete." Maybe so. But at the same time, the Buddha Śākyamuni himself is still doing zazen somewhere, only half finished with his practice. Even when Chao-chou settled down to teach, at the age of eighty, he felt presumptuous and ashamed of himself. Sometimes I'm anxious to wander like a fool, completely unknown, sitting here and there in famous dōjōs seeking interviews with accomplished masters. Let's just say it this way: "If you can see into this clearly, and make it your own, then you have the whole picture. Now all you have to do is to clarify it and enrich it for the rest of your life."

Wu-men's verse begins: "Present a sword if you meet a swordsman." When I worked on this line with Yamada Rōshi, he remarked: "A true swordsman will know whether your sword is sharp." Some time ago I read a little piece by I. A. Richards reminiscing about his meeting with Walter De la Mare. Richards was one of the great critics of his time; De la Mare was a British poet whose folkloric quality was much admired. When the two met, De la Mare was very old and Richards was a youth, introduced as a psychologist. "May I ask you a question that means a lot to me?" asked De la Mare. "Do you think that in the next world I may meet Hamlet?"[8] Whatever you may think of Walter De la Mare's poetry, you'll have to agree that on that occasion his sword was sharp. Present your mind when you meet a Zen person. Nothing is more rewarding for you and your friend. It will be clear who has the sharper sword—or maybe both swords will dissolve in the ambrosia of pure laughter. Kuei-shan and Yang-shan will beam with approval.

"Don't offer a poem unless you meet a poet." Nothing is more degrading than a discussion of poetry or religion with someone who's not really interested. Louis Armstrong's comment about jazz comes to mind here: "If you don't know, I can't tell you." Recently I was talking about this kind of caution with one of my students, a Christian priest. We were speaking about the injunction of Jesus, "Don't cast your pearls before swine," and he said, "Yes, because they will eat them, and then they'll come after you!" And their weapons will be your very words.

"When speaking say one-third of it; / don't give the whole thing at once." The point is that with saying "Not mind, not Buddha" Ma-tsu pointed to something we already know. We sense it in common. In pointing there is clarity, realization. But saying too much degrades your virtue.

Nan-ch'üan: Mind and Buddha

THE CASE

Nan-ch'üan said, "Mind is not Buddha; wisdom is not the Tao."

WU-MEN'S COMMENT

I must say that Nan-ch'üan got old and knew no shame. He opened his stinking mouth a bit and revealed the family disgrace. Only a few can acknowledge his great kindness.

WU-MEN'S VERSE

The sky clears, the sun shines brightly;
rain falls, the earth gets wet.
He fully opens his heart and expounds the whole secret;
but I fear he is little appreciated.

Nan-ch'üan appears here for the fourth time—a measure of his importance for Wu-men and for us all. He was, you will recall, the teacher of Chao-chou and a disciple of Ma-tsu, the Dharma Master of Cases 30 and 33. He lived in the ninth century at the time of the great flowering of Zen in the T'ang period. Apparently the saying "Mind is not Buddha; wisdom is not the Tao" was current then:

Chao-chou asked Nan-ch'üan, " 'Mind is not Buddha; wisdom is not the Tao.' Is this faulty?"

Nan-ch'üan said, "Yes, it is."

Chao-chou said, "Where does the fault lie? Please, Master, tell me."

Nan-ch'üan said, "Mind is not Buddha; wisdom is not the Tao."[1]

Nan-ch'üan's game with faults is the game of Zen itself. Chao-chou played it in turn:

Chao-chou said, "I don't like to hear the word Buddha."
A monk asked, "Then how will Your Reverence teach?"
Chao-chou said, "Buddha! Buddha!"[2]

Another time a monk asked, "What is Buddha?"
Chao-chou said, "The one in the shrine."
The monk said, "The one in the shrine is only a clay figure. What is Buddha?"
Chao-chou said, "The one in the shrine!"[3]

Dai'ō Kokushi explains:

Wishing to entice the blind,
the Buddha has playfully let words escape his golden mouth;
Heaven and Earth are ever since filled with entangling briars.[4]

Mind, Buddha, wisdom, the Tao—all these are briars, faulty expressions that can lead us astray, yet eminently useful in guiding us if we are prepared for them. Most of us aren't ready, unfortunately, so even the best of the old teachers created confusion. "A jungle of monks at sixes and sevens / is your fault after all," as Wu-men admonishes Bodhidharma.[5]

With preparation, however, the divine accident can come about. Once a disciple of Hakuin, an older woman, rushed to him and exclaimed, "Amitābha Buddha has crashed into my body. Mountains, rivers, grasses, all shine brightly. Splendid! Marvelous!" And she jumped about with joy.

Hakuin said, "How about the shit in the hole?"
The woman pushed at him and said, "Don't you know about that, Rōshi?"[6]

The shit in the hole! The one in the shrine! Clear as a bell! Let's call it Mind! Let's call it Buddha!

So the old teachers plunged ahead using "mind, Buddha, wisdom, Tao" incisively and cogently. "Mind," for example, with "heart" as its etymology, was much more than the human faculty of understanding, the function of the brain. It was much more than the faculty of compassion. Huang-po said:

> There is only the One Mind and not a particle of anything else on which to lay hold, for this Mind is the Buddha. If you students of the Way do not awaken to this Mind substance, you will overlay Mind with conceptual thought, you will seek the Buddha outside yourselves, and you will remain attached to forms, pious practices and so on, all of which are harmful and not at all the way to supreme knowledge.[7]

Mind is Buddha after all. In playfully opening his mouth, Huang-po might seem to be placing mind beneath or behind or beyond things. He needs to be read with Yün-men and Chao-chou and other worthies whose "mind" could be salty or gritty—or with Ma-tsu who points to something that is unnamable only because it is not separate. Mind is not Buddha, but Buddha or anything else comes forth as essential mind itself. Dōgen plays the exquisite harmony of mind against its vast emptiness:

> Mountains, rivers, Earth, the sun, the moon, and stars are mind. At just this moment, what is it that appears directly in front of you? When we say "mountains, rivers, and Earth" we do not merely mean the mountains, rivers, and Earth where you are standing. There are various kinds of mountains such as Great Sumeru and Small Sumeru; some mountains extend widely, some rise up steeply. A billion worlds and innumerable lands can be found in a mountain. There are mountains suspended in form; there are mountains suspended in emptiness.[8]

Great Sumeru, according to Indian Buddhist mythology, is the center of the spiritual world; I don't know about Small Sumeru. Following this passage, Dōgen goes on to make comments about rivers, earth, sun, moon, and stars which are similar to his remarks about mountains. In effect he is saying that mind is the awesome mystery which cannot be named—yet it can be spoken of, even vividly delineated:

Little trotty wagtail, he waddled in the mud,
And left his little footmarks, trample where he would.
He waddled in the water-pudge, and waggle went his tail,
And chirrupt up his wings to dry upon the garden rail.[9]

As he is! And as for "Wisdom is not the Tao," the point is the same. Let's take wisdom to begin with:

A monk asked Chih-men, "What is the function of enlightened wisdom?"
Chih-men said, "The rabbit conceives her young."[10]

Enlightened wisdom indeed! And for the Tao:

Pa-ling asked rhetorically, "What is the Tao?"
Answering himself he said, "A clear-eyed person falls into a well."[11]

Resonating to the furthest reaches of the Milky Way—with no trace of mind, Buddha, wisdom, or the Tao!

The story of Kobori Nanrei Rōshi and a Christian priest bears repeating in this connection. The priest asked the meaning of the saying, "Form is emptiness." Kobori Rōshi said, "I don't know. It's from an old sutra."[12] Was the rōshi just playing dumb? Well, in a way, he was. But more fundamentally he was answering the question directly and incisively. I presume that John Clare didn't know about emptiness being form, either, or about any of the other Buddhist buzzwords or buzz ideas. He just showed the wagtail, waddling in the water-pudge—nothing missing, nothing left over!

Wu-men comments: "I must say that Nan-ch'üan got old and knew no shame." When people get old, they do tend to say anything and everything, right up front, with no shame at all. But Wu-men is implying something else. Nan-ch'üan hadn't merely grown old—he had become timeless. He is so old that he's sitting right here on your cushion.

"He opened his stinking mouth a bit and revealed the family disgrace." It seems rude of Wu-men to say that Nan-ch'üan's mouth stank, but he's driving at something important—the stink of Zen. Zen stink is Zen overdone. Even Dōgen's memorable remark—"I have returned from China with empty hands. I only know that my eyes are horizontal and my nose is vertical"—gets smelly after a while.[13]

"He revealed the family disgrace." This is reminiscent of Wu-men's verse to Case 22: "Elder brother calls, younger brother answers—the family disgrace." See into Wu-men's irony. But he is also being straightforward. The way some people (myself included) ramble on about such expressions as "Mind is not Buddha; wisdom is not the Tao" is really a scandal.

"Only a few can acknowledge his great kindness." Take Wu-men to heart! He is talking to all of us. Why don't you get it?

Wu-men's verse begins: "The sky clears, the sun shines brightly, / rain falls, the earth gets wet." When the persimmon is completely ripe, it will fall straight down. Very naturally. What is your response to these natural events? How do you respond when the sky clears or when the rain falls? In such a grateful mood, you can appreciate Nan-ch'üan's "Mind is not Buddha; wisdom is not the Tao."

"He fully opens his heart and expounds the whole secret; but I fear he is little appreciated." Here Wu-men repeats the message of the last part of his comment. Again he is challenging us. Why don't you get it?

The monk Seikan Hasegawa, author of *The Cave of Poison Grass*, remarked in a letter to me that kōan practice is self-limiting when it is used as an aesthetic device for the appreciation of symmetry. That's a comment which could only be made by a person of true realization and insight. The words of Nan-ch'üan are deceptively simple if understood only as expressions of symmetrical form. They are neat statements, and we can take pleasure in presenting their content in the interview room. But to express them as Nan-ch'üan would is another matter. To appreciate Nan-ch'üan, Chao-chou, and the other old worthies is the way of transformation. It is to become equally worthy. Kōans are not riddles but ways to open out one's bodhisattva nature. To paraphrase Yamada Rōshi: "The way of Mu is the perfection of character."

CASE 35

Wu-tsu: "Which Is the True Ch'ien?"

THE CASE

Wu-tsu asked a monk, "The woman Ch'ien and her spirit separated. Which is the true Ch'ien?"

WU-MEN'S COMMENT

If you realize the true one, then you'll know that emerging from one husk and entering another is like a traveler putting up at an inn. If this is still not clear, don't rush about recklessly. When you suddenly separate into earth, water, fire, and air, you'll be like a crab dropped into boiling water, struggling with your seven hands and eight legs. Don't say I never told you.

WU-MEN'S VERSE

The moon and the clouds are the same;
mountains and valleys are different.
All are blessed, all are blessed.
Is this one? Is this two?

If kōans are the folk stories of Zen, then here we have a folk story as a kōan. As such it is not unique in our study. Case 42, "Mañjuśrī and the Young

Woman in Samādhi," is another—but that is a Buddhist folk story, while this case emerges straight from the lay Chinese tradition. The teacher who placed the story before his students was Wu-tsu (Goso), whose name means "Fifth Ancestor." Don't confuse him with the traditional Fifth Ancestor, who lived in the seventh century. This Wu-tsu lived in the Sung period at Mount Wu-tsu and during his time was greatly revered. He was the teacher of Yüan-wu, the editor of *The Blue Cliff Record*, and Wu-men himself was directly in his line several generations later. Like Nan-ch'üan he appears in *The Gateless Barrier* four times.

As a young man Wu-tsu studied Buddhist philosophy, and one day a fellow student challenged their teacher with the words, "If subject and object are one, how can that fact be realized?" The teacher responded, "It is like drinking water and knowing personally whether or not it is warm or cold." Wu-tsu said to himself, "I know about warm and cold, but I don't know about personally."

His teacher could not explain it to him, and suggested that he take up Zen practice. Accordingly he wandered from temple to temple, finally settling in the assembly of Pai-yün (Haku'un). One day he heard the master give the following teishō: "There are several Zen monks from Mt. Lu who have had satori. If you have them speak, they give beautiful talks. If you ask them regarding kōans, they answer clearly. If you ask them to write pithy commentaries, they do so nicely. Yet they have not attained it."[1] Wu-tsu was dumbfounded by this. Ultimately, though, he realized it personally and tangibly. The present case is grounded on that personal and tangible vantage.

The full story appears in a number of versions which are summarized by Lafcadio Hearn in his piece "A Question in the Zen Texts." This essay, first published in 1898, is one of the earliest references in English either to Zen or to Wu-men's collection of classic cases:

I

My friend opened a thin yellow volume of that marvelous text which proclaims at sight the patience of the Buddhist engraver. Movable Chinese types may be very useful; but the best of which they are capable is ugliness itself when compared with the beauty of the old block-printing.

"I have a queer story for you," he said.

"A Japanese story?"

"No—Chinese."

"What is the book?"

"According to Japanese pronunciation of the Chinese characters
of the title, we call it 'Mu-Mon-Kwan,' which means 'The Gateless
Barrier.' It is one of the books especially studied by the Zen sect, or
sect of Dhyāna. A peculiarity of some of the Dhyāna texts—this
being a good example—is that they are not explanatory. They only
suggest. Questions are put; but the student must think out the answers for himself. He must think them out, but not write them. You
know that Dhyāna represents human effort to reach, through meditation, zones of thought beyond the range of verbal expression; and
any thought once narrowed into utterance loses all Dhyāna quality. . . . Well, this story is supposed to be true; but it is used only
for a Dhyāna question. There are three different Chinese versions of
it; and I can give you the substance of the three." Which he did as
follows:

II

The story of the girl Ch'ien, which is told in the "Lui-shwo-li-hwan-
ki," cited by the "Ching-tang-luh," and commented upon in
the "Wu-men-kwan" (called by the Japanese "Mu-Mon-Kwan"),
which is a book of the Zen sect:

There lived in Han-yang a man called Chang-Kien, whose child-
daughter, Ch'ien, was of peerless beauty. He had also a nephew
called Wang-Chau—a very handsome boy. The children played together, and were fond of each other. Once Kien jestingly said to his
nephew: "Some day I will marry you to my little daughter." Both
children remembered these words; and they believed themselves
thus betrothed.

When Ch'ien grew up, a man of rank asked for her in marriage;
and her father decided to comply with the demand. Ch'ien was
greatly troubled by this decision. As for Chau, he was so much an-
gered and grieved that he resolved to leave home, and go to another
province. The next day he got a boat ready for his journey, and after
sunset, without bidding farewell to any one, he proceeded up the
river. But in the middle of the night he was startled by a voice calling
to him, "Wait!—It is I!"—and he saw a girl running along the bank
toward the boat. It was Ch'ien. Chau was unspeakably delighted.

She sprang into the boat; and the lovers found their way safely to the province of Chuh.

In the province of Chuh they lived happily for six years; and they had two children. But Ch'ien could not forget her parents, and often longed to see them again.

At last she said to her husband: "Because in former times I could not bear to break the promise made to you, I ran away with you and forsook my parents—although knowing that I owed them all possible duty and affection. Would it not now be well to try to obtain their forgiveness?"

"Do not grieve yourself about that," said Chau. "We shall go to see them." He ordered a boat to be prepared; and a few days later he returned with his wife to Han-yang.

According to custom in such cases, the husband first went to the house of Kien, leaving Ch'ien alone in the boat. Kien welcomed his nephew with every sign of joy and said:

"How much I have been longing to see you! I was often afraid that something had happened to you."

Chau answered respectfully: "I am distressed by the undeserved kindness of your words. It is to beg your forgiveness that I have come."

But Kien did not seem to understand. He asked: "To what matter do you refer?"

"I feared," said Chau, "that you were angry with me for having run away with Ch'ien. I took her with me to the province of Chuh."

"What Ch'ien was that?" asked Kien.

"Your daughter Ch'ien," answered Chau, beginning to suspect his father-in-law of some malevolent design.

"What are you talking about?" cried Kien, with every appearance of astonishment. "My daughter Ch'ien has been sick in bed all these years—ever since the time when you went away."

"Your daughter Ch'ien," returned Chau, becoming angry, "has not been sick. She has been my wife for six years; and we have two children; and we have both returned to this place only to seek your pardon. Therefore please do not mock us!"

For a moment the two looked at each other in silence. Then Kien arose, and motioning to his nephew to follow, led the way to an inner room where a sick girl was lying. And Chau, to his utter amazement, saw the face of Ch'ien—beautiful, but strangely thin and pale.

"She cannot speak," explained the old man; "but she can understand." And Kien said to her, laughingly: "Chau tells me that you ran away with him, and that you gave him two children." The sick girl looked at Chau, and smiled; but remained silent.

"Now come with me to the river," said the bewildered visitor to his father-in-law. "For I can assure you—in spite of what I have seen in this house—that your daughter Ch'ien is at this moment in my boat."

They went to the river; and there, indeed, was the young wife, waiting. And seeing her father, she bowed down before him, and besought his pardon.

Kien said to her: "If you really be my daughter, I have nothing but love for you. Yet though you seem to be my daughter, there is something which I cannot understand. . . . Come with us to the house."

So the three proceeded toward the house. As they neared it, they saw that the sick girl—who had not before left her bed for years—was coming to meet them, smiling as if much delighted. And the two Ch'iens approached each other. But then—nobody could ever tell how—they suddenly melted into each other, and became one body, one person, one Ch'ien—even more beautiful than before, and showing no sign of sickness or of sorrow.

Kien said to Chau: "Ever since the day of your going, my daughter was dumb, and most of the time like a person who had taken too much wine. Now I know that her spirit was absent."

Ch'ien herself said: "Really I never knew that I was at home. I saw Chau going away in silent anger; and the same night I dreamed that I ran after his boat. . . . But now I cannot tell which was really I—the I that went away in the boat, or the I that stayed at home."

III

"That is the whole of the story," my friend observed. "Now there is a note about it in the 'Mu-Mon-Kwan' that may interest you. This note says: 'The fifth patriarch of the Zen sect once asked a priest—"In the case of the separation of the spirit of the girl Ch'ien, which was the true Ch'ien?"' It was only because of this question that the story was cited in the book. But the question is not answered. The author only remarks: 'If you can decide which was the real Ch'ien, then you will have learned that to go out of one envelope and into another is merely like putting up at an inn. But if you have not yet reached this degree of enlightenment, take heed that you do not wander aimlessly about the world. Otherwise, when Earth, Water, Fire, and Wind shall suddenly be dissipated, you will be like a crab with seven hands and eight legs, thrown into boiling water. And in that time do not say that you were never told about the Thing.' . . . Now the Thing—"

"I do not want to hear about the Thing," I interrupted—"nor about the crab with seven hands and eight legs. I want to hear about the clothes."

"What clothes?"

"At the time of their meeting, the two Ch'iens would have been differently dressed—very differently, perhaps; for one was a maid, and the other a wife. Did the clothes of the two also blend together? Suppose that one had a silk robe and the other a robe of cotton, would these have mixed into a texture of silk and cotton? Suppose that one was wearing a blue girdle, and the other a yellow girdle, would the result have been a green girdle? . . . Or did one Ch'ien simply slip out of her costume, and leave it on the ground, like the cast-off shell of a cicada?"

"None of the texts says anything about the clothes," my friend replied: "so I cannot tell you. But the subject is quite irrelevant, from the Buddhist point of view. The doctrinal question is the question of what I suppose you would call the personality of Ch'ien."

"And yet it is not answered," I said.

"It is best answered," my friend replied, "by not being answered."

"How so?"

"Because there is no such thing as personality."[2]

Lafcadio Hearn was born on the Ionian island of Santa Maura of a Greek mother and an Irish father, a surgeon major in the British army. He was raised by his Irish grandmother, filled we may be sure with folk stories and fairy tales. He became an essayist and a storyteller who wandered the world and finally settled in Japan, married a Japanese woman, and took Japanese citizenship under the name Koizumi Yakumo. He was an important interpreter of Japan to the English-speaking world, and today his stories are read in English by Japanese people who are interested in the culture of their great-grandparents. Throughout his life he devoted himself to these folk stories and wrote many of his own. Yet he did not always see into their mythic configurations. On this occasion, rather than listen to his friend, who must have had some Zen eye, Hearn was off on his question about the clothes. The question is ridiculous and really unlike Hearn, who was quite capable of suspending belief. Off he went flashing his wit and intellect, as people sometimes do in the interview room, flashing history or philosophy or psychology. I can't help feeling that he was resisting the suggestion that he look deeper than the surface.

Wu-men comments: "If you realize the true one, then you'll know that emerging from one husk and entering another is like a traveler putting up at an inn." Once Yamada Rōshi asked a student of the Diamond Sangha, "What do you think of death?" She replied, "Why, it's like when a bus stops before you—you get on and go." He approved that answer and Wu-men would too, I think. The young woman Ch'ien separated and rejoined. Can you identify her? It is not enough to say they were one from the beginning. Where is the real Ch'ien?

"If this is still not clear, don't rush about recklessly." Wu-men is admonishing you not to flit from teacher to teacher, from doctrine to doctrine, from practice to practice. More than that, Wu-men is kindly advising you not to rush about with interpretations and analysis. Just settle patiently into your practice.

"When you suddenly separate into earth, water, fire, and air, you'll be like a crab dropped into boiling water, struggling with your seven hands and eight legs." The image is all too vivid. A crab is cooked by placing the live animal in boiling water. It doesn't die right away, but struggles against the lid of the pot. What will be your reaction when that lid comes down over you? This question is reminiscent of the question by Tou-shuai (Tosotsu): "When you have seen into your true nature, you will be free of birth and death. How will you free yourself when your eyes are darkening for the last time?"[3] At such a time, says Wu-men, "Don't say I didn't warn you."

Dying well, in the Victorian phrase, is more than going calmly. Surely, it is a great adventure. I noticed an interview with Ram Dass in the newspaper recently in which he spoke of dying as "a great creative act."

It is living well, however, that is Wu-tsu's lesson. In his teishō on this case, one of my long-time students points out that living a divided life is debilitating. It laid the woman Ch'ien out completely. And there is more than one way of being divided. Seated at my desk, I long to be on the line protesting the destruction of the habitat. Thus I cannot be effective in either place. The man who takes a mistress slights both his family and his new love. His spirit divided, he dissipates his potential as an integrated person.

Wu-men's verse begins: "The moon and the clouds are the same." Ch'ien living with her husband and children; Ch'ien pining at home— aren't these the same Ch'ien? All your actions, cleaning the bathtub, crossing the street, paying bills, are movements in separate circumstances of the same essential you. In the context of the story, how are moon and clouds the same?

"Mountains and valleys are different." Ch'ien was wife and mother in the far city. Ch'ien was a sick daughter at home. They were widely separated in every way. These are interpretations of the story, of course. You must see the application of these two lines in your own life.

"All are blessed, all are blessed." The blessed outcome! "Is this one? Is this two?" Now about this *thing*—what do you say? Two Ch'iens? One Ch'ien? Can the true one be two?

CASE 36

Wu-tsu: Meeting Someone
Attained in the Tao

THE CASE

*Wu-tsu said, "When you meet someone attained in the Tao on the road, do not make
your greeting with words or with silence. How will you make your greeting?"*

WU-MEN'S COMMENT

*If you become intimate with this matter, you are certainly to be warmly congratu-
lated. If it is not yet clear, then you must be alert to every single thing.*

WU-MEN'S VERSE

> *Meeting someone attained in the Tao on the road,
> don't make your greeting with words or with silence;
> a punch in the jaw!
> If you want to realize—just realize.*

Again we encounter Wu-tsu. In this case, he takes up a verse traceable to
Hsiang-yen, the T'ang period teacher who put you up a tree in Case 5:

Clear, lucid, with no hindrance whatsoever;
standing all by yourself, you don't rely on anything.
If you meet a man or woman of the Tao on the road,
make your greeting with neither words nor silence.[1]

Several years ago I heard a story of Yasutani Rōshi meeting Asahina Sō-gen Rōshi on the stone steps leading to Matsugaoka Library. This is the library that Dr. D. T. Suzuki established soon after World War II in Kita-kamakura. Asahina Rōshi was the eminent master of Enkakuji, the great monastery in Kitakamakura where Dr. Suzuki and Senzaki Sensei trained. He had at one time been the teacher of Kyōzō Yamada, who went on to be Yamada Kōun Rōshi under the guidance of Yasutani Rōshi.

Asahina Rōshi stared at Yasutani Rōshi in astonishment, crying out "Oh! Oh!" Then he laughed heartily.

Yasutani Rōshi bowed with a smile and said, "It's been a long time since we met, Rōshi."

Is this the kind of meeting Wu-tsu challenges us to carry through? In any case, it was certainly a great test of their humanity for those old masters. There on the stone steps through the bamboo grove, each dipped his colors to the other forthrightly with great good humor. Each day, each of us is similarly tested.

Once the Koko An Sangha held a joint meeting with the two Tibetan Sanghas of Honolulu. At the end of that meeting, Anne Aitken and I went to Nechung Rinpoché's room to make our farewells. The last thing he said to us was, "See you again!" Don't suppose that he was just being polite. Indeed, now that Nechung Rinpoché has died, I meet him again when I visit his Wood Valley Temple at Pahala, Hawai'i—and on stone steps, too, which he himself built from the dormitory to the temple.

I wonder if you can appreciate the mind that Asahina Rōshi, Yasutani Rōshi, and Nechung Rinpoché expressed in their words of greeting and farewell. Turning to Zen literature, we find many cases that deal overtly with speech and silence. In Case 24, Feng-hsüeh quotes a poem when challenged to transcend speech and silence, subject and object. In Case 32 the Buddha presents his gracious silence in response to a similar question. In *The Blue Cliff Record* we find three cases of Pai-chang asking his attendants in turn, "How would you say something with your lips and throat closed?"[2]

Lin-chi explores the matter further and cautions us not to fling muddy water on such an occasion: "Meeting someone attained in the Tao on the road, above all don't take up the Tao."[3] A slightly different point, but worth exploring nonetheless. Pao-fu got the same lesson from Ch'ang-ch'ing:

> Ch'ang-ch'ing and Pao-fu were wandering in the hills. Pao-fu pointed to the top of the hill where they were standing and said, "Right here is the top of Mount Sumeru."
> Ch'ang-ch'ing said, "Yes, that's true, but a pity."[4]

Since Mount Sumeru is the center of paradise, Pao-fu's comment could be rendered, "Right here is the peak of paradise." In his comment on this case, Yüan-wu quotes Chao-chou:

> A monk asked Chao-chou, "What is the lone summit of Mount Sumeru?"
> Chao-chou said, "I won't answer that question of yours."
> The monk asked, "Why won't you answer my question?"
> Chao-chou said, "I'm afraid that if I answered you, you would fall to flat ground."[5]

You would lose your sense of configuration, in other words. On that absolute peak of "paradise," everything is immobile and undifferentiated, like a bowl of mayonnaise, and there is no room for questions and answers.

We must cultivate a good balance, a sense of proportion, at all times. If our zazen has no application in daily life, then we are simply indulging in cultist tricks. Unless the new bearings we find on our cushions govern our Sangha relations—both within our training center and in everyday contacts at home, at school, and at work—attainment on the cushions is only relative. In this case the dōjō is merely a place where we restore ourselves after dealing with the exigencies of everyday life.

Those exigencies are tough. If you are working in the world, you know this can be a cruel, acquisitive society. But if you treat the dōjō only as a sanctuary, then your delight, harmony, and tranquility are just a small fraction of your life. The Three Poisons of greed, hatred, and foolishness dominate the rest. The place where the true sons and daughters of the Buddha dwell is not like this. With all the comings and goings of our busy life, there is something that does not come or go, something that does not move. Make your greetings there.

Bashō has the verse:

> Seeing off,
> being seen off—the outcome:
> autumn in Kiso.[6]

"Outcome" could also be translated "upshot." In the bustle of being seen off, the ground of Bashō's mind was the autumn of Kiso where he and his friends were making their greetings. He recalled this season on the busiest holiday—New Year's Day:

> New Year's Day!
> when I reflect—
> lonely autumn evenings.[7]

The dragon enjoys its jewel. Bashō's enjoyment is somber, but it is pleasure nonetheless—royal solitude.

What kind of responses do you make to family members and Dharma friends? When I used to speak of the importance of being decent to others, people would sometimes say, "Isn't it dishonest to say one thing and feel something else?" It is no more dishonest to practice decency than it is to practice zazen. Zazen is the practice of harmony at the source of responsibility. Being decent is simply the practice of harmony in a wider context.

Wu-tsu did not have the advantage of knowing from psychological research how childhood traumas carry over into the adult world. Nonetheless, he knew very well about immaturity. With his challenge, he can be said to be pointing to the seasoned way of Yün-men—whose responses, it is said, fit situations as a lid fits its box:

> Monk: "What is my true self?"
> The Master: "Play in the mountains, play in the waters."
> Monk: "What is your true self, Master?"
> The Master: "Fortunately, the monitor isn't here."[8]

It is play! It is play! Yün-men was lucid and clear, not relying on anything or anybody, turning the Dharma Wheel all by himself. When meeting a student of the Tao, he did not make his greetings in any relative manner—

with speech or silence—but came forth zestfully from the ground of his joyous mind.

Wu-men comments: "If you become intimate with this matter, you are certainly to be warmly congratulated." Intimacy is realization. When there is no intimacy, you are separate from your kōan and separate from everything else. Realization is that place of harmony from which you greet the man or woman of the Tao with the delight of intimacy.

"If it is not yet clear," Wu-men says, "then you must be alert to every single thing." Moreover, when you are working with Mu, then everything will be alert to you. At this moment the cardinal, the wind, the candle, all are giving their full attention to you. Listen! Look!

On this short staff which Yamada Rōshi gave me, he inscribed: "The Dharma, the Dharma majesty, is just this!"[9] We are exposed to a succession of phenomena—this, this, this—and we tend to focus on the sequence. Thus we become preoccupied with generalizations and mindsets, fixed attitudes, and concepts. This (*crack!*) gives life. This (*crack!*) saves all beings.

Wu-men's verse begins: "Meeting someone attained in the Tao on the road, / don't make your greeting with words or with silence." Do you think Wu-men is repeating himself here? I don't. He is saying it for the first time.

"A punch in the jaw!" Perhaps the tranquil mind, the mind of dwelling nowhere, might come forth with a punch in the jaw. Mu-chou broke Yün-men's leg in just the right place.[10] Ma-tsu twisted Pai-chang's nose and Pai-chang wept with joy.[11] Shōju Rōjin kicked Hakuin down his front steps to Hakuin's eternal gratitude.[12]

"If you want to realize—just realize." Don't make it difficult. Some writers criticize Wu-men's verse as being too rough. It is rough, all right, but it's not self-indulgent. Like heaven and earth, the Buddha is merciless.

Chao-chou: The Oak Tree in the Courtyard

THE CASE

A monk asked Chao-chou, "What is the meaning of Bodhidharma's coming from the West?"

Chao-chou said, "The oak tree in the courtyard."[1]

WU-MEN'S COMMENT

If you can see intimately into the essence of Chao-chou's response, there is no Śākyamuni in the past and no Maitreya in the future.

WU-MEN'S VERSE

Words do not convey the fact;
language is not an expedient.
Attached to words, your life is lost;
blocked by phrases, you are bewildered.

Bodhidharma brought Dhyāna Buddhism from India to China, where it became Ch'an Buddhism and then, in Japan, Zen. What was Bodhidharma's mind as he journeyed from India to China? He made the hazardous trip by boat, it is believed, very near the end of his long life. He came with the message that one cannot depend upon words, and he urged seeing into true nature for the attainment of Buddhahood.

That may have been his message, but we must distinguish this from his meaning, his essence of mind. If you are familiar with that fundamental ground, then Chao-chou's response will also be intimate. Lin-chi, too, was intimate with the matter. But when asked the same question, he responded in a very different way. He said, "If Bodhidharma had had any meaning he could not have saved even himself."[2] This was also true of Chao-chou. If Chao-chou had had any meaning, there would be no such thing as a Zen path. It is also true of Wu-men. If Wu-men had had a meaning, he could never have composed his great book.

Then is Chao-chou's answer designed to show "no-meaning"? Not exactly. The point is that "meaning" is a word that invites a presentation of your heart of hearts and there are two basic ways to do this—as in Ma-tsu's two responses to questions about Buddha. In Case 30 Ma-tsu says, "This very mind is Buddha." In Case 33 he turns around and says, "Not mind, not Buddha." Positively: "Oak tree in the courtyard." Negatively: "If he had had any meaning, he could not have saved even himself." Positive and negative are not opposites here; each *includes* the other. They are the meaning of Bodhidharma's coming from the West, now by land, now by sea. Lin-chi presented the fact of the oak tree in the courtyard with his words, "If he had had any meaning, he could not have saved even himself." Likewise, Chao-chou presented Lin-chi's point.

Dōgen says in his *Genjō Kōan* that we are confirmed by the ten thousand things.[3] "Confirmed" is perhaps not a strong enough expression:

A monk asked Yün-men, "What was Niu-t'ou after he met the Fourth Ancestor?"

Yün-men said, "The moth in the flame swallows the tiger."[4]

You might say that Niu-t'ou (Gozu) was "enlightened" when he met the Fourth Ancestor, but Yün-men would clobber you if you used such a stale expression. Even his word "swallows" is not clear enough. The moth in the flame *devours* the tiger and begins to roar! Take it in! Take it in!

I have heard that an American teacher who no longer encourages kōan practice has said something like this: "It is easy enough to realize the oak tree, but how is this experience relevant to daily life?" I agree that our task is to embody kōans at home and on the job—this is our life work. But the first part of that teacher's statement is incorrect. I do not realize the oak tree. Quite the contrary, in fact. If the practical implications of this intimacy are not as plain as day for you, then you are not yet a teacher of religion.

Once again Wu-men abbreviates the original story, which has the monk continuing the dialogue after Chao-chou's initial response:

> "Please don't teach me with reference to outside things."
>
> Chao-chou said, "I don't teach you with reference to outside things."
>
> The monk said, "What is the meaning of Bodhidharma's coming from the West?"
>
> Chao-chou said, "The oak tree in the courtyard."[5]

The monk thought he knew enough to understand that Zen practice is a matter of looking within. Chao-chou's first response seems to answer his question with reference to his environment. What is happening here? The monk couldn't understand. Don't suppose that the resolution of this point lies in the identity of inside and outside. That is philosophy. What is the true fact?

Monks at that time were quite preoccupied with Chao-chou's response. After his death, Fa-yen asked Chao-chou's disciple Hui-chiao (Ekaku) about it:

> "I have heard that your late master had a saying: 'The oak tree in the courtyard.' Is that correct?"
>
> Hui-chiao said, "No."
>
> Fa-yen said, "Anyone who has been around will say that a monk asked him about the meaning of Bodhidharma's coming from the West, and that he answered, 'The oak tree in the courtyard.' How can you maintain that he didn't say it?"
>
> Hui-chiao said, "He really didn't say that. Please don't slander him."[6]

We can trust Hui-chiao. He was a formidable master, nicknamed "Iron Beak Chiao," and during his lifetime and thereafter he had a splendid reputation—some teachers even declare that he surpassed his master.[7] He was Chao-chou's faithful attendant during his teacher's later years, so of course he knew all about the oak tree. Then what was his meaning when he said, "He really didn't say that. Please don't slander him"?

There's a wonderful Japanese story relating to this case that involves Shidō Munan (though it is sometimes attributed to Hakuin, his famous grandson in the Dharma): Munan had collected a large sum of gold for the establishment of a monastery and was returning home on foot with the money. A bandit, skilled in detecting travelers carrying valuables, followed him to an inn where both put up for the night. When all was quiet, the bandit came to Munan Zenji's room and slipped open the sliding door. To his amazement he didn't find a monk snoozing under his quilts but an enormous oak tree, rooted in the tatami mat, pushing its branches against the ceiling and walls! Trembling and confused, he withdrew to his own room.

Next day, as the two men set out again, the bandit approached Munan and said, "I am a great bandit. I know in one glance when someone has gold or jewels concealed on his person. I can steal such valuables without my victim feeling a thing. But last night I met my master. I found that you had disappeared and an oak tree was growing there instead. I realize that I am your inferior. I beg you to accept me as your disciple."[8] Munan accepted him and the bandit went on to become a great monk. He knew true intimacy when he saw it.

Regarding this case Kanzan, the founder of Myōshinji, said: "The kōan of the oak tree has the function of a bandit. It steals everything from you."[9] Kanzan was a marvelous Zen master who became the emperor's teacher, but he left no writings at all and only this one saying is recorded of him. When Yin-yüan (Ingen), founder of the Ōbaku sect in Japan, came from China several centuries later, he visited Myōshinji and was told this story. Prostrating himself before Kanzan's image he said, "This one saying is superior to ten thousand volumes of teishōs."[10] When I was a young student I visited Myōshinji with Nakagawa Sōen Rōshi. We were told the story about Kanzan and Yin-yüan, but it made little impression on me. Sōen Rōshi, however, got very excited, and bowed over and over to Kanzan's image. He took it in, and I did not. If there was ever anyone rooted, who walked like a tree, it was Sōen Rōshi.

Wu-men comments: "If you can see intimately into the essence of Chao-chou's response, there is no Śākyamuni in the past and no Maitreya in the future." Maitreya Buddha is the Buddha who is waiting in the Tusita

Heaven to appear in the world. Your body, your mind, inside, outside, the years between Chao-chou and yourself, the miles between China and Hawai'i, the personages of past and future—all fall away and disappear. What remains?

> A monk asked Chao-chou, "Has the oak tree Buddha nature?"
> Chao-chou said, "Yes, it has."
> The monk said, "When does the oak tree attain Buddhahood?"
> Chao-chou said, "Wait until the great universe collapses."
> The monk said, "When does the universe collapse?"
> Chao-chou said, "Wait until the oak tree attains Buddhahood."[11]

The great universe itelf finds everything stolen away by this one kōan, "Oak tree in the courtyard." Wait until the oak tree attains Buddhahood indeed! If everything is truly stolen away, the universe has collapsed right there.

Wu-men's verse begins: "Words do not convey the fact."[12] That's true, isn't it? In the pungent English proverb "Fine words butter no parsnips," the word "butter" is neither smooth nor salty. "The oak tree in the courtyard" does not convey the real oak tree.

"Language is not an expedient." That's true too—as Hui-chao hinted. "Oak tree in the courtyard" is not a device which Chao-chou summoned up to enlighten a monk. Don't slander the great master.

"Attached to words, your life is lost." Yes. Words are the keys which program most people. Such people are used by words instead of using words. Their understanding is not experiential but merely verbal; instead of coming from life and using words, they act on the basis of concepts, which can destroy life.

Follow Simone Weil's way in dealing with this kōan: "Contemplating an object fixedly with the mind, asking myself, 'What is it?' without thinking of any other object or relating it to anything else for hours on end."[13] It is in this way that you must work on "The oak tree in the courtyard," or on Mu, or on counting your breaths.

"Blocked by phrases, you are bewildered." That's not altogether bad. How else can one practice? "The oak tree in the courtyard"—bewildered by that, you have a great chance.

CASE 38

Wu-tsu's Buffalo Passes
Through the Window

THE CASE

Wu-tsu said, "It is like a buffalo that passes through a latticed window. Its head, horns, and four legs all pass through. Why can't its tail pass through as well?"

WU-MEN'S COMMENT

If you can get upside down with this one, discern it clearly, and give a turning word to it, then you can meet the Four Obligations above and give comfort to the Three Existences below. But if it is not yet clear, pay close attention to the tail and you will resolve it at last.

WU-MEN'S VERSE

Passing through, falling in a ditch;
turning beyond, all is lost.
This tiny little tail—
what a wonderful thing it is!

Here we meet Wu-tsu again, the Sung dynasty teacher featured in Cases 35 and 36. He appears often in our kōan study, each time with an original, distinctive, and profoundly humorous presentation.

Like all Zen cases, this one about the tail of the buffalo is metaphorical.

Your task is to understand the metaphor and then resolve the question it poses. To start with, you need to know about the buffalo. This is the water buffalo or water ox, an important member of the household for farming families throughout Asia. It pulls the plow through the mud of the rice fields and enriches them with its manure. Its power and placid disposition give it a place in the Buddhist pantheon with the lion of Mañjuśrī and the elephant of Samantabhadra. Its figure is sometimes found with Buddhas and bodhisattvas on Zen Buddhist altars—on the altar at the Sanun Zendō, for example, in Kamakura. The water buffalo is the ox of the Ten Oxherding Pictures, a series of symbolic images found in a number of English Zen texts. In that series the ox represents essential nature. It is sought, followed, glimpsed, captured, tamed, and ultimately forgotten, and in the tenth picture the herdsman has become Pu-tai entering the marketplace with bliss-bestowing hands, his bag full of candy and toys for children.[1] Wu-tsu's ox is the one in the final picture, but you can't see him. The ox has become Pu-tai, too, teasing you with that tail.

To the point: Your head, horns, and four legs all have passed through the gate of Zen practice. But something doesn't pass. A Zen master I have known for more than thirty years tells his students, "I have never passed Mu." Well, as you know, Mu is the first kōan for most Zen students. My friend has taught the entire Zen curriculum for decades and many of his students have completed their study with him. Yet he says that he himself has not yet passed the first gate—not entirely, that is. His tail has not yet passed through. He has, however, passed this kōan about the tail. As Dō-gen says: "When the Dharma does not fill your whole body and mind, you think it is already sufficient. When the Dharma fills your body and mind, you understand that something is missing."[2] In his celebrated passage cited earlier in Case 12, Dōgen helps to clarify what is missing:

> To study the Buddha Way is to study the self. To study the self is to forget the self. To forget the self is to be confirmed by the myriad things. To be confirmed by the myriad things is to cast off the body and mind of the self as well as those of others. No trace of realization remains and this no-trace is continued endlessly.[3]

Each of these five sentences forms a step in Zen practice—the five oxherding pictures, so to speak, the Five Modes of Tung-shan: mustering body and mind, forgetting the self in the practice, finding confirmation with birdsong and the morning star, dying to the self with this confirmation, continuing for all time. The final sentence, "No trace of realization remains and this no-trace is continued endlessly," refers to the fact that *anuttara-samyak-sambodhi*, peerless omniscient wisdom, is still incomplete. It is commonly said in Zen monasteries that Śākyamuni is only halfway there and is still sitting hard in the Tusita Heaven. In other words, with *anuttara-samyak-sambodhi* you finally realize that there is nothing to be gained—and instead of taking yourself in hand and making the practice happen, it is yourself as *anuttara-samyak-sambodhi* that continues it. This evokes Pu-tai's broad smile.

Such fulfilling experiences as catching sight of the ox and entering the marketplace with bliss-bestowing hands are complete in themselves, however. Dōgen wrote: "The Dharma Wheel turns from the beginning. There is neither surplus nor lack. The whole universe is moistened with nectar and the truth is ready to harvest."[4] The truth is ready to harvest *before* our practice, but we harvest it *through* our practice. It is with practice that we study and understand the Buddha Way. It is with practice that we cast off body and mind. And it is with practice that this casting off is continued endlessly in our delight. All this, however, is just "making something," as one of my Zen colleagues is fond of saying. Wu-tsu's question is: "Why can't the tail pass through too?" How do you respond?

Wu-men comments: "If you can get upside down with this one, discern it clearly, and give a turning word to it, then you can meet the Four Obligations above and give comfort to the Three Existences below." In this one sentence Wu-men sets forth the whole of formal Zen study. The first step is to get upside down: to look south at the tail when all this while you have been looking north at the ox. This is a personal resolution—an "aha!" experience. The second step is to discern it clearly. After you have brought this matter of the tail home to yourself, you will see why it doesn't pass through the latticed window. The final step is to give a turning word—say something or do something that will enlighten others about that tail. I wrote a haiku long ago that might help you to stand on your head for Wu-tsu:

> The station at evening:
> no one gets on or off;
> the autumn wind.

Then with your experience, your discernment, and your talent for efficacious hints—your words and conduct will meet your obligations, which teachers like Wu-men view as four: parents, country, all beings, and the Three Treasures of Buddha, Dharma, and Sangha.

Do you feel obliged to your parents? Some people feel that they have taken the brunt of their parents' egregious mistakes. But their parents took the brunt of their parents' mistakes in turn, and so on back. No parents, no life whatsoever, and no practice.

Some people do not feel that their country poses any kind of obligation. But actually your geographical, cultural, political, and economic place is your dōjō, your seat of enlightenment. If you deny this seat, you are wandering in mind and body. "When," as Huang-po asked, "can you meet today?"[5]

The third obligation—all beings—confirms your true nature as you open your serene and receptive mind to them. And they do much more, of course.

Finally, the Three Treasures, so difficult to encounter, bring us understanding, the Way, and supportive religious friends. With your realization, your clear discernment of its many facets, and your skillful means to guide others—everything you do or say will be the Bodhisattva Samantabhadra graciously bowing and saying thank you. And don't stop there.

The Three Existences below are the world of desire, the world of color and form, and the world of no-color and no-form. Wu-men uses the words "above" and "below" the way we would say "on the one hand, the Four Obligations; on the other, the Three Existences." Giving comfort to the Three Existences really means fulfilling our first vow: to save the many beings. Everywhere, at all times, we express our gratitude and love.

Wu-men's verse begins: "Passing through, falling in a ditch." Passing through is yourself going through the window. What is falling in a ditch? This is a metaphor about your continuing practice.

"Turning beyond, all is lost." This is the ditch beyond the ditch. Compounding the fall! The English proverb reads, "Pride goes before a fall." In Zen we would turn this around and say, "Pride goes after a fall."

"This tiny little tail—/ what a wonderful thing it is!" Indeed! Nothing more wonderful, nothing more subtle, nothing more exquisite in the whole universe!

Yün-men: "You Have Misspoken"

THE CASE

A monk said to Yün-men, "The radiance serenely illumines the whole universe . . ."

Before he had finished the line, Yün-men interrupted him and asked, "Aren't those the words of Chang-cho?"

The monk said, "Yes, they are."

Yün-men said, "You have misspoken."

Later, the master Ssu-hsin took up this matter and asked, "Tell me, where did the monk misspeak?"

WU-MEN'S COMMENT

If you can see the uncompromising and rigorous operation of Yün-men's method and how the monk misspoke, then you qualify as teacher of people and devas. If it is not yet clear, then you cannot save even yourself.

WU-MEN'S VERSE

A line is cast in the waters;
the greedy will be caught;
if your mouth opens just a bit,
your life is completely lost.

Yün-men appears many times in *The Gateless Barrier*, *The Blue Cliff Record*, and elsewhere in kōan study. He is one of the most eminent teachers of T'ang Zen, and his marvelous dialogues survive and influence all of East Asian Buddhism. In particular, his teaching is embedded in *The Blue Cliff Record*, whose compiler, Hsüeh-tou, was his great-grandson in the Dharma.

Each of the greatest teachers is remembered for a particular method: Lin-chi for his shout, Te-shan for his stick, Chao-chou for his welcoming spirit, and so on. Yün-men is remembered especially for his capacity to teach in the broadest context, cutting off the student's preoccupations, and following up appropriately on the student's question or presentation. He realized and practiced the ideal of all Zen masters.

Here a monk begins a quotation from the government official Chang-cho (Chōsetsu), a prominent lay student of Zen in earlier times. His enlightenment poem runs as follows:

> The radiance serenely illumines the whole universe;
> the ignorant, the wise, all beings are in my abode.
> When no thought rises, the whole is revealed;
> if the six sense organs move even a little, it is obscured by clouds.
> If you cut off your ignorance your ailment will increase;
> if you look for the truth you are wrong.
> Living in accord with things of the world you have no obstructions;
> Nirvana and life-and-death are like colors in a dream.[1]

The monk was probably going to ask Yün-men a question about this poem. If Yün-men had waited for the question, the dialogue would have been very different. I don't know of other Zen cases where the teacher actually interrupts a student. Usually the questioner is allowed full scope to ask a question or make a presentation—though the rug may be yanked thereafter, of course. Yün-men's interruption in this case is quite instructive. By the time the monk reached the end of Chang-cho's long poem, he might have been full of pride about his appreciation of the lofty words. "Can't let this go on," Yün-men probably thought. "Stop right there!"

Consider the purpose of your own questions. Do they inquire about the Dharma? Or are they intended to establish a point? Take a look at Case 15 for an example of Yün-men giving Tung-shan Shou-ch'u an extended opportunity to come forth with something interesting. "Where did you come from? Where were you during the summer? When did you leave there?" Only with the third feeble response did he jerk on the rug: "I spare you sixty blows!" As Hakuin wrote:

> How sad that people ignore the near
> and search for truth afar.[2]

"Oh, you rice bag! Do you go about in such a way, now west of the river, now south of the lake?"

Dōgen said, "Don't permit haphazard talk."[3] Nakagawa Sōen Rōshi paraphrased this with his caution, "Don't use rootless words." No one was more patient with the chatter of students than Sōen Rōshi, and no one was more careful of his own words.

Another example of a student quoting someone when speaking with a teacher is found in Case 40 of *The Blue Cliff Record*. In that story, Nan-ch'üan lets Lu-keng complete his quotation before giving him his come-uppance:

> As Lu-keng was talking with Nan-ch'üan, he said, "The Dharma Master Chao said, 'Heaven and earth and I have the same root. The myriad things and I are one.' This is quite marvelous."
> Nan-ch'üan called Lu and pointed to a flower in the garden, say-ing, "People these days see this flower as if they were in a dream."[4]

"People these days" is a polite form of direct address in Chinese. He really means, "*You* see this flower as if *you* were in a dream." Sometimes "dream" is a positive word referring to the state of the world, but that wasn't Nan-ch'üan's meaning here. His point was this: "You quote the Dharma Master Chao and rhapsodize over his beautiful expression, but you don't really see what he's talking about. You don't even see this flower under your nose! Erase that dream—now what becomes vividly clear?"

When I quote Yün-men, you might stop me and ask, "Aren't those the words of Yün-men?" I could say yes. Would that be misspeaking? As I mentioned in my comment on Case 24, Chao-chou frequently quoted from a verse attributed to Seng-ts'an: "The Supreme Way has no diffi-culties; / it is simply a matter of not choosing."[5] He then invited questions or presentations. What if one of his students had asked him, "Aren't those the words of Seng-ts'an?" How would Chao-chou reply? Suppose I were to quote, "Speak the speech I pray you, as I pronounce it to you, trippingly on the tongue. But do not mouth your words as many of your players do, or I'd as lief the town crier spoke my lines." Aren't those the words of William Shakespeare? Or are they the words of Hamlet, Prince of Denmark? Those of my generation might ask, "Aren't they the words of Maurice Evans?"

Why should Yün-men and Wu-men make such an issue of all this? Surely they are not just demanding that we follow some rule about studying books. Let me digress for a moment. Many contemporary Japanese Zen teachers advise their students to avoid reading, at least when they're working on Mu, and some Zen teachers in the West take the same position. I think this advice can become counterproductive. Some "Zen" books are very misleading, and I don't hesitate to criticize them pointedly. But everyone should have the privilege of browsing in a good bookstore or library. Wise words in a text can resonate as profoundly as a great temple bell.

The question for teachers of Yün-men's time, and for us today, has been how to help people avoid getting lost in the beautiful words—manufacturing all kinds of ignorant elaborations on the Dharma. Ta-hui (Dai'e) burned the printing blocks of *The Blue Cliff Record*, the basic textbook of Zen edited by his teacher Yüan-wu, "because he observed that the enthusiasm for the beauty and eloquence of expression was hindering people from directly experiencing enlightenment on their own."[6]

The point is well taken. But Western students do not live in a culture that is permeated by Zen thought. Even after finishing kōan study, the advanced Western student needs to prowl the bookstores and libraries and, if possible, to learn Japanese or Chinese and begin reading texts in the original and trying to translate them.

If you are working on Bassui's kōan—"Who is hearing that sound?"—your understanding will be enriched and deepened not only by steady zazen but also by studying Bassui's own writings—and then studying the words of other teachers in English, noticing how often they enhance those of Bassui.[7] Gradually you will find your vision expanded. You will be looking with new delight at the words of the Buddha and all his successors. You will be looking with new delight, too, at Shakespeare and Lady Murasaki. Freed into vast dimensions, your kōan will have profound implications not just for human development but also for comets, clouds, and birds. New kōans for Western students will appear in time.

Even if you haven't yet begun kōan study, it's useful to read in conjunction with your zazen practice. You can trust yourself to smell out the right books. "This one seems too advanced, this one seems too occult, but *this* one!" Get the book. You will find out where you stand in your practice. You will also find points that will stretch you. Even if you don't understand parts of the book, it still can be very helpful. It might be, say, Christopher Cleary's *Swampland Flowers.*[8] Take five minutes and read a section aloud to yourself every evening—or to a close friend if he or she can bear it. The words will imprint—just as the King James Version of the Bible imprinted in the minds of your forebears around the fire in the living room when they were young. Out they came as literate adults. Out you will come a student of Zen.

Back to the case. When the monk innocently affirms that those were indeed the words of Chang-cho, Yün-men says, "You have misspoken." Although that's the end of the dialogue, it reverberates—probably in the mind of that monk, but also in the halls of other monasteries and in the minds of other Zen students. Ssu-hsin (Shishin) takes up the case two hundred years later and asks, "Tell me, at what point did the monk misspeak?" That's the key question.

Some students say that the monk misspoke when he said, "The radiance serenely illumines the whole universe." Everything was complete before he spoke. That's true, of course. It is also true of all the thousands of kōans, all the volumes of the Tripitaka, not to mention this teishō. Colossal misspeaking.

Some students say that the monk misspoke when he replied in the affirmative to Yün-men's question. Quotations can obscure the vivid fact itself. I would find it distracting if someone quoted Wordsworth when I was admiring a rainbow. But if the monk had replied in the negative, would that have been correct? After all, they were indeed Chang-cho's words.

Wu-men comments: "If you can see the uncompromising and rigorous operation of Yün-men's method and how the monk misspoke, then you qualify as teacher of people and devas." If you can see where Yün-men was diverting the flow of the dialogue, then you are resolutely independent, a teacher of humans and angels. You are not dependent upon the words of others but can use them as Yün-men did, as all great teachers do, intimately, personally.

"But if it is not yet clear, then you cannot save even yourself." And certainly you cannot save other people. No intimacy, no wisdom, no love, no creativity.

Wu-men's verse begins: "A line is cast in the waters." In the flow of the dialogue Yün-men casts a bit of bait: "Aren't those the words of Chang-cho?"

I would dare to respond to Yün-men, "The thrush said it, the Melodious Laughing Thrush." He would certainly have a riposte. "Farfetched!" I think he would say.

"The greedy will be caught." How about Yün-men? Suppose there was a great Zen master lurking there in the deep pool when Yün-men cast in his line? The fish would catch the greedy fisherman. He would pull Yün-men into the water, and that would be no more than he deserves—always trying to save somebody!

"If your mouth opens just a bit, / your life is completely lost." Just "The radi . . ."—and you have given yourself away completely. Whose words are those, anyway!

CASE 40

Kuei-shan Kicks Over
the Water Bottle

THE CASE

When Kuei-shan was with Pai-chang's assembly, he was cook of the monastery. Pai-chang wanted to choose a founding teacher for Mount Ta-kuei. He invited all his monks to make a presentation, saying, "The outstanding one will be sent." Then he took a water bottle and set it on the floor, and said, "Don't call this a water bottle. What would you call it?"

The head monk said, "It can't be called a wooden clog."

Pai-chang then asked Kuei-shan his opinion. Kuei-shan kicked over the water bottle and walked out.

Pai-chang laughed and said, "The head monk loses." Kuei-shan thereupon was made the founding teacher at Mount Ta-kuei.

WU-MEN'S COMMENT

Though Kuei-shan was altogether valiant, he could not leap out of Pai-chang's trap. If you scrutinize what happened next, you'll see that he accepted the heavy and rejected the light. How? Look! *Removing his sweatband, he shouldered an iron yoke.*

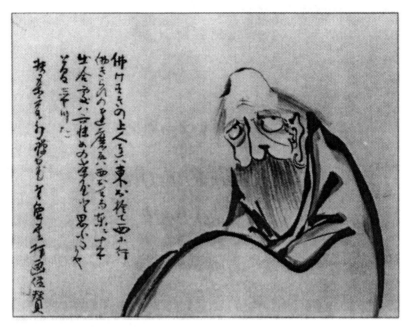

PLATE 7: *Bodhidharma*. Courtesy of The Idemitsu
Museum of Arts. (Cases 4 and 41)

Sages who love Buddha leave East and go West;
Mr. Bodhidharma who hates Buddha leaves West to
    go East;
I thought they might meet at the Teahouse of
    Repose;
it was just a dream.

WU-MEN'S VERSE

Tossing bamboo baskets and ladles away,
he swept all impediments before him;
Pai-chang's severe barrier cannot interrupt his rush;
thousands of Buddhas come forth from his toes.

Kuei-shan (Isan) lived from 770 to 853 and was cofounder of the Kuei-yang school with his disciple Yang-shan. He became a monk at the age of fifteen and began Zen study with Pai-chang when he was twenty-four. One late evening he was sitting up in the dark and was accosted by Pai-chang:

"Who is it sitting here in the dark?"
Kuei-shan said, "It's Ling-yu, Master."
Pai-chang said, "Rake up the hearth."
Kuei-shan arose, stepped to the hearth, and searched for live coals but found none. "The fire has gone out," he said.
Pai-chang then took up the tongs and deep in the ashes he found a small, live ember. Holding it up he said, "What is this?"

With that, Kuei-shan could acknowledge the live coal of his own nature and was deeply enlightened.[1] He remained with Pai-chang for further training, and at the time of this story he was cook of the monastery, a very responsible position. He was in middle life, perhaps forty-seven or so.

A friend of Pai-chang, an itinerant monk who knew geomancy, visited the monastery and reported that he had found a fine mountain ideal for the establishment of a new monastery. Its orientation was propitious, its configuration perfect. He suggested that Pai-chang send someone there to be the founder. Pai-chang agreed it would be a good idea, but who should he send?

"How about me?" said Pai-chang.
"No," said the Geomancer, "You are too little and ascetic. This is a broad mountain that needs someone large and vigorous."
Just then the head monk came in. "How about him?" said Pai-chang.
The Geomancer turned to the head monk and said, "Cough." The head monk coughed. "Take a few steps." The monk paced about.
"Not qualified," the Geomancer said. Pai-chang then sent for

Kuei-shan, and as soon as he saw him, the Geomancer announced, "Here is the man for Mount Ta-kuei!"

Pai-chang agreed, and in a private interview he advised Kuei-shan that he was selected. When this was announced, the head monk protested, saying that since he was the leader of the assembly, he should get the job. To keep the peace and to keep matters clear, Pai-chang arranged a contest.[2]

Gathering his assembly, he set a water bottle on the floor and said, "Don't call this a water bottle. What would you call it?" The water bottle was a kind of canteen, an important piece of the monk's equipment in those days of no running water.

Pai-chang liked this kind of kōan. Indeed, there are three cases in *The Blue Cliff Record* in which Pai-chang charged his attendants: "Say something without moving your lips or tongue."[3] He gags everybody in a slightly different way here, but the bind is the same.

The head monk stepped forward and said, "It cannot be called a wooden clog." Various translations are offered for the Chinese ideograph I render as "wooden clog," including "wedge" and "stump." Never mind. It doesn't really matter what it can't be called.

Yamada Rōshi used to say that the head monk's answer is not too bad, but it still shows traces of intellectual association. His mind is not free of thinking—he is still bound by the binary computer of the human cortex: this is not that, male is not female, birth is not death, the sage is not an ordinary person. Well, these "certain certainties" are true enough, but not sufficient.

When our son was about six years old, I asked him, "Suppose you couldn't say that your name is Tom. How would you call yourself?" He said, "That's a very hard question." A better answer than the head monk's, I think. When I told this story in the early days of the Maui Zendō, one of the members went home and asked his five-year-old son, "If you weren't Mischa, what would you be?" Mischa said, "A tree." Another good one.

In any case, without showing any reaction, Pai-chang turned to Kuei-shan and asked his opinion. Kuei-shan stepped forward, tipped over the water bottle with his foot, and went out. There is a marvelous painting of this scene ascribed to Kano Motonobu which R. H. Blyth reproduced in his *Mumonkan*. The water bottle is on its side and Kuei-shan is walking out—leaving Pai-chang grinning and the monks agape.[4]

When Kuei-shan stepped to the bottle and tipped it over, what was in his mind? The *Diamond Sutra* says: "Dwell nowhere and bring forth that mind."⁵ Kuei-shan was not restricted by any thoughts of winning or losing. He was completely free from all relative thought. His mind was empty—and thus he could act with rigorous rightness. His essential being took essential action. The complication of the water bottle and its name was shattered forever. His walking out is also full and complete: nothing missing, nothing left over.

In Case 2, Pai-chang's student Huang-po responded by slapping his face. Kuei-shan tipped over the water bottle. Pai-chang approved each with a hearty laugh and approving words. Here he says "The head monk loses" and makes Kuei-shan the founder of a monastery. Suppose that you were that head monk. How would you respond to Pai-chang's laughter? Would you be able to take the joke? As Dōgen says in a completely different context:

> There is an ocean of bright clouds;
> there is an ocean of solemn clouds.⁶

At kōan review sessions in the old days at the San'un Zendō, we would take turns around a circle presenting our understanding of cases for colleagues to hear. Even though we had all completed our kōan study, we'd miss an appropriate response now and then. At that point Yamada Rōshi would ask for another opinion, and someone would chime in with something more to the point. Everyone, including the old-timer who had missed the point, would approve. When this happened to me, I'd feel regretful for a moment, and then for a moment I'd feel regretful about my reaction. Finally I would come to and smile at myself. I wondered at the time if I'd ever reach the point where I could simply accept a mistake at the moment it happened.

When I reject a student's response to a kōan, sometimes the student goes back to the dōjō and frets about personal inadequacy and the rōshi's unreasonableness—only to return with a response that is worse than the first one. Again I ring my little bell. The student returns to the dōjō and enters a dreadful whirlpool of anger and disappointment. That's really too bad. The head monk of Pai-chang's monastery went on to become a well-respected master in his own right.⁷ He was worthy of his office. And if you and I are worthy students of the Dharma, we will accept such challenges, taking the solemn clouds with the bright, going forward openly and gracefully: "Yes, that's right. Your response was better than mine. I must go deeper. Step by step I will be more clear and more intimate."

Though it seems that Kuei-shan was well accepted as a promising student from the outset of his practice, still it took him several years to find his bit of hot coal. He too must have found himself often in a frame of mind where he could confess, "I am certainly not adequate to this challenge. I must devote myself more sincerely to my practice." If you can take yourself in hand as he did and use the frustrations that inevitably appear, then you have a chance for the same freedom that he finally enjoyed.

Wu-men comments: "Though Kuei-shan was altogether valiant, he could not leap out of Pai-chang's trap." Pai-chang snared him for the top position at what would be a great monastery. Not only could he not leap out of Pai-chang's trap, he put his foot right into it.

"If you scrutinize what happened next, you'll see that he accepted the heavy and rejected the light. How? *Look!* Removing his sweatband, he shouldered an iron yoke." Leaving his relatively light job of cook, he accepted the iron yoke of responsibility for establishing a monastery. *Look!*—indeed! The demons lurking in such an enterprise might overpower even a great master like Kuei-shan.

At the top of Mount Ta-kuei, Kuei-shan built a hut of mud, branches, and straw. He ate chestnuts and berries, made friends with monkeys and birds. But nobody came. Eight years passed. Finally he said to himself, "This doesn't make sense. I'm supposed to be the founder of a great monastery, but here I am all by myself in a miserable hut, talking to monkeys. I'm going back to civilization where I can be more effective."

So he packed his gear and started down the mountain. On the path he met a tiger. In one version of the story the tiger grasped him by the sleeve. In any case, Kuei-shan reflected, "This tiger seems to be telling me something." So he turned around and went back to his hut. And sure enough, soon after, three monks appeared and helped him.[8] Finally, with imperial assistance, he was able to build a great temple that later would have fifteen hundred disciples. Quite a blaze from that tiny bit of live coal!

Wu-men's verse begins: "Tossing bamboo baskets and ladles away, / he swept all impediments before him." Tossing away his vegetable basket and his soup ladles, tossing away everything, his mild action of tipping over the bottle and walking out destroyed the weeds of delusion of all time, like the great laugh of Pu-tai.

"Pai-chang's severe barrier cannot interrupt his rush." Pai-chang's injunction was complicated, but Kuei-shan sliced it as neatly as he did the great radishes he prepared every day in his kitchen. Take that! Take that!

In teaching this case, one of my successors asks a checking question about Wu-men's last line, "Thousands of Buddhas come forth from his toes." How do you show *that* in your daily life? he asks. That's a good question to leave you with.

Bodhidharma Pacifies the Mind

THE CASE

Bodhidharma faced the wall. The Second Ancestor stood in the snow, cut off his arm, and said, "Your disciple's mind has no peace as yet. I beg you, Master, please put it to rest."

Bodhidharma said, "Bring me your mind, and I will put it to rest."

The Second Ancestor said, "I have searched for my mind, but I cannot find it."

Bodhidharma said, "I have completely put it to rest for you."

WU-MEN'S COMMENT

The snaggletoothed foreigner came complacently a hundred thousand miles across the sea. It was like raising waves where there is no wind. Finally he cobbled together a single disciple, and a crippled one at that. Barbaric! Hsieh-san-lang does not know four words.

WU-MEN'S VERSE

Coming from the West and directly pointing—
all the trouble springs from this;
the jungle of monks at sixes and sevens
is your fault after all.

Bodhidharma, it is said, was the third son of an Indian king. He became a monk and studied with Prajñātara, twenty-seventh successor of the Buddha Śākyamuni, and after a lifetime career of teaching in India he journeyed to China about A.D. 520. On arriving in the Kingdom of Liang, he had an audience with the Emperor Wu. This emperor was a devout Buddhist; he expounded upon sutras, had many spiritual experiences, and sometimes wore the robes of a monk, but he couldn't make much sense of his talk with the old master. I gave part of their dialogue in my comment to Case 4. Here it is in full:

> The emperor asked, "I have endowed temples and authorized ordinations—what is my merit?"
> Bodhidharma said, "No merit at all."

Merit is *te* or *toku*, the virtue and responsibility one accumulates by yielding wisdom, treasure, and power. This yielding is a matter of giving so completely that there is nothing left for the donor. In classical Buddhism, this yielding is called *dāna*, roughly translated "charity." Dāna Pāramitā is the Perfection of Charity, the first of the Six Perfections that the devoted Buddhist tries to fulfill. *Dāna* is first of all our expression of gratitude for the Buddha Dharma—gifts of housing, food, clothing, and medicine to those who teach and maintain it. *Dāna* is also the way to embody the interdependence of all things, with all beings giving to all beings. The one who gives wisdom, treasure, and power to others clarifies the Dharma and gains natural authority for more clarifying. This is "merit"—it is itself passed on through the *dāna* given in turn by those who receive it. Of course, merit was also considered to be spiritual credit for an auspicious rebirth. The emperor understood this multifaceted doctrine very well, but perhaps he was too preoccupied with it.[1]

But Bodhidharma says, "No merit at all." Oops! As Yüan-wu remarks, with this response Bodhidharma poured dirty water over His Imperial Majesty.[2] What a shock! His foundations were shaken. No merit? No *dāna*? No interdependence? In his next question he wants to get to the bottom of this:

> The emperor asked, "What is the first principle of the holy teaching?"
> Bodhidharma said, "Vast emptiness, nothing holy."

The emperor had held many deep discussions of Buddhism with advisors and teachers. He knew the conventional truth that things exist and the esoteric truth that things do not exist—further, he knew that these two truths are the same. It is this one truth, he knew, that is the first principle, at the heart of all doctrine, underlying *dāna* itself. But what is this principle?

With Bodhidharma's response, the curtain is whipped aside. And nothing is behind it! The silent universe is dark and infinite. Abstruse principles, religious concepts, imperial vanity—all are invalidated! The emperor was upset and asked,

> "Who is this confronting me?"
> Bodhidharma said, "I don't know."

The emperor is asking: Who are you—in your elegant robes, at your advanced age, with your distinguished reputation—to say that the first principle of the holy teaching is vast emptiness with nothing holy about it?

Each response by Bodhidharma touches the central point of the Buddha Dharma: the first with regard to karma, the second with regard to metaphysics, and the third, "I don't know," with regard to the self. "Nothing to gain" becomes "nothing out there" becomes "nothing in here." Yet standing here is the red-bearded Barbarian in his clerical robes with his particular view and particular bearing. He has embodied the vast unknown.

Bodhidharma thought he might show the emperor the way of no-majesty, and that this realization might trickle down and enlighten the whole country. It didn't work. After three rounds Bodhidharma gave up, crossed the Yellow River, and journeyed deep into the Kingdom of Wei in northwestern China. There he found a ruined temple, Shao-lin-ssu (Shōrinji), and set himself up in a cave behind it—and there he was sitting, facing the wall, when our story opens.[3]

The practice of facing the wall is retained literally in the Sōtō sect today and in spirit by all earnest Zen students. This is not merely to avoid distraction. (In Senzaki Sensei's apartment I used to sit facing a bookcase, and I had all the titles memorized.) Whatever you are facing can be the wall. Your eyes go out of focus, and the wall is no other than your practice: your breath-counting, your shikantaza, your kōan. As the wall comes closer and closer, it becomes more and more intimate. At last it is the wall itself sitting on your cushions, and the practice is doing the practice. This is practice before kenshō and after kenshō—it is Bodhidharma's practice.

At the time of Bodhidharma's appearance, Buddhism had flourished in China for more than four hundred years. Probably brought by foreign merchants, envoys, and refugees, it gradually spread in intellectual circles. The first Buddhist monastery was established in China very early, perhaps during the first century A.D.[4] So Bodhidharma was another in a long line of Indian and Central Asian missionaries.

Shen-kuang (Shinkō), who became the Second Ancestor after Bodhidharma, was a forty-year-old monk whose childhood and youth, it seems, were not very different from those of monks in later times: reading and roaming about in nature, then ordination, followed by rigorous study of Buddhist texts and years of hard practice. Finally, in the midst of his studies, Shen-kuang was visited by a spirit who advised him that his practice was ripe: he was ready to move on. Knowing about Bodhidharma, he felt encouraged to seek him out. The story of their encounter is almost certainly inaccurate historically, but it is a myth that empowers our practice like few others:

> It was winter. Day and night, Shen-kuang stood before Bodhidharma's cave, beseeching him for instruction. The Old Barbarian, however, sat in zazen and paid no attention. One night there was a snowstorm, but Shen-kuang stood there unmoving, and the snow reached his knees. Finally, Bodhidharma said, "You have been standing there a long time in the snow. What is it that you want?"
>
> Shen-kuang said, 'I beseech you, Master, open the gate of the Dharma and save all of us beings."
>
> Bodhidharma said, "The incomparable truth of the Buddhas can only be attained by constant striving—practicing what cannot be practiced, bearing the unbearable. How can you, with your small virtue and wisdom, and your easy-going and conceited mind, dare to aspire to the true teaching?"
>
> With this, it is said, Shen-kuang drew a knife, cut off his hand, and presented it to Bodhidharma, who relented at last, and accepted him as a disciple, giving him the name by which he is known today, Hui-k'o (Eka, Light of Wisdom).[5]

Sesshū, the great Zen artist, painted a glorious picture of Hui-k'o confronting his master. It is a black and white painting, but there is a delicate line of red around the severed wrist. Bodhidharma is sitting facing the wall, looking out of the corner of his eye at his new disciple. The scene is very peaceful: Hui-k'o presenting the hand folded into a napkin as an of-

fering.[6] At times of extreme crisis, Asian people have traditionally cut off fingers or even hands to demonstrate sincerity. The nun who presides at the Kuan-yin Temple in Honolulu is missing a part of one finger. She tells the story that her parents in Hong Kong would not allow her to become a nun so she severed the end of her ring finger by way of indicating that she had no intention of marrying. Thus they were persuaded.

The anguish of Hui-k'o facing Bodhidharma and this determined young woman facing her parents in Hong Kong—this is the anguish of the heroes and heroines of fairy stories and folktales who must strive constantly, practicing that which cannot be practiced, bearing the unbearable. This is a treasure of the Path disguised as sheer misery. This treasure is found in all religions worthy of the name. It is the "dark night of the soul" experienced by Ch'ing-shui, solitary and destitute, in Case 10. Hui-k'o had no choice but to enter this dark night. We have no choice either.

Some Zen teachers try to induce this condition artificially by deliberately frustrating their students. Philip Kapleau gives a spirited account of this kind of programming at Hosshinji.[7] I have heard of instances where the head monk says, "Get in there and see the rōshi!" The rōshi says, "What are you doing in here! Get out!" The head monk then says, "What are you doing out here so soon? Get back in there!" The student is bewildered and upset. I have many doubts about such methods.

Don't be literal! Bodhidharma as a historical figure is shadowy at best. His virtue for us is his archetype, and the myth of his challenges to Hui-k'o are expressions of challenges we feel naturally in our own experiences of the dark night.

Here they are in the vivid reminiscences of Flora Courtois in her book *An Experience of Enlightenment*:

> It was as if I were being pulled down into the vortex of a maelstrom within me, pulling me ever further down and away from everyday life and involving me in an all-consuming life-or-death struggle. Although I never completely lost touch with other people around me I began to wonder if I would ever be in close communication with other human beings again. Their lives and daily preoccupations seemed so remote from mine. The simplest tasks distracted me, and took an excessive amount of time. I remember standing over an ironing board and concentrating so intently on the question: What is the ground of reality? that it took me all afternoon to do a small ironing.[8]

Well, read the book: Ms. Courtois's story, like this case, has a happy ending. My point is simply that you needn't be a monk in ancient China to experience the dark night and to pass through it. Flora Courtois walked this path alone without even knowing the word Zen. Shibayama Rōshi quotes the poem of another teacher:

> The snow of Shao-lin is stained crimson;
> let me dye my heart with it
> as humble as it may be.[9]

Probably after some time had passed, Hui-k'o said: "Your disciple's mind has no peace as yet. I beg you, Master, please put it to rest." Bodhidharma said, "Bring me your mind, and I will put it to rest."

Again, probably some time passed. In this interval, Hui-k'o fervently continued his search. "Where is this mind? What is this mind?" Finally, he returned to his master and said, "I have searched for my mind, but cannot find it." This is very interesting. How do you see the Second Ancestor here?

Bodhidharma said, "There, I have completely put it to rest for you." Yes, settled at last. Nothing more to be said. On this perennial path, Hui-k'o and his master reach the denouement. The rest that Bodhidharma confirmed in the heart-mind of his disciple is the same rest he sought to confirm in the heart-mind of Emperor Wu with his words "I don't know." The emperor, to his profound regret, did not understand. After Bodhidharma died, the emperor mourned him and personally wrote an inscription for his monument:

> "Alas! I saw him without seeing him;
> I met him without meeting him;
> I encountered him without encountering him;
> now as before I regret this deeply."[10]

Practice hard so that you do not share this regret.

The Old Barbarian was just as uncompromising with Hui-k'o as he was with the emperor—and, at bottom, just as compassionate. Bodhidharma is not usually depicted as gracious and compassionate. In fact, he sits in a little chair on the altar of the Koko An Zendō looking quite gruff. In a certain light, however, after several days of sesshin, you may see him smile.

Wu-men comments: "The snaggletoothed foreigner came compla-

cently a hundred thousand miles across the sea." It wasn't a hundred thousand miles, it was hardly a step.

"It was like raising waves where there is no wind." A modern analogy would be a commercial artist pointing to a painting by Rembrandt and crying out, "That's it! That's what we should be doing!"

"Finally he cobbled together a single disciple, and a crippled one at that." More loving talk on Wu-men's part. Cobbled with care! Bodhidharma made absolutely sure that his successor would be a worthy vessel for the lifeblood he had inherited from the Buddha Śākyamuni. This single worthy disciple, it is said, had just a few disciples in turn, and on through the generations the Dharma of facing the wall was a tiny movement. Finally the stream reached Ma-tsu and Yüeh-shan—and suddenly there were dozens, and then hundreds, of wonderful Zen teachers all over T'ang China. This is the way to enlighten the country.

Meanwhile Wu-men continues on his sarcastic way: "Barbaric! Hsieh-san-lang (Shasanrō) does not know four words." The folkloric figure Hsieh-san-lang was a superb fisherman who was illiterate. Again Wu-men calls our attention to the failure of words and abstraction. Ananda K. Coomaraswamy makes the point that humanity suffered a great loss with the development of literacy,[11] for concepts get in our way. Like Coomaraswamy himself and Bodhidharma, however, we learn to use them, and then they no longer can turn around and bite us.

Wu-men begins his poem: "Coming from the West and directly pointing"—melding two classic sayings. The first is the popular question "Why did the Ancestral Teacher come from the West?" The second, "directly pointing," comes from the co-called Four Principles of Bodhidharma (which were not set forth until much later):

> A special transmission outside sutras;
> no dependence on words or phrases;
> directly pointing to the human mind;
> seeing into one's nature and attaining Buddhahood.[12]

"All the trouble springs from this; / the jungle of monks at sixes and sevens / is your fault after all." All the confusion in Zen centers about realization and its embodiment in daily life can be traced directly to you, Bodhidharma. You have a heavy load of karma, and so we offer incense to you at every period of zazen.

Mañjuśrī and the Young Woman
in Samādhi

THE CASE

Once Mañjuśrī went to a place where many Buddhas had assembled with the World-Honored One. When he arrived, all the Buddhas had returned to their original dwelling place. Only a young woman remained, seated in samādhi, near the Buddha's seat.

Mañjuśrī addressed the Buddha and asked, "How can the young woman get near the Buddha's seat when I cannot?"

The Buddha replied to Mañjuśrī, "Awaken this young woman from her samādhi and ask her yourself!" Mañjuśrī walked around the young woman three times, snapped his fingers once, took her to the Brahma Heaven and exerted all his supernatural powers, but he could not bring her out.

The World-Honored One said, "Even a hundred thousand Mañjuśrīs cannot awaken her. Down below, past twelve hundred million lands, as innumerable as sands of the Ganges, lives the Bodhisattva of Delusive Wisdom. He will be able to bring her out of her samādhi."

Instantly the Bodhisattva of Delusive Wisdom emerged from the earth and made bows before the World-Honored One, who gave him his imperial order. Delusive Wisdom stepped before the young woman, snapped his fingers once, and at this she came out of samādhi.

PLATE 8: *The Bodhisattva Mañjuśrī*. Courtesy of The
Idemitsu Museum of Arts. (Cases 25 and 42)

For past Buddhas surely a teacher;
for present Buddhas surely a resource;
this Mañjuśrī is not Mañjuśrī;
on the tips of a million hairs, a million lions.

WU-MEN'S COMMENT

Old Śākyamuni put on a disorderly comedy this time, no better than a child. Mañjuśrī is teacher of the Seven Buddhas—why couldn't he bring the young woman out of samādhi? Delusive Wisdom is a bodhisattva at the beginning level. How could he bring her out? If you can see into this intimately, then in the flurry of karma and discrimination you are a dragon of great samādhi.

WU-MEN'S VERSE

One can bring her out, the other cannot;
both of them are free.
A god mask; a devil mask—
the failure is an elegant performance.

The Gateless Barrier is made up of sayings and dialogues for the most part, but it also includes dreams, memories, and myths. This case involving the Buddha and Mañjuśrī is a myth taken from a Chinese sutra that was published around A.D. 300.[1] Although it is not a historical account, it is more relevant than Caesar crossing the Rubicon back in 49 B.C. History becomes myth and so you can speak of crossing your own Rubicon. History as history traces changes in human society and its environment; myth is the drama of my life and yours. Each character is myself acting out a part of my nature and interacting with other aspects of myself within my own context.

Mañjuśrī, a nameless young woman, and the Bodhisattva of Delusive Wisdom (Jāliniprabhah) are the characters here. The Buddha directs the play and offers comments. It is a *nantō*, or "difficult-case" kōan, which for us means a kōan that is especially effective in revealing essential nature.

Mañjuśrī, as noted earlier, is the incarnation of wisdom and usually presides over the zendō in large Zen temples. Sometimes he is the main figure of a smaller temple, as he is here in our Palolo Valley Zen Center.[2] He is usually seated on a lion, which is sometimes recumbent, sometimes standing—expressive of his master's spiritual power and incisiveness. Mañjuśrī is known as the teacher of the Seven Buddhas, who appeared in the dimmest of the remote past, one by one, with immeasurable spaces of time between them. Śākyamuni was the seventh of these august personages, so in this story the Buddha is confronting his own teacher.

The person sitting near the Buddha's throne is identified as a young woman. Why a woman? In the time of the Buddha, sad to say, women were not generally considered to be spiritual. In India they were held to be impure, and in East Asia they have simply been considered inferior. In both contexts they were thought to be dangerous—ready and able to seduce the spiritual man from his holy path. However malicious and mistaken such views may be, we still can make good use of the metaphor. Take the "young woman" as simply someone you might not expect to be near the Enlightened One, someone deep in zazen and rather stuck there.

The other character in this play is the Bodhisattva of Delusive Wisdom, who lives down below, past twelve hundred million lands, at the first level of bodhisattvahood. There are twelve such levels (twelve hundred million, if you wish), the highest occupied by the Buddha. Delusive Wisdom is like you and me when we start off in Zen Buddhist practice—very diligent, perhaps, but full of dualistic ideas.

Now for the setting of this mythological play: it is your own dōjō, your own zafu, your own robe. It is your own sacred setting. Mañjuśrī shows up at the conference after being excluded at first, and all the Buddhas have disappeared. You may think this is just a narrative device to simplify the action. Not at all. It is the first point of the case as a kōan. No one is there, and Śākyamuni stays around only for a give-and-take with his old teacher.

If you understand the assembly's disappearing, you have the rest of the case in the bag. If not, the entire matter will remain obscure. Why aren't Buddhas present when Mañjuśrī arrives? They have returned to their original dwelling place. Only a single person remains, sitting near the Buddha's throne. If you are free of concern about her gender, you'll find that the key word here is "near"—the virtue Mañjuśrī recognizes when he asks, "How can the young woman get near the Buddha's seat when I cannot?" That's the next question.

"How is it that the wisest being in the universe, the teacher of the Seven Buddhas, cannot get near the Buddha when some student who is stuck in her practice can sit there quite readily?" Yamada Rōshi used to say, in commenting on this kōan, "Mañjuśrī cannot fly an airplane."

Now the Buddha speaks up: "Awaken this young woman from her samādhi and ask her yourself!" Here again, you may suppose this is a narrative device designed to carry the story along. But the Buddha is actually answering Mañjuśrī's question directly. He is not passing the buck. "How

can that person get near and I can't?" "Wake her up and ask her yourself."
Waking and nearing hang together. The one illuminates the other.

But Mañjuśrī can't wake her. He walks around her three times, snaps
his fingers once, takes her to the Brahma Heaven, and exerts all his supernatural power but can't bring her out. Why not? The Buddha explains
what is by now obvious: "Even a hundred thousand Mañjuśrīs cannot
awaken her." Even a hundred thousand Mañjuśrīs cannot get near the Buddha's seat. But down below, past twelve hundred million lands as innumerable as the sands of the Ganges, lives the Bodhisattva of Delusive Wisdom. "He is far, far away, completely removed from our dimension. He is
many, many levels below us," the Buddha is saying to his teacher.

Instantly the Bodhisattva of Delusive Wisdom appears. He is not way
down there twelve hundred million lands below, but is right here, one
with us all. Remember Hui-neng's words: "With an enlightened thought
you are an enlightened person. With an ordinary thought you are an ordinary person."[3] What difference is there between the Bodhisattva Mañjuśrī and the Bodhisattva of Delusive Wisdom?

After receiving the Buddha's imperial order, Delusive Wisdom steps
before the young woman, snaps his fingers once, and suddenly she emerges
from her samādhi. How could Delusive Wisdom bring the young woman
from her samādhi when Mañjuśrī could not? How could the young woman
get near the Buddha when Mañjuśrī could not? Where had all the Buddhas
gone when Mañjuśrī appeared? Cut one, cut all!

Wu-men comments: "Old Śākyamuni put on a disorderly comedy this
time, no better than a child." In fact, it *is* a little disorderly. If Mañjuśrī is
so wise, why can't he answer his own question?

The point is that the actor knows the butler did it, but he doesn't let on.
If he did there wouldn't be any play. The play's the thing. Without it, the
old teachers could never have presented the Dharma. Once Nechung Rinpoché was asked in a public meeting about emptiness. He said he couldn't
answer the question because if he did, then his audience would suppose
that emptiness is something, whereas it is really nothing at all. To know
emptiness, you must experience emptiness; to know death, you must experience death; to know realization, you must experience realization. The
Zen play is a presentation of experience.

Wu-men then takes up Mañjuśrī's failures and says that if you see into
them intimately, "then in the flurry of karma and discrimination you are

a dragon of great samādhi." The flurry of karma and discrimination is our everyday life—the flurry of inadequate relationships, responsibilities unmet, misunderstandings, physical pain sometimes. It is the very cliff-edge of birth and death. There you enjoy a samādhi of frolic and play.[4]

What is samādhi? As a technical term, it is a deep zazen condition. But more broadly, all conditions are samādhi. Samādhi really means "one with the universe." People in mental hospitals are in samādhi. They are not completely out of touch. The trees, the grass—all are in samādhi. Like animals and birds, they are one with the universe. Then what is "*great* samādhi"? It is the samādhi of no obstructions. The dragon of great samādhi takes pleasure in the vast and fathomless Dharma of shells and lichen and smiling children.

"If you can see into this intimately"—if you shed history, philosophy, and logic and come naked to this kōan, making it your own, then you are Mañjuśrī himself or herself, though you are surrounded by Delusive Wisdoms and wonder about yourself sometimes.

Wu-men's verse begins: "One can bring her out, the other cannot; / both of them are free." In your samādhi of frolic and play, now you bring out the prize, now you don't. Is there anything beyond this samādhi?

"A god mask; a devil mask"—I bring out a devil mask, and the children scream with delight; I bring out a god mask, and their parents run away. What do the masks mask? I don't think they mask anything. God mask and devil mask, Mañjuśrī and Delusive Wisdom, each one unique, each one saving and being saved, just as they are.

"The failure is an elegant performance." Going to the Brahma Heaven and doing all his miraculous tricks—what a marvelous show Mañjuśrī puts on for us! Failure, as Jesus so vividly showed, can be apotheosis. What a fine failure Mañjuśrī created!

Shou-shan's Short Bamboo Staff

THE CASE

*The priest Shou-shan held up his short bamboo staff before his assembly and said,
"You monks, if you call this a staff, you're entangled. If you don't call this a staff,
you ignore the fact. Tell me, what do you call it?"*

WU-MEN'S COMMENT

*Call it a short staff and you're entangled. Don't call it a short staff and you ignore
the fact. You cannot use words. You cannot not use words. Speak quickly! Speak
quickly!*

WU-MEN'S VERSE

*Holding up a short staff—
faithfully giving and taking life;
entangling and ignoring interweave;
Buddhas and Ancestors beg for their lives.*

Shou-shan (Shuzan) was a great-great-grandson of Lin-chi in the Dharma
and a student of Feng-hsüeh, who transcended subject and object in Case
24. Shou-shan was ordained as a boy and noted for his natural dignity
throughout his life. Though little is recorded of his teaching, he is cred-

ited with reviving the Lin-chi school in the tenth century after it had gone through a period of decline. When he was about to die, he took the high seat before his monks and delivered the following verse:

> A golden body in a silver world!
> sentient and nonsentient are of one truth;
> at the extremity of light and dark
>   all practice is transcended;
> the sun reveals its true body in the afternoon.[1]

"A golden body in a silver world." Can you relate this to the challenge he makes with his staff?

"Sentient and nonsentient are of one truth." Stones and birds have the same message: "Here I am!"

"At the extremity of light and dark all practice is transcended." This is the samādhi of frolic and play: "The stone man bows; the bare pillar claps."[2]

"The sun reveals its true body in the afternoon." The sun appears after days of cloudy weather. The farm wife looks up from her chores to enjoy it. Everything drops away.

It is presentation that Shou-shan is concerned about. The sun presents itself; sentient and nonsentient beings present themselves. Shou-shan presents a question as he holds up his short staff.

Wu-men abbreviated the original case, as he did several others in his collection. The story continues:

> The monk Kuei-sheng snatched the short staff from Shou-shan, dashed it to the floor, and cried out, "What is this!"
>   Shou-shan shouted, "Blind!" With this, Kuei-sheng was enlightened.[3]

"Blind!" Like Te-shan exposed to total darkness by Lung-t'an, Kuei-sheng went completely blind.[4]

The short staff itself is the *chu-pi* (*shippei*)—about three feet long, it is shaped like a broken bow, from which it takes its name. It is one of the traditional implements of a Zen master. When Shou-shan holds it up he says in effect: If you call this a short staff, you get entangled with it as a thing; if you don't call it a short staff, you ignore its virtue as such. Can you cut through this dichotomy and respond directly to Shou-shan?

Kuei-sheng was like Kuei-shan, the monk who tipped over the water bottle when presented with a similar challenge: "You may not call this a water bottle. What do you call it?"[5] Those two old worthies responded with decisive action. How would you respond?

During World War II, I was interned in Japan, and that was the occasion of my meeting R. H. Blyth and my introduction to Zen Buddhism. In the camp, my friends and I often talked about the novel ideas that Zen seemed to offer. Once, one of those friends took a pencil and broke it into two by way of showing decisive Zen action. Since pencils were not easy to come by in those circumstances, I thought his behavior was inappropriate, but I couldn't say why. Now I understand that when Kuei-sheng cast the staff to the floor before Shou-shan, he was not taking "Zen action" as a display but grasping the very wheel that Shou-shan had set into motion and giving it a most forthright turn.

> Ma-yü came to see Lin-chi. He spread his mat and asked, "Which is the true face of the twelve-faced Kuan-yin?"
>
> Getting down from the rope-bottomed chair, the Master seized the mat with one hand and with the other grabbed hold of Ma-yü. "Where has the twelve-faced Kuan-yin gone?" he asked.
>
> Ma-yü jerked himself free, and tried to sit in the chair.
>
> The Master picked up his stick and hit at him. Ma-yü seized the stick, and holding it between them, they entered the Master's room.[6]

Grabbing the stick and holding it together with his teacher and leaving the room—this is Ma-yü's masterful presentation: caught by his teacher yet free of him. Your task is to drive through Shou-shan's complications while holding his short staff with him all the way. What is it after all!

Wu-men goes over Shou-shan's ground: "Call it a short staff and you're entangled. Don't call it a short staff and you ignore. You cannot use words. You cannot not use words." And he adds, "Speak quickly! Speak quickly!" Stop pressing me, old Wu-men! Let me think about this a little. After all, the World-Honored One himself didn't reply to such a question.

Still the problem is that if you don't say it, you won't express yourself. If you do say it, you will say too much. This is not merely a philosophical dilemma, it's an ordinary dilemma too. My dad thought he was resolving such a dilemma when he laid out the details of procreation for his sons. It didn't work because he said too much. Be careful! Actually, Shou-shan's question is no different from the one you hear in the interview room: "What is Mu?" Personalize the matter and your words will flow forth naturally, like those of a clerk at the grocery counter when asked about the price of bread.

Wu-men begins his verse: "Holding up a short staff, / faithfully giving and taking life." It is the job of the Zen teacher to give life to realization and death to delusions. Shou-shan requited his deep obligation to Feng-hsüeh and all his ancestors by holding up his short staff and challenging us.

"Entangling and ignoring interweave." Wu-men carries on where Shou-shan left off. How do you realize this interweaving? If you quote the *Heart Sutra* here—"Form is emptiness . . ."—Shou-shan will whack you with his stick. No deviating!

"Buddhas and Ancestors beg for their lives." It is not that they are merely defeated but that they no longer have any reason for being. It's all been said with that interweaving. That's it! But it—the *thing* that Lafcadio Hearn objected to,[7] perhaps feared—can be a formidable barrier, the wall faced by Bodhidharma himself. He didn't shilly-shally, thank goodness. Stay with your barrier, stay with Mu, and the little stream that ran past Shou-shan's veranda will murmur its secret. "Here I am!"

CASE 44

Pa-chiao's Staff

THE CASE

The priest Pa-chiao said to his assembly: "If you have a staff, I will give you a staff. If you have no staff, I will take a staff from you."

WU-MEN'S COMMENT

It helps you to cross the stream when the bridge is broken down. It guides you back to the village on a moonless night. If you call it a staff, you enter hell like an arrow.

WU-MEN'S VERSE

*The depths and shallows of the world
are all in his grasp;
it supports the heavens and sustains the earth—
everywhere it enhances the doctrine.*

Since Pa-chiao's name is rendered Bashō in Japanese, he is sometimes confused with Matsuo Bashō, the Japanese haiku poet. They were two altogether different people who lived at different times and places. This Pa-chiao was a Korean who studied Zen in late ninth-century China and ultimately settled and taught there in the Kuei-yang lineage. His successor was Ch'ing-jang who explained about the nonattained Buddha in Case 9. One of Pa-chiao's recorded dialogues goes like this:

A monk asked Pa-chiao, "What is the water of Pa-chiao?"
Pa-chiao said, "Warm in winter, cool in summer."[1]

Pa-chiao's name means "banana tree"—which, as those who have cut one down will know, is full of water. So the monk is asking: "What is the content of Pa-chiao?"

"Warm in winter, cool in summer—my ordinary mind is quite constant," Pa-chiao is saying. Constancy is equanimity, the virtue of Zen Buddhist practice.

In the present case, Pa-chiao is presenting two configurations of practice by way of checking his students and the rest of us. But before examining just what it is he's presenting, let's look at the staff he holds before us. Every Zen master has a staff that he cuts for himself in the mountains. It is about seven feet long, perhaps with some of its twigs left untrimmed, and is quite ungainly in appearance. This is the staff which Pai-chang used to poke out the dead body of a fox in Case 2.[2] It is a symbol of the master's status as mountain steward—for every Zen temple is a mountain and has a mountain name, even those located in the heart of busy cities. The master has cut his staff from wild nature in the wild mountains, which is no different from the essential nature set forth by the Buddha Śākyamuni.

On ceremonial occasions in the Lin-chi school, the master enters the main hall with his staff, and at appropriate moments he thumps the floor with it to punctuate the ceremony. It has no fancy carving and is really a very ordinary thing. But at the same time there is no thing more precious, as you will see on visiting any Zen monastery in Japan. Each monastery has a Kaisandō—a "Founder's Hall," Kaisan meaning "One Who Opens the Mountain." There is an image of the founder enshrined there with some of his memorabilia, always with his staff.

At Ryūtakuji, where I trained many years ago, there are three nearly life-size figures in the Kaisandō. Hakuin Ekaku, the nominal founder, is in the center. Actually, he visited the monastery only a couple of times, and his disciple, Tōrei Enji, was the de facto first master there. He occupies a seat to one side of Hakuin, while Seijō Genshi, teacher of Yamaoka Tesshū and rebuilder of the monastery in the nineteenth century, sits on the other side. It is awesome to step into that little room and feel the fierce gaze of those three great masters upon you. Behind each statue is the staff which that particular rōshi used—long withered sticks in grotesque shapes. The statue is the presence of the teacher. The staff is the presence of his teaching and that of all the Buddhas before him.

So Pa-chiao took up this potent staff and said: "If you have a staff, I will give you a staff. If you have no staff, I will take a staff from you." What is this giving? What is this taking? Chao-chou gave and took away too:

> Yen-yang said, "I don't bring a single thing. How about that?"
> Chao-chou said, "Put it down."
> Yen-yang said, "If I don't bring a single thing, what should I put down?"
> Chao-chou said, "In that case, carry it away."[3]

Chao-chou takes away when he says, "Put it down." He gives (a little) when he says, "In that case, carry it away." Generous, compassionate Chao-chou! Another pertinent example:

> San-sheng said to Hsüeh-feng, "When the 'golden scales' has passed through the net, I wonder what it should eat."
> Hsüeh-feng said, "I will wait for you to pass through the net, and then I'll tell you."
> San-sheng said, "You are the teacher of fifteen hundred people, yet you don't know what to say."
> Hsüeh-feng said, "I have many complicated affairs to deal with as abbot."[4]

As Yüan-wu says in his comment to Hsüeh-feng's final remark, "He let his move go." Like a careless chess player, Hsüeh-feng gave away his rook while fiddling with a pawn. But, Yüan-wu goes on to remark, "The final statement was most poisonous."[5] History does not relate what San-sheng said or did at the end of the dialogue. I suspect he bowed in acknowledgment. The pawn became a queen. Checkmate!

Both giving or taking away in this context are altogether deadly. When Chao-chou said, "Then carry it away"—there was sand in the rice and thorns in the mud. When Hsüeh-feng gave up his move, the burglar alarm went off. Likewise Pa-chiao was ill-tempered and ruthless in his giving and taking. See through his metaphors and show me his intention!

This is not just a matter to be talked about. When I meet with relatives or old friends who are not involved in Zen Buddhist practice, they frequently refer to my work as philosophy. I have nothing against philosophy; in fact several friends in the field of Buddhology are my teachers.

Where would I be without Thomas Cleary or Hee-Jin Kim! But I am not a philosopher, and neither were Pa-chiao, Hsüeh-feng, or Chao-chou. Those old worthies were not merely discussing the way Zen students drop off body and mind. They were not merely explaining how to die to the self. In their great improvisations with their students, the old teachers dropped off everything themselves and died right there with everybody.

Wu-men's comment is really a poem: four lines of five ideographs per line. The first two lines—"It helps you to cross the stream when the bridge is broken down; / it guides you back to the village on a moonless night"— are quotations from an earlier teacher.[6] For me they are among the loveliest lines in Zen literature. I recall the Twenty-Third Psalm: "Thy rod and thy staff, they comfort me." At the extremity, when it's clear that the only way to cross the stream is to break down the bridge, the staff shows its true function.

"It guides you back to the village on a moonless night." When everything is equal in total darkness, the road is the same as the ditch, the pond is the same as the meadow. Then the precious staff will be your guide. A stick with night vision!

"If you call it a staff, you enter hell like an arrow." This is like the previous kōan, when Shou-shan challenged us, "If you call this a short staff, you are entangled," and Wu-men's comment on that challenge, "You cannot use words; you cannot not use words." Although the two cases seem linked, ultimately their points differ.

What is it to fall into hell? It is to become entangled with self-serving concepts. Yung-chia wrote, "If you don't seek an invitation to hell, never slander the Tathāgatha's true teaching."[7] Dwelling in ideas of having something or having nothing you are bound to the wheel of birth and death. When can you find your true freedom? As Wu-men says elsewhere, "If you argue right and wrong, you are a person of right and wrong."[8] If you argue staff or no staff, then that's the kind of person you are.

Wu-men's verse begins, "The depths and shallows of the world / are all in his grasp." They are all in Pa-chiao's grasp as he holds forth his staff and delivers his challenge. What are the depths and shallows of the world?

"It supports the heavens and sustains the earth—/ everywhere it enhances the doctrine." Without that staff, Buddhism would be empty formulations and empty moral injunctions. It not only enhances the doctrine, it is the doctrine itself. But don't knock formulations and injunctions. They trace the configuration of the Great Fact.

Wu-tsu: "Who Is That Other?"

THE CASE

Wu-tsu said, "Śākyamuni and Maitreya are servants of another. Tell me, who is that other?"

WU-MEN'S COMMENT

If you can see this other and distinguish him or her clearly, then it is like encountering your father at the crossroads. You will not need to ask somebody whether or not you're right.

WU-MEN'S VERSE

Don't draw another's bow;
don't ride another's horse;
don't discuss another's faults;
don't explore another's affairs.

Wu-tsu is the Sung period master who was teacher of Yüan-wu and great-great-grandfather in the Dharma of Wu-men.[1] In Case 35 I recount his doubts on hearing the words, "It is like drinking water and knowing personally whether or not it is warm or cold." Realizing that his philosophical studies would not bring him an experience of the personal, he switched careers and became a monk. After a time he became a disciple of Pai-yün and found his own understanding at last.

In the present case Wu-tsu tells us that Śākyamuni and Maitreya are servants of another, and challenges us to identify that other by personal experience. Śākyamuni is the great founder of our Way. After years of hard practice he realized that all beings are the Tathāgata and only their delusions and preoccupations keep them from testifying to that fact. Maitreya is the Buddha still to be born. In Chinese iconography Maitreya is indistinguishable from Pu-tai, the so-called Laughing Buddha, with a big belly, his arms raised in the air, his generous mouth stretched in a warm smile. In the Ten Oxherding Pictures, Pu-tai or Maitreya is the figure in the final frame: entering the marketplace with bliss-bestowing hands, consorting with publicans and prostitutes, and enlightening them all. Arrived at last![2]

These marvelous Buddhist figures are servants of another. Wu-tsu means that Bodhidharma, Ma-tsu, Pai-chang, Nan-ch'üan, Chao-chou, Ch'ang-sha, Huang-po, Yün-men, Lin-chi, Tung-shan, Dōgen, Keizan, Ikkyū, Bankei, Bassui, Munan, Hakuin, and all our other teachers are servants of another. Tell me, who is that other? Consider this question in the Confucian context of nobles, commoners, and servants. The most noble of all teachers are servants of somebody—making that somebody the noblest of all. Who is that?

Both Yamada Rōshi and Shibayama Rōshi quote a student of Wu-tsu who replies to his challenge—"Who is that other?"—with the equivalent of "John! Mary!"[3] A clever disguise. Standing on your own two feet, with Śākyamuni, Maitreya, and the others nowhere to be seen, you can gently lift the mask these teachers put in place and make a much more pointed identification.

Wu-men comments: "If you can see this other and distinguish him or her clearly, then it is like encountering your father at the crossroads." Seeing the other clearly—no question! Once thirty years ago I met Nakagawa Sōen Rōshi in the underground passage between Tokyo Station and the Marunouchi Building. He was coming from his temple in Mishima, and I was returning to my place in Kamakura. Ha! Ha! We bowed and continued on to our destinations.

I recall also meeting my grandfather, not at a crossroads, but in the brochure of a bank. This was a mailing from a large company that owns a number of banks in California, including the Bank of Upper Lake, where my grandfather had been a trustee. The bit of stock in the Bank of Upper Lake which I inherited became stock in the big company, so this is how I came to get the mailing. On the back page was a tiny photograph showing the front entrance of the Bank of Upper Lake in the 1920s. Entering the bank was a barely discernible figure—perhaps an eighth of an inch high on the page—but it was my grandfather, no mistake, even though his back was to the camera. I knew it personally.

"You will not need to ask somebody whether or not you're right." Though Yamada Rōshi rushed to Yasutani Rōshi after his clear perception of the other, he certainly knew that he had already passed his barrier. Yet he rushed to him. It is not necessary to ask somebody. Yet at the same time it is very important to ask somebody. If you are convinced that you have realized something important, run, do not walk—telephone, do not write—to the nearest Zen master. This is a crucial time. If you do not consult with a good teacher, you may fall into fixed assumptions about your experience and its implications that will be hard to uproot later. Remember that in one sense Zen practice *begins* with realization. Yamada Rōshi used to say that a person with a new kenshō is like an infant needing lots of nurturing.

Wu-men begins his verse: "Don't draw another's bow; / don't ride another's horse." You must be your own archer. You must be your own rider. I think of Yasutani Rōshi's wonderful mime of "Don't ride another's horse." You could hear the galloping hoofs. He was mounted on his own horse, taking charge, with General Kuan's sword at his belt. He had taken Wu-tsu's challenge to heart.

One day when I was out for a walk on Maui, I passed a horse in a field. She eyed me speculatively, so I walked over and petted her. Suddenly there was a sharp whistle from some distance away. I looked up but couldn't see anyone. It reminded me, however, that some people don't like to have their animals touched by strangers. Wu-men's point is that you should ride your own horse, pet your own horse, draw your own bow, stand on your own feet, as the Buddha did when he announced, "Above the heavens, below the heavens, only I, the World-Honored One!"

The next two lines of the verse extend the first two: "Don't discuss another's faults." If you are standing on your own feet, how do you handle the mistakes that your friends and family members keep making? The precept becomes a kōan: "I take up the way of not discussing faults of others."[4] Does this mean that you overlook them? Surely your friend's tendency, say, to use coarse language on inappropriate occasions is a fault. If you are a friend, you need to do something. How do you handle it? It's your turn to take Wu-tsu's challenge to heart.

"Don't explore another's affairs." This is the same kind of point. You cannot live in this world without dealing with the affairs of friends and family members. Suppose your friend is obviously in the throes of an addiction. Do you say, "None of my business?" The disaster that is inevitable will bring you down too.

Mutual interdependence, the primary teaching of the Buddha Śākyamuni, is also mutual support. We get at the truth of this responsibility on our cushions in zazen, and we cultivate our ability to respond in daily life.

The human development movement can offer responses to Wu-men's admonitions. Some people mock this movement as "touchy-feely," but at best its programs can be very effective in turning the Dharma Wheel. Do you use that disparaging term "touchy-feely"? Are you avoiding the other? Intimacy is our practice.

What is the Tao of intimacy? In his comment on this last line of Wu-men's verse, Shibayama Rōshi quotes lines from Dōgen that by now are familiar. All the questions of self and other come to this:

> To study the Buddha Way is to study the self;
> to study the self is to forget the self;
> to forget the self is to be confirmed by the ten thousand things.[5]

Shih-shuang: "Step from the Top of the Pole"

THE CASE

The priest Shih-shuang said, "How do you step from the top of a hundred-foot pole?"

Another eminent master of former times said:

> You who sit on the top of a hundred-foot pole,
> although you have entered the Way, it is not yet genuine.
> Take a step from the top of the pole
> and worlds of the Ten Directions are your total body.

WU-MEN'S COMMENT

Stepping forward, turning back—is there anything to reject as ignoble or unworthy? Be that as it may, how do you step from the top of a hundred-foot pole? Sah!

WU-MEN'S VERSE

> He darkened the eye in his forehead
> and clung to the mark on the scale.
> Throw away body and discard life,
> and the blind one leads the blind.

Shih-shuang (Sekisō) is the name of a Lin-chi monastery in South China that had a succession of teachers who took its name. This one is probably Shih-shuang Ch'u-yüan (Sekisō Sōen), who lived in the eleventh century. He began his Zen study very young and had a remarkable career, though he died rather young at the age of fifty-three. He left many prominent successors, among whom was Yang-ch'i (Yōgi), whose line of Lin-chi Zen has survived as modern Rinzai Zen in Japan.

The present case is an example of how kōans develop. Shih-shuang revived an old case from Zen literature involving Ch'ang-sha and his friends. Later Wu-men included it in *The Gateless Barrier*. Now, 765 years after Wu-men, 865 years after Shih-shuang, and 1090 years after Ch'ang-sha, the case as a kōan is still vital. Show me how you step from the top of a hundred-foot pole!

No history is involved. Yet history and biography are nonetheless instructive: Ch'ang-sha and the monk Hui trained together under Nan-ch'üan. In due time these two brother monks became independent. Ch'ang-sha became abbot of a large training center. Hui went to live in a hermitage in the mountains.

"How is brother Hui getting along these days?" Ch'ang-sha wondered. He sent a monk to call on him with instructions about what to say.

The monk arrived and asked Hui, "What about when you had not yet met Nan-ch'üan?" Hui sat quietly.

The monk asked, "What about after you met Nan-ch'üan?"

Hui said, "Nothing special." The monk returned to Ch'ang-sha and told him what had happened.

Ch'ang-sha said,

> You who sit on the top of a hundred-foot pole;
> although you have entered the Way, it is not yet genuine.
> Take a step from the top of the pole
> and worlds of the Ten Directions are your total body.

This story is given in full in the *Book of Serenity*,[1] but it seems that Shih-shuang thought this portion would be enough for the purposes of his students.

Hui was in the condition of "nothing special." He had entered the Way—he had realized equality and emptiness, where nothing happens. There are no sages and no ordinary people. There are no animals, trees, deserts, or mountains. There is no eye, ear, nose, tongue, body, mind. Saving others is out of the question.

So Ch'ang-sha said, "It is not yet genuine." Śākyamuni under the Bodhi Tree was not yet genuine. He was sitting there enjoying his realization, but meantime his former disciples were feeling abandoned in the big city. He needed to step out and give them the word.

In Cases 13 and 28, I discussed the character of Te-shan, who felt most at home in emptiness—he only popped out to give his students a swat, and then hurried back. Ch'ang-sha was a different breed. He had a clear view of the void, of course, but he was a man of the world and made his home there. Once he visited Yang-shan, who later went on to help establish the Kuei-yang school but was at that time a young monk.

> During the evening they were strolling under the full moon, and Yang-shan said, "All people have *this*, but they do not use it."
>
> Ch'ang-sha said, "How true. Won't you please use it?"
>
> Yang-shan said, "How would you use it?" Ch'ang-sha seized him by the lapels of his robe, threw him to the ground, and trampled on him.
>
> Yang-shan got to his feet, dusted himself off, and said, "What a tiger you are!" Thereafter Ch'ang-sha Ching-ts'en was known as Ts'en, the Great Tiger.[2]

Yang-shan was not equal to Ch'ang-sha's challenge. He dithered and just said, "How would you use it?" Ch'ang-sha then showed him how to step forward as *this*. He makes this point again in one of his teishōs: "The entire universe is in your eye; the entire universe is your total body; the entire universe is your own luminance; the entire universe is within your own luminance. In the entire universe there is no one that is not your own self."[3]

Here Ch'ang-sha recasts the last line of his message to Brother Hui. "The worlds of the Ten Directions are your total body" becomes "The entire universe is in your eye." This one phrase sums up thirty-nine chapters of Hua-yen metaphysics. My eye and yours are holograms, every being is a hologram: each leaf, each bird, each flower, each child, is a chalice containing all. Realizing yourself as such a chalice is your luminance.

Apart from this case and the verse from Ch'ang-sha that Wu-men uses in Case 12, the only other case involving Ch'ang-sha appears in *The Blue Cliff Record*. After Mu, this is one of the most important kōans:

Ch'ang-sha one day went on a stroll in the mountains. When he returned to the gate, the head monk asked, "Where has Your Reverence been wandering?"

Ch'ang-sha said, "I have come from strolling about in the hills."

The head monk said, "Where did you go?"

Ch'ang-sha said, "First I went following the scented grasses, then I came back following the falling flowers."

The head monk said, "That is the spring mood itself."

Ch'ang-sha said, "It is better than the autumn dew falling on the lotus flowers."

Hsüeh-tou commented, "I am grateful for that answer."[4]

When I worked on this kōan with Yamada Rōshi, he told me that the expression about the scented grasses and falling flowers is often used during the eulogy at a monk's funeral. The implication is: "Coming and going, you enjoyed the scented grasses and falling flowers. Thus you lived a fulfilled life."[5]

What do you make of Ch'ang-sha's saying that spring is better than the autumn dew falling on the lotus flowers? This is the key to Ch'ang-sha's character, and to all mature human character. It relates to the way he reacted to Brother Hui's "Nothing special" and to Yang-shan's equivocation. It's true that spring and autumn can be called the same—but that is just a kind of entry to the Way; it is not yet genuine. In autumn there is no sun warming the earth after a long winter, no grasses or flowers. Spring is the time for strolling about in the hills, leisurely going and coming, with the scented grasses and falling flowers becoming one's entire body. So Hsüeh-tou comments that he is grateful to Ch'ang-sha for his response. Let us all be grateful.

Grateful because Ch'ang-sha is our teacher of Zen in this age of grave danger to the earth and its music, art, animals, and everything else. He is urging that we move off our seats and transform our attitudes and our systems. If everything is one, as Brother Hui knew, then it is also vital that we show that fact in our conduct. Worlds of the Ten Directions are indeed my total body and yours, and we neglect this primordial truth to our peril.

Wu-men comments: "Stepping forward, turning back—is there anything to reject as ignoble or unworthy?" Stepping forward and turning back, going and coming, we find that scented grasses are very special indeed. Strolling through them we realize our intimacy with them. Turning back through falling flowers, we delight in the total body they create. Brother Hui is depriving himself and depriving the world, dithering there atop his pole! "Be that as it may, how do you step from the top of a hundred-foot pole? *Sah!*" Let's see you try it!

Wu-men's verse begins: "He darkened the eye in his forehead." What is meant here? There is a lot of nonsense written about the third eye. I think Wu-men is simply referring to the eye of understanding, of realization. He is harking back to Brother Hui perched up there in emptiness. Forty years or so ago a book was published that purported to be the autobiography of a great Tibetan master. It stated that Tibetan children who were considered to be future teachers would have a circle of bone removed from their foreheads to make their third eye more sensitive. When we told our teacher Senzaki Sensei about this, he shouted, "Fake! Fake!" We were amazed. How could he be so sure? It turned out that the book was in fact written by someone in England who had never been to Tibet. Even after this exposure, though, some people continue to believe the story, saying that the author was remembering something from his previous life. Nonsense. The third eye is a metaphor and a profoundly instructive one. But "roses in her cheeks" does not mean the American Beauty is sprouting there.

"And clung to the mark on the scale"—he was mistaking the measure for the weight. It is true that empty equality is the touchstone of realization. Unless you see it clearly, you cannot deepen your practice. But once you do see it, don't neglect what comes next.

"Throw away body and discard life." Give up, once and for all, and shed that "nothing special."

"And the blind one leads the blind." Wu-men did not know about the English proverb. He was referring to something else. Sort out the meanings here.

Tou-shuai's Three Barriers

THE CASE

The priest Tou-shuai set up three barriers in order to examine his students:

"You make your way through the darkness of abandoned grasses in a single-minded search for your self-nature. Now, honored one, where is your nature?"

"When you have realized your self-nature, you are free of birth and death. When the light of your eyes falls, how are you free?"

"When you are free of birth and death, you know where to go. When your four elements scatter, where do you go?"

WU-MEN'S COMMENT

If you can rightly give the three turning words here, you will be master in all the varied circumstances and will deal with your affinities in accord with the Buddha Dharma. If you have not resolved the matter yet, the food you bolt down won't sustain you. Chew it well, and you won't be hungry.

WU-MEN'S VERSE

One nien *sees eternity;*
eternity is equal to now;
if you see through this one nien
you see through the one who sees.

The priest Tou-shuai (Tosotsu) was an eleventh-century Lin-chi master in the Huang-lung line, a contemporary of Wu-tsu. It is said that he suffered from overconfidence as a young monk, but the rebuke of an older colleague changed his attitude completely. Later he gave up his position as master and returned to the life of a monk in training in order to deepen his understanding. He died young, at the age of forty-eight, and left no Dharma successors.

Tou-shuai's Three Barriers form one of the best-known kōans in Zen study. Lin-chi teachers place it toward the end of formal practice—immediately preceding Tung-shan's Five Modes of the Universal and the Particular. Harada Rōshi, however, included it among the Introductory Kōans which the student, fresh from realization, must face very early. It deals with the three most important matters in our lives: how to realize true nature, how to die, and where one goes after death.

If you see Mu clearly and are serious in your purpose, then these three matters are not barriers in the ordinary sense at all—they simply clarify the understanding that is already present. If, however, you do not see Mu so clearly, then they are useful in pointing the way to practice. The three questions derive from fundamental human purposes. Most people who come to introductory Zen Buddhist meetings are clearly caught up in anxiety about realizing their true nature. Others are preoccupied with death and the afterlife. Some people, however, have other concerns which they hope they can take up in their zazen: illness, family disruption, career failure, self-doubt, injustice. You might find that these concerns dominate your zazen at first. A good teacher will never deny their importance. But eventually you will see that the three issues raised by Tou-shuai underlie all problems.

A few people are so preoccupied with secondary matters that eventually they find their practice to be meaningless because, it seems to them, nothing in zazen addresses, say, illness or injustice directly. This is too bad. For there beneath the Buddha's seat is the ground of healing and the foundation of justice. *Duhkha*, the anguish of dissatisfaction, is the universal human condition. At the heart of this anguish are Gauguin's questions: "What are we? Where do we come from? Where are we going?"[1] All other concerns follow. With Mu these concerns are addressed and perhaps resolved. What is Mu after all? What is your true nature after all? What is all this talk about life after death?

"You make your way through the darkness of abandoned grasses in a single-minded search for your self-nature." Darkness can sometimes refer to the essential side of reality where there are no distinctions. But here it means chaos—the clashing of thoughts and emotions. Abandoned grasses refers to the wild quality of the everyday mind: higgledy-piggledy, at sixes and sevens, like the mind of the youth in the first of the Ten Oxherding Pictures who sees only the forest and hears only the singing of insects.[2]

"Now, honored one," continues Tou-shuai, right now, not looking ahead, accepting your nobility as an agent of realization, "where is your nature?" Never forget that however higgledy-piggledy you may be, you are the honored one! With his imperative question, Tou-shuai has erected a barrier all right. But the barrier itself is the point, as it always is. "Virtue is its own reward" has implications beyond morality.

"When you have realized your self-nature, you are free of birth and death. When the light of your eyes falls, how are you free?" Your true nature does not come into being or go out of being. But as the *Heart Sutra* says, "There is no old age and death, and also no end to old age and death."[3] There is nothing to be born and nothing to die, yet there is forever senility and passing away. It is this dimension of no-birth and no-death that you realize on discerning your self-nature. You find that it is not separate from your mortality.

In Case 35, you are asked to identify the real Ch'ien: the one sick in bed at home or the healthy one in a distant city. Wu-men comments on that imperative: "If you know which was the real one, then you will know that leaving one husk and taking on another is like putting up at an inn." This is true freedom. The test comes when everything starts to get dark, and you know it will not get light again.

"When you are free of birth and death, you know where to go. When your four elements scatter, where do you go?" The four elements are earth, water, fire, and air—the basic units of Chinese biology. Perhaps you have found complete freedom in your realization that life and death are the same as no-life and no-death. Then where do you go after you die? Please don't say, "Nowhere." Don't say, "Right here." Don't say, "In my grave." All of these responses may be true from an ordinary point of view. Inquire further.

Wu-men comments: "If you can rightly give the three turning words here, you will be master in all the varied circumstances and deal with your affinities in accord with the Buddha Dharma." What is the Buddha Dharma? Regarding the first barrier—searching for true nature—it might be compared to a scholar in pursuit of something that is unclear. Once when I was living with my grandfather, the astronomer Robert G. Aitken, he told me that he had spent the entire morning verifying the middle initial of one of the Herschels. He said, "I suppose you think that was a great waste of time." He is my inspiration when I settle into zazen and focus on that little word Mu.

Now for the second barrier: How will you free yourself at the ultimate point? Everyone who has ever lived is put to this test. Yamada Rōshi told me that Lung-t'an, teacher of Te-shan, died crying out, "It hurts! It hurts!" Was he dealing with it?

And finally the destination: "When you are free of birth and death, you know where to go. When your four elements scatter, where do you go?" Several years ago one of our members, an old friend and college classmate, was dying of cancer. I had been away and came back just two days before she died. I called on her and was taken into her sick room. She was blind with her illness by this time. I took her hand and she said, "Bob, where am I going?"

I said, "Wherever your toes will lead you." She took a big sigh and smiled, repeating the words for herself: "Wherever my toes will lead me, wherever my toes will lead me." I think she died expectantly.

Recall the condolence story I cite in connection with Case 19:

Chien-yüan rapped on the coffin and asked, "Living or dead?"
    Tao-wu said, "I won't say living; I won't say dead."
    Chien-yüan asked, "Why won't you say?"
    Tao-wu said, "I won't say! I won't say!"[4]

Later Chien-yüan finally realized "I won't say." Tou-shuai, however, demands that you do say.

"If you have not resolved the matter yet, the food you bolt down won't sustain you. Chew it well, and you won't be hungry." This needs no further comment. Chewing well in Zen practice is a matter of examining closely. Examine Tou-shuai's Three Barriers closely. Examine Mu closely.

Wu-men's verse begins: "One *nien* sees eternity." One *nien* (*nen*) is one frame of thought in the sequence of the thought movie. In that frame is all of eternity—past, present, and future, from the top of heaven to the bottom of hell. Please show *that*.

"Eternity is equal to now." All those places between the top of heaven and the bottom of hell are right here in this thought-moment. Show this!

"If you see through this one *nien* / you see through the one who sees." If you take a step from this realization of the universe in one *nien*—and one *nien* containing the universe—then worlds of the Ten Directions will be your total body. You will see what your body is and show it. Tou-shuai will find that he has a successor after all.

CASE 48

Kan-feng's One Road

THE CASE

A monk asked the priest Kan-feng, "'Bhagavats in the Ten Directions, one straight road to nirvana.' I wonder where that road is."

Kan-feng lifted up his staff, drew a line in the air, and said, "Here it is."

Later a monk asked Yün-men about this. Yün-men held up his fan and said, "This fan jumps up to the Heaven of the Thirty-three and strikes the nose of the deity Śakradevendra. Give a carp of the Eastern Sea one blow, and the rain comes down in torrents."

WU-MEN'S COMMENT

One goes deep—deep to the bottom of the sea—and winnows the mud and pumps up the sand. The other goes high—high to the top of the mountain—and raises foaming waves that spread over the entire sky. Maintaining, releasing, each using but one hand, they safeguard the vehicle of the Tao. They are like two children, running from different directions, who collide with each other. In this world, there is almost no one who can touch the true essence. In the view of the true eye, even these two ancient worthies do not know the road.

WU-MEN'S VERSE

Before you take a step, you are already there;
before your tongue has moved, your teishō is finished.
Though your every move is ahead of the last,
remember the vast all-encompassing crater.

The priest Kan-feng (Kempō) is less well known than other teachers we have studied. Active in the tenth century, he was a successor of Tung-shan Liang-chieh and thus Ts'ao-shan's brother in the Dharma and a contemporary of Hsüeh-feng and Yen-t'ou. The scene is probably the nightly confrontation of teacher and students. The teacher makes a statement or asks a question; students step forward and respond. We can imagine that sacred occasion: the monks gathered in the dim light, the master at the altar offering incense and then taking the high seat to face his students, saying a few words, and inviting responses.

A monk steps up, makes bows, and quotes from the *Śūrangama Sūtra*: " 'Bhagavats in the Ten Directions, one straight road to nirvana.' " Perhaps Kan-feng had just quoted that passage during his presentation. A Bhagavat is a holy one or a Buddha. The Ten Directions is shorthand for the whole universe. Figuratively the term means "throughout space and time." The holy ones are everywhere, past, present, and future. And as for the one straight road, there is, the *Śūrangama Sūtra* says, just one way to enlightened rest, just one correct way to the mind of Prajñā Pāramitā, to the completed wisdom of all the holy ones.

"I wonder," muses the monk aloud, "where that road is." In one of his early teishōs at the Koko An Zendō, Yamada Rōshi said, "When your mind is crystal clear like a still mountain lake, then anything will do as a medium of enlightenment." Anything can turn out to be the correct way.

In the *Transmission of Light*, we have the case of Sanghanandi and Gayaśāta:

At the sound of copper bells at the corners of the temple Sanghanandi asked, "Do the bells ring, or does the wind ring?"

Gayaśāta said, "It is not the wind, it is not the bells, it is my mind that rings."

Sanghanandi said, "Well, then, who is that mind?"

Gayaśāta said, "Only because the mind is solitary and calm."[1]

In the present case, when the monk asked where that road might be, Kan-feng did not just sit quietly with his mind at rest. It is true that a mind solitary and calm mirrors the mountains and stars, but Kan-feng came forth from that calm and presented it. He drew a line in the air, saying "Here it is!"

A single horizontal line in Chinese is the ideograph for the numeral one, but I don't think that Kan-feng had oneness in mind. The thrush singing in the early morning would answer the monk's question just as well, but Kan-feng did not mime the thrush. He drew a line in the air. That was his "one straight road."

If that monk's mind were clear like a still mountain lake, perhaps the divine accident might have occurred and the Dharma Wheel would have made an additional turn. Kan-feng put himself forward—he showed his holy mind—and this is what we all must do. He came forth with stick in hand as we come forth with pick, hammer, kettle, pen, or calculator in hand as Kuan-yin. This is the vital act of responsibility.

"Here it is!" Here is your supper! Here is your contract! Here is your newly spaded garden! Here is your conjugation of *aller*. Here is your (*crack!*). This is the basic point of work—of sweeping the garden, striking the bell, washing the pots after breakfast.

When we established the Koko An Zendō, Nakagawa Sōen Rōshi showed me how to use the small signal bell. "Loud and clear," he said. "*That* is your teaching."

At the end of Case 7 I quoted the master Chin-niu (Kingyū), who would appear at the door of the zendō at mealtimes with a tub of cooked rice and dance and laugh loudly, shouting, "Little bodhisattvas, come and eat your rice!" That was his teaching. And as Ch'ang-ch'ing said a long time later, "It was a kind of grace before the meal."[2] It was a kind of one straight road.

Yün-men held up his fan and said, "This fan jumps up to the Heaven of the Thirty-three and strikes the nose of the deity Śakradevendra." Lifting his fan instead of his staff, Yün-men evokes the richness of Indian cosmology. The Heaven of the Thirty-three is centered at the summit of Mount Sumeru, where Śakradevendra (Indra) rules with the help of thirty-two devas. All deities and their entourages in countless multitudes, all the holy ones throughout space and time, are included in the perfected wisdom of one moment, as Yün-men lifts his fan. For cosmic wit, nobody beats Yün-men.

"Give a carp of the Eastern Sea one blow, and the rain comes down in torrents." The Chinese metaphor is "the rain comes down like tipping over a pan of water." The rain comes down in buckets. Wonderful. When our big bell rings, our neighbor looks up. You don't need Śakradevendra up there to turn the Dharma Wheel. What greater miracle can there be?

Wu-men comments: "One goes deep—deep to the bottom of the sea—and winnows the mud and pumps up the sand." That is Kan-feng and his staff, stirring everything up at the very source.

"The other goes high—high to the top of the mountain—and raises foaming waves that spread over the entire sky." That is: the worlds of the Ten Directions as Yün-men's total body.

"Maintaining, releasing, each using but one hand, they safeguard the vehicle of the Tao." Kan-feng grasps it firmly. Yün-men tosses it around. Yün-men grasps it firmly; Kan-feng tosses it around.

"They are like two children, running from opposite directions, who collide with each other." And collapse laughing!

"In this world, there is almost no one who can touch the true essence." Do you think Kan-feng and Yün-men are truly realized? Not so. "In the view of the true eye, even these two ancient worthies do not know the road." Like the Buddha himself, they are still working at it.

Wu-men explains in his verse: "Before you take a step, you are already there; / before your tongue has moved, your teishō is finished." That is the view of the nirvana eye. There is no knowing or not knowing from the beginning. There are no steps on that road.

"Though your every move is ahead of the last, / remember the vast all-encompassing crater." Though you move along, kōan after kōan, milestone after milestone, graduating, getting your first job, getting married, having children, remember the timeless crater of no dimension that includes everything.

Kan-feng showed how the step-by-step road to nirvana is a single gesture. Yün-men went to nirvana and poked the loftiest deity in the nose with his fan. These two old worthies, Kan-feng and Yün-men, joined hands to show how "eternity is in love with the productions of time"—how *this* gesture of *this* moment includes heaven and earth, past, present, and future. And that is our purpose too, our practice, and our realization.

Wu-men's Postscript

I follow the precedent of Buddhas and Ancestral Teachers in offering these comments—like passing judgment on the confessions of criminals—without a single superfluous word. For your sake, I have removed the lid of my skull and bulged out my eyeballs. Please take hold of the matter directly, and do not preoccupy yourself otherwise.

If you are a competent, realized person, you will see the point clearly as soon as you hear a bit of my discourse. There will be no gate to enter—no stairs to climb. You will pass through the barrier with your arms folded firmly, not even asking permission of the guard. Remember the words of Hsüan-sha: "No-gate is the gate of liberation; no-mind is the mind of the wayfarer." Remember too the words of Pai-yün: "Clearly, clearly, the Tao is known. It is just this. Why don't you pass through?"

These remarks of mine are like smearing milk on red soil. If you can pass through the Gateless Barrier, you make a fool of Wu-men. If you cannot pass through, you are insensible to yourself. It may not be so difficult to realize the so-called mind of nirvana, but it is hard to realize the wisdom of differentiation. When you realize the wisdom of differentiation, then your nation is naturally at peace.

The first year of Shao-ting (1228)
five days before the end of the summer retreat
respectfully inscribed by the monk Wu-men Hui-k'ai
eighth descendant of Yang-ch'i

Wu-men's Cautions

With Comments by Robert Aitken

To maintain standards and follow rules is to tie yourself up without a rope.

When I met with Yamada Rōshi and Miyazaki Kan'un Rōshi about the latter's prospective visit to Hawaii, I said that I expected Miyazaki Rōshi to be of help to us with our procedures. Yamada Rōshi said, "Procedures are for the sake of practice, not practice for procedures." In this spirit Miyazaki Rōshi made helpful corrections to our ritual.

To indulge freely without restraint is to behave like heretics and demons.

Restraint is the practice of the Eightfold Path: right views, right thought, right speech, right conduct, right livelihood, right lifestyle, right recollection, right zazen—"right" when the step is taken with clear awareness of how all things pass quickly away and how all things are innately in harmony. Without this or a similar practice, you are dissipating yourself, chattering rootlessly, pursuing bright lights and confetti. The adult who behaves wantonly is a danger to the world, and so Wu-men uses the strong word "demon."

To maintain the mind in solitary depths is the specious Zen of quietism.

The Way of the Buddha is established in the dōjō, the *bodhimanda*, the sacred ground of enlightenment. The Buddha himself was tempted to remain there after his realization, but he arose to work with others. He became his own dōjō, walking, sitting, speaking. Thus he is our original teacher. Don't tarry!

To give rein to the will and ignore karma is to fall into the pit.

When all your concerns are upon your individual self, it is natural for you to respond to your personal whims, to be rude to others, and to come and go without feeling any need to be grounded. I know this path very well. The more you try to be happy, the more miserable you become. Practice goodwill and you will find goodwill. This is karma.

To be alert and never unclear is to wear chains and an iron yoke.

I dropped off those fetters long ago, thank goodness! I find it so pleasant to go to the beach, to look at the clouds, to gossip with children! In a dim state of mind I rise and wash. Sitting in the interview room I lose track of time. Now I must go to the dōjō. Let's see, where is my stick? Ah! here it is, right here in my hand!

To think good and evil is to belong to heaven and hell.

As Wu-men says elsewhere, the one who argues right and wrong is a person of right and wrong. To belong to heaven and hell is to belong to the world of sage and ordinary person, sweet and sour, birth and death. If you think Wu-men is approving license here, you belong to the world of license.

To have a Buddha view and a Dharma view is to be enclosed by two iron mountains.

The Buddha view is that all is empty. The Dharma view is that all is karma. One is the First Principle, the other the Second Principle. You are caught in principles. What is the way out? The eucalyptus trees stand motionless in the night air. Only a faraway rooster can be heard.

To treat each thought as realization is to trifle with your spirit.

This is advice to beginners who regard every little intimation as something important. But it also applies to old-timers, who despite long training become enchanted with odd thoughts. I'm sure that the Buddha himself had trouble with this tendency. We share his humanity.

To cultivate samādhi is to practice in a haunted house.

The Buddha Way is the way of realization. All the words of the founding teachers are based on experience. Mere absorption is not enough. Unless human thirst for realization is involved, zazen is the practice of the stone image. It just sits there getting more and more quiet. Very eerie.

To proceed is to stray from the truth.

You sit in the Buddha's dōjō itself. Your body is the Buddha herself or himself. Don't try to proceed—remain on target, come what may. You say you are stuck, but this is not possible. The mango is not stuck on the mango tree. Something of the utmost importance is happening.

To retreat is to violate the Tao.

This goes without saying. But don't load that word "violate" with condemnation. Over the years I have known several people who retreated. They stopped zazen—and then, perhaps years later, returned again. All of us have experienced retreat many times. We dawdle off on some preoccupation while on our cushions and then come back. To retreat is human. To return is humanity at its best.

Neither to proceed nor to retreat is to be a corpse with breath.

Wu-men is like a mad director of traffic. No left turn, no right turn, no U turn, no advancing, no reversing, no parking. He denies us all options—and this is the best place to be in our practice.

Now tell me, what do you do?

When all your options are exhausted, what do you do? That's easy. Muuu!

Work hard for realization in this life, or you will have regrets eternally.

This is a short life with even shorter episodes. But don't be diverted by your anxiety about eternal regrets. Use your anxiety. It is precious energy.

Notes

ACKNOWLEDGMENTS

1. Kōun Yamada, *Gateless Gate* (Los Angeles: Center Publications, 1979); Katsuki Sekida, *Two Zen Classics: Mumonkan and Hekiganroku* (New York: Weatherhill, 1977).

2. Yamada, *Gateless Gate*, and Zenkei Shibayama, *Zen Comments on the Mumonkan* (New York: Harper & Row, 1974); Shibayama, *Kunchū Mumonkan* [*The Gateless Barrier* explicated] (Tokyo: Kichūdō, 1954).

3. Ruth Fuller Sasaki, *The Recorded Sayings of Ch'an Master Lin-chi Hui-chao of Chen Prefecture* (Kyoto: Institute for Zen Studies, 1975).

4. See Case 4, n. 9.

5. Honzanban Shukusatsu, ed., *Shōbōgenzō* (Tokyo: Kōmeisha, 1968).

6. Seizan Yanagida and others, eds., *Zen no Goroku* [*Analects of Zen*], 20 vols. projected (Tokyo: Chikuma Shōbō, 1969–).

INTRODUCTION

1. The etymology of *kōan*, "universal/particular," is discussed by Norman Waddell and Masao Abe, "*Shōbōgenzō Genjōkōan*," *Eastern Buddhist*, new series, vol. 5, no. 2, October 1972, p. 130.

2. Case 23. See Mou-lam Wong, trans., *The Sutra of Hui Neng*, in *The Diamond Sutra and the Sutra of Hui Neng* (Berkeley: Shambhala, 1969), p. 21; and Philip B. Yampolsky, *The Platform Sutra of the Sixth Patriarch* (New York: Columbia University, 1967), p. 134.

3. See Case 5, my comment.

4. Robert Aitken, *Taking the Path of Zen* (San Francisco: North Point Press, 1982); Haku'un Yasutani, "Introductory Lectures on Zen Training," in *The Three Pillars of Zen*, ed. Philip Kapleau (Boston: Beacon Press, 1965), pp. 26–62.

5. Arthur Braverman, trans., *Mud and Water: A Collection of Talks by the Zen Master Bassui* (San Francisco: North Point Press, 1989), pp. 101–104.

PREFACE

1. The year 1228.
2. Wu-men's story is told in several Zen books in English: D. T. Suzuki, *Essays in Zen Buddhism: Second Series* (New York: Samuel Weiser, 1976), pp. 264–265; Isshū Miura and Ruth Fuller Sasaki, *Zen Dust: The History of the Koan Study and Koan Study in Rinzai (Lin-chi) Zen* (New York: Harcourt, Brace & World, 1966), pp. 203–205; Yamada, *Gateless Gate*, p. 6; Shibayama, *Zen Comments on the Mumonkan*, pp. 10–11.
3. Cited by R. H. Blyth, *Zen in English Literature and Oriental Classics* (New York: Dutton, 1960), p. 19.
4. Suzuki, *Essays in Zen Buddhism: Second Series*, p. 265.

CASE 1: *Chao-chou's Dog*

1. The modern standard Chinese pronunciation is "Wu"; the Cantonese pronunciation is "Mu." The word probably moved from T'ang period Chinese to Japanese as "Mu."
2. Shibayama, *Zen Comments on the Mumonkan*, p. 21.
3. Yamada, *Gateless Gate*, p. 15.
4. See *Meditations on the Tarot* [anonymous] (New York: Amity House, 1985), pp. 3–4.
5. Hee-Jin Kim, trans., *Flowers of Emptiness: Selections from Dōgen's Shōbōgenzō* (Lewiston, N.Y.: Edwin Mellon Press, 1985), p. 66.
6. Yasutani, "Introductory Lectures," p. 32.
7. William F. Powell, trans., *The Record of Tung-shan* (Honolulu: University of Hawaii Press, 1986), p. 63.
8. Ira Progoff, trans., *The Cloud of Unknowing* (New York: Julian Press, 1957), p. 148.
9. Kazuaki Tanahashi, trans., *Shinjin Gakudo* ("Body-and-Mind Study of the Way"), in *Moon in a Dewdrop: Writings of Zen Master Dōgen* (San Francisco: North Point Press, 1985), p. 89.
10. D. T. Suzuki, *Sengai: The Zen Master* (Greenwich, Conn.: New York Graphic Society, 1971), pp. 46–47.

CASE 2: *Pai-chang's Fox*

1. Thomas Cleary and J. C. Cleary, *The Blue Cliff Record*, 3 vols. (Boulder: Shambhala, 1977), 2:357.
2. "His" attendant. Confucian standards pervaded the monasteries of Chinese Buddhism, and no woman, however enlightened (and there were many), was

formally recognized as a Zen teacher. This discrimination has broken down to some degree in modern Japan, and the West has several women rōshis.

3. Yasutani, "Introductory Lectures," p. 28.

4. This comment by Hakuin is handed down from teacher to student and forms a traditional part of the study of the case.

5. Shibayama, *Zen Comments on the Mumonkan*, p. 39.

6. Yamada, *Gateless Gate*, p. 24.

CASE 3: *Chü-chih Raises One Finger*

1. See, for example, Oliver Statler, *Japanese Pilgrimage* (London: Pan Books, 1984), p. 22, and Walter Scott, "The Two Drovers," in *The Oxford Book of Short Stories*, ed. V. S. Pritchett (New York: Oxford University Press, 1981), p. 4.

2. Cleary and Cleary, *Blue Cliff Record*, 1:194.

3. For Lu-tsu (Roso), see Thomas Cleary, *Book of Serenity* (Hudson, N.Y.: Lindisfarne Press, 1990), p. 100.

4. Norman Waddell, trans., *The Unborn: The Life and Teachings of Zen Master Bankei* (San Francisco: North Point Press, 1984).

5. Case 14.

6. For Mu-chou (Bokushū), see Yamada, *Gateless Gate*, p. 81.

7. For Te-shan (Tokusan), see D. T. Suzuki, *Essays in Zen Buddhism: First Series* (York Beach, Me.: Samuel Weiser, 1985), p. 276.

8. Ibid., p. 295.

9. Cleary and Cleary, *Blue Cliff Record*, 1:3.

CASE 4: *Huo-an's Beardless Barbarian*

1. Cleary and Cleary, *Blue Cliff Record*, 1:xxii.

2. Shibayama, *Zen Comments on the Mumonkan*, p. 50.

3. For Fu Ta-shih (Fu Daishi), see Miura and Sasaki, *Zen Dust*, p. 49.

4. Wallace Stevens, *The Palm at the End of the Mind: Selected Poems and a Play*, edited by Holly Stevens (New York: Random House, 1972), p. 353.

5. Inscribed on the board drum at the Koko An Zendō, Honolulu.

6. For Shih-t'ou Hsi-chien (Sekitō Kisen), see Suzuki, *Essays in Zen Buddhism: Second Series*, p. 231.

7. Cleary and Cleary, *Blue Cliff Record*, 1:1.

8. Suzuki, *Essays in Zen Buddhism: Second Series*, pp. 231–232.

9. Haku'un Yasutani's *dokugo* ("musings") on the *Mumonkan*, the *Hekiganroku*, the *Shōyōroku*, the *Denkōroku*, and the *Goi, Sanki, Sanju, Jūjūkinkai* were published in Tokyo by the Sanbō Kōryūkai from 1956 to 1964.

CASE 5: *Hsiang-yen: Up a Tree*

1. The other cofounder of the Kuei-yang school was Yang-shang (Kyōzan), who figures later in Hsiang-yen's story.

2. Suzuki, *Essays in Zen Buddhism: First Series*, pp. 242–243. Kuei-shan's question is a kōan derived from words attributed to the Sixth Ancestor, Hui-neng. See my Introduction.

3. Nan-yang Hui-chung (Nanyō Echū), also known as Chung Kuo-shih (Chū Kokushi), Chung, the National Teacher, who lived a century earlier, an eminent successor of Hui-neng, the Sixth Ancestor. See Case 17.

4. R. H. Blyth, *Mumonkan*, vol. 4 of *Zen and Zen Classics* (Tokyo: Hokuseido, 1966), pp. 69–70.

5. Ibid., p. 70.

6. Ibid.

7. Chung-yuan Chang, *The Original Teachings of Ch'an Buddhism* (New York: Random House, 1969), p. 220.

8. Ibid., p. 221.

9. The "high seat" is a kind of giant highchair perhaps four feet from the floor. From there the rōshi delivers his teishō, facing the Buddha, to the monks lined up on each side below him, listening in zazen. The teishō format in Western Zen centers is derived from this traditional arrangement.

10. Nyogen Senzaki, "101 Zen Stories," in *Zen Flesh Zen Bones*, comp. Paul Reps (Rutland, Vt.: Charles Tuttle, 1970), pp. 38–39.

11. For a discussion of *duhkha*, the Four Noble Truths, and the Eightfold Path, see Richard A. Gard, *Buddhism* (New York: Braziller, 1962), pp. 106–135; Walpola Rahula, *What the Buddha Taught* (New York: Grove Press, 1959), pp. 16–50.

12. See Case 28.

CASE 6: *The World-Honored One Twirls a Flower*

1. Suzuki, *Manual of Zen Buddhism*, pp. 155, 158. This is the birth-cry of humanity: "Here I am!" It is also the "royal aloneness" of Wu-men and Suzuki (Wu-men's Preface, comment). It is echoed in the kōan "Sitting Alone at Ta-hsuing Peak." See Case 12, comment, and Cleary and Cleary, *Blue Cliff Record*, 1:172.

2. Suzuki, *Manual of Zen Buddhism*, pp. 155, 158.

3. Miura and Sasaki, *Zen Dust*, pp. 151–152.

4. Ibid., pp. 229–230.

5. Kajitani Sōnin, ed., *Shūmon Kattōshū* [The Traditional Tangled Wisteria Collection] (Tokyo: Hōzokan, 1982), p. 86.

6. Susanne Langer, *Philosophy in a New Key* (Cambridge: Harvard University Press, 1976), pp. 79–102.

7. See Tanahashi, *Moon in a Dewdrop*.

8. "Hakuin Zenji's 'Song of Zazen' "; see Aitken, *Taking the Path of Zen*, p. 113.

9. Yung-chia (Yōka), *Cheng-tao ko* (*Shōdōka*); see Nyogen Senzaki and Ruth Strout McCandless, *Buddhism and Zen* (San Francisco: North Point Press, 1987), p. 54.

10. Cleary and Cleary, *Blue Cliff Record*, 3:506.

11. R. H. Blyth, *Haiku*, 4 vols. (Tokyo: Hokuseido, 1950), 2:334; retranslated from the Japanese text.

12. Charles Luk, *Ch'an and Zen Teaching*, 3 vols. (London: Rider, 1960–1962), 2:187.

13. "Hakuin Zenji's 'Song of Zazen' "; see Aitken, *Taking the Path of Zen*, p. 112.

14. A. F. Price, trans., *The Diamond Sutra*, in *The Diamond Sutra and the Sutra of Hui Neng* (Berkeley: Shambhala, 1969); see also Case 8, n. 7.

15. Kōun Yamada, "The Stature of Haku'un Yasutani," *Eastern Buddhist*, new series, vol. 7, no. 2, October 1974, pp. 108–120.

16. Dōgen Kigen, *Genjō Kōan* ("Actualizing the Fundamental Point"); see Tanahashi, *Moon in a Dewdrop*, p. 70.

17. Cleary and Cleary, *Blue Cliff Record*, 1:1.

18. Thomas Cleary, *Transmission of Light* (San Francisco: North Point Press, 1990), pp. 6, 10, 16, 20.

CASE 7: *Chao-chou: "Wash Your Bowl"*

1. Cleary and Cleary, *Blue Cliff Record*, 3:500.

2. Yamada, *Gateless Gate*, p. 46.

3. Ibid., pp. 46–47.

4. Blyth, *Mumonkan*, p. 83.

5. Cleary and Cleary, *Blue Cliff Record*, 1:154.

6. Chin-niu (Kingyū); ibid., 2:490.

CASE 8: *Hsi-chung Builds Carts*

1. Shibayama, *Zen Comments on the Mumonkan*, p. 72.

2. Yamada, *Gateless Gate*, p. 49.

3. D. H. Lawrence, "Making Pictures," *Selected Essays* (Middlesex: Penguin, 1969), pp. 300–301.

4. See, for example, Shibayama, *Zen Comments on the Mumonkan*, p. 74.

5. Christmas Humphreys, "Some Observations on Zen Buddhism for the West," *Eastern Buddhist*, new series, vol. 1, no. 2, September 1966, pp. 78ff.
6. Here I strike the lectern with my stick.
7. See Akira Hirakawa and others, eds., *Japanese-English Buddhist Dictionary* (Tokyo: Daito Shuppansha, 1965), p. 255.
8. Price, *Diamond Sutra*, pp. 29, 41, 53, 65.

CASE 9: *Ch'ing-jang's Nonattained Buddha*

1. Cleary, *Book of Serenity*, pp. 163, 324.
2. The Buddha Mahābhijñā Jñānābhibhu (Ta-t'ung Chih-sheng, Daitsū Chisō).
3. Bunnō Katō and others, eds., *The Three-Fold Lotus Sutra: Innumerable Meanings, The Lotus Flower of the Wonderful Law, and Meditation on the Bodhisattva Universal Virtue* (Tokyo: Kōsei, 1987), pp. 145–149.
4. Sasaki, *Recorded Sayings of Ch'an Master Lin-chi*, English text p. 36, Chinese text p. 19.
5. Ibid., English text pp. 36–37, Chinese text p. 19.
6. Wu-men is quoting from Yüan-wu, who in turn is paraphrasing Hsüeh-tou (Setchō); see Cleary and Cleary, *Blue Cliff Record*, 2:300.
7. Flora Courtois, *An Experience of Enlightenment* (Wheaton, Ill.: Theosophical Press, 1986), particularly pp. 43–57.

CASE 10: *Ch'ing-shui: Solitary and Destitute*

1. For a discussion of the origin of the name of the Ts'ao-tung school, see Miura and Sasaki, *Zen Dust*, p. 166.
2. Ibid., pp. 62–72.
3. David Hume, "Of the Sceptical and Other Systems of Philosophy," in *The Age of Enlightenment*, ed. Isaiah Berlin (New York: New American Library, 1956), p. 256.
4. Yamada, *Gateless Gate*, p. 59.
5. Blyth, *Haiku*, 3:414.
6. Gempō Yamamoto, *Mumonkan Teishō* (Tokyo: Daihōrin, 1960), p. 133.
7. Raymond Bernard Blakney, *Meister Eckhart: A Modern Translation* (New York: Harper & Brothers, 1941), p. 228.
8. Yamada, *Gateless Gate*, p. 60.
9. Ibid., pp. 60–61.
10. Dominique Lapierre, *The City of Joy* (New York: Warner Books, 1986).

CASE 11: *Chao-chou and the Hermits*

1. Shibayama, *Zen Comments on the Mumonkan*, p. 87.

2. Nyogen Senzaki, "The Gateless Gate," unpublished translation and commentary, Diamond Sangha, Honolulu, and Zen Center of San Francisco, pp. 35–37.

3. "His" fist. There were female hermits, both lay and clerical, but the Chinese compilers of Zen cases always identified them as such. Thus the Chinese hermits in this case are male.

4. Yamada, *Gateless Gate*, pp. 64–65.

5. Chang, *Original Teachings of Ch'an Buddhism*, p. 166.

6. Yamada, *Gateless Gate*, p. 65.

CASE 12: *Jui-yen Calls "Master"*

1. Cleary, *Book of Serenity*, p. 316.

2. Shibayama, *Zen Comments on the Mumonkan*, p. 95.

3. Yamada, *Gateless Gate*, p. 70.

4. Tanahashi, *Moon in a Dewdrop*, p. 70.

5. Cleary and Cleary, *Blue Cliff Record*, 1:172.

6. Cleary and Cleary, *Blue Cliff Record*, III:553; see Case 2, my comment.

7. Haku'un Yasutani, *Hekiganshū Dokugo* [Musings on the *Blue Cliff Record*] (Tokyo: Sanbō Kōryūkai, 1960), p. 152.

8. Senzaki, "Gateless Gate," p. 38.

9. Shibayama, *Zen Comments on the Mumonkan*, p. 94.

10. Nicholas Herman [Brother Lawrence], *The Practice of the Presence of God* (Springdale, Pa.: Whitaker House, 1982), p. 36.

11. Dōgen misquotes, as he so often did for his purposes, in his *Semmen* [Washing the face] in Honzanban Shukusatsu, *Shōbōgenzō*, p. 509. See also Yūhō Yokoi, *Shōbō-genzō* (Tokyo: Sankibō Buddhist Bookstore, 1986), pp. 594–595; and Hee-Jin Kim, *Dōgen Kigen: Mystical Realist* (Tucson: University of Arizona Press, 1987), p. 174. For the original Chinese, see Heng Tsai and others, trans., *Flower Adornment Sūtra: Pure Conduct, Chapter 11* (Talmage, Calif.: Dharma Realm Buddhist University, 1982), pp. 140–141.

12. Robert Aitken, *The Dragon Who Never Sleeps: Verses for Zen Buddhist Practice* (Monterey, Ky.: Larkspur Press, 1990), p. 4.

13. Miura and Sasaki, *Zen Dust*, p. 275. Ch'ang-sha is also responsible for the kōan about the hundred-foot pole (Case 46).

14. "Hakuin Zenji's 'Song of Zazen' "; see Aitken, *Taking the Path of Zen*, p. 112. The Six Worlds are the realms of devils, hungry ghosts, animals, titans, humans, and celestial beings through which one constantly transmigrates.

CASE 13: *Te-shan: Bowls in Hand*

1. Heinrich Dumoulin, *Zen Buddhism: A History* (New York: Macmillan, 1988), 1:169.

2. Chang, *Original Teachings of Ch'an Buddhism*, p. 49.
3. Kōun Yamada, unpublished teishō, Diamond Sangha, Honolulu; see also Chang, *Original Teachings of Ch'an Buddhism*, p. 262.
4. See Charles Luk, trans., *The Vimalakīrti Nirdeśa Sūtra* (Boston: Shambhala, 1990), pp. 64–65; Robert A. F. Thurman, trans., *The Holy Teaching of Vimalakīrti* (University Park: Pennsylvania State University Press, 1976), pp. 42–43.
5. Cleary, *Book of Serenity*, p. 60.
6. The original Chinese can be read "the last phrase."
7. Case 42, Wu-men's Verse.

CASE 14: *Nan-ch'üan Kills the Cat*

1. Lu-keng (Rikkō); retold from Miura and Sasaki, *Zen Dust*, p. 280.
2. Yoel Hoffman, *Radical Zen: The Sayings of Jōshū* (Brookline, Mass.: Autumn Press, 1978), p. 17.
3. Cleary and Cleary, *Blue Cliff Record*, 2:407.
4. Robert Aitken, *A Zen Wave: Bashō's Haiku and Zen* (New York: Weatherhill, 1978), pp. 153–154.
5. Cleary and Cleary, *Blue Cliff Record*, 2:407.
6. Hsüan-sha (Gensha) and Hsia-t'ang (Shōtō); see Cleary, *Book of Serenity*, p. 346.

CASE 15: *Tung-shan's Sixty Blows*

1. Cleary and Cleary, *Blue Cliff Record*, 3:554.
2. Yamada, *Gateless Gate*, p. 81.
3. Chang, *Original Teachings of Ch'an Buddhism*, p. 269.
4. Yamada, *Gateless Gate*, p. 82.
5. Chang, *Original Teachings of Ch'an Buddhism*, p. 299.

CASE 16: *Yün-men: The Sound of the Bell*

1. Yamada, *Gateless Gate*, p. 88.
2. "Mealtime Sutras," unpublished leaflet, Diamond Sangha, Honolulu, n.d.
3. Paraphrased from "*Mahā Prajñā Pāramitā Hrdaya Sūtra*: The Heart Sutra"; see Aitken, *Taking the Path of Zen*, pp. 110–111.
4. See Wu-men's Preface and my comment; Miura and Sasaki, *Zen Dust*, pp. 203–204.
5. It was Nakagawa Sōen Rōshi who told me that Munan Zenji was really the central figure of this story. Usually it is attributed to Hakuin Ekaku, his grandson in the Dharma, who is better known. I changed the name accord-

ingly and rephrased a bit from Nyogen Senzaki, "101 Zen Stories," in Reps, *Zen Flesh Zen Bones*, p. 22.

6. See Plate 3; also Case 5, my comment.

7. Suzuki, *Essays in Zen Buddhism: First Series*, pp. 242–243.

8. Tanahashi, *Moon in a Dewdrop*, p. 68.

9. Powell, *Record of Tung-shan*, p. 26.

10. Miura and Sasaki, *Zen Dust*, pp. 47–49.

11. Shibayama, *Zen Comments on the Mumonkan*, p. 124.

12. Haku'un Yasutani, "Why Do We Recite Sutras?" *Diamond Sangha*, vol. 3, no. 2, March–April 1963.

CASE 17: *Kuo-shih's Three Calls*

1. See Case 5, my comment, and Plate 3.

2. Yamada, *Gateless Gate*, p. 92.

3. Cleary and Cleary, *Blue Cliff Record*, 3:628.

4. Ibid., 1:115; Miura and Sasaki, *Zen Dust*, pp. 267–268.

5. Senzaki, "Gateless Gate," pp. 51–53.

6. This part of the case seems quite important on first reading, and indeed it can be related to experiments conducted by Japanese psychologists back in the 1960s. They lined up veteran monks on one side of the room and a control group of medical students with no meditation experience on the other, and hooked them all up to brain-wave machines. They told the monks to do zazen and the students just to sit there with their eyes closed. Alpha waves appeared on the charts on both sides. When experimenters set up a clicking sound every fifteen seconds or so, interruptions to the alpha waves appeared on all the charts. But whereas the control group showed a pattern of habituation—a big jump the first time, followed by successively smaller responses, and finally no response at all—the monks showed the same alpha breaks at each click. This outcome was very interesting for the psychologists. Though the clicks were the same in quality, each sound was fresh and new for the monks, whereas those in the control group became inured and didn't notice them after awhile. See Yoshiharu Akishige, "A Historical Survey of the Psychological Studies on Zen," in *Kyushu Psychological Studies*, no. 5, 1968, pp. 36–37.

7. Cleary and Cleary, *Blue Cliff Record*, 1:39.

8. For the ideograph rendered as "ungrateful," see Shibayama, *Kunchū Mumonkan*, p. 53, n. 2; see also R. H. Mathews, *Mathews' Chinese-English Dictionary: Revised American Edition* (Cambridge: Harvard University Press, 1969), p. 515.

9. Kuei-tsung (Kisu) and Ma-ku (Mayoku); Cleary and Cleary, *Blue Cliff Record*, 2:434.

10. Ta-kung-wang (Taikōbō), Katō, Totsudō, *Mumonkan*, vols. 13–15, in *Hekiganroku Daikōza* [A complete course of study of the *Hekiganroku* (*Blue Cliff Record*)] (Tokyo: Heibonsha, 1940), 14:50.

11. Nyogen Senzaki and Ruth Strout McCandless, *The Iron Flute* (Rutland, Vt.: Tuttle, 1981), p. 13.

CASE 18: *Tung-shan's Three Pounds of Flax*

1. Tetsuo Suzuki, *Chūkoku Zenshū Jimmei Sakuin* [An index of Chinese Zen personages] (Nagoya: Kikōdō Shōten, 1975), p. 274.

2. Zenkyō Komagata, *Sōtōshū Yōten* [Principal rituals of the Sōtō sect] (Honolulu: Sōtōshū Betsuin, 1959), pp. 81–82.

3. *Fo-ming ching* (*Butsumyōkyō*); Genmyō Kono, ed., *Busshō Kaisetsu Daijiten* [Complete bibliography of Buddhist books], 12 vols. (Tokyo: Daitō Shuppansha, 1933), 9:339.

4. Thomas Cleary, trans., *The Flower Ornament Scripture*, 3 vols. (Boulder: Shambhala, 1984–1987), 1:125.

5. Cleary and Cleary, *Blue Cliff Record*, 1:82.

6. Senzaki, "Gateless Gate," p. 55.

7. Case 7, Wu-men's Verse.

8. Blyth, *Haiku*, 4:243.

9. See Case 6, my comment; Cleary and Cleary, *Blue Cliff Record*, 3:506.

10. Yamada, *Gateless Gate*, p. 97.

11. Here I strike the lectern with my stick.

CASE 19: *Nan-ch'üan: "Ordinary Mind Is the Tao"*

1. Wu-men's Comment and the placement of this dialogue in the various records indicates that it occurred early in Chao-chou's study with Nan-ch'üan, but Harada Sogaku Rōshi believed that it occurred when Chao-chou was a mature monk clearing up his final doubts. See Sogaku Harada, *Mumonkan Teishōroku* (Fukui-ken, Obama-shi: Dai'unkai, 1959), p. 123; also Yamada, *Gateless Gate*, p. 101, and Shibayama, *Zen Comments on the Mumonkan*, p. 141.

2. D. T. Suzuki, *The Training of the Zen Buddhist Monk* (Berkeley: Wingbow Press, 1974), p. 133.

3. Bruce Chatwin, *The Songlines* (London: Pan Books, 1988), p. 215.

4. Kōgen Mizuno, *Buddhist Sutras: Origin, Development, Transmission* (Tokyo: Kōsei, 1982), pp. 52–55.

5. A contemporary teacher, Kobori Nanrei Rōshi, includes Confucianism

among the antecedents of Zen: "Zen is, so to speak, a strange dragon with a Taoist torso, Confucian feet, and the Buddhist enlightenment-experience for eyes." See Nanrei Kobori, "The Ripening Persimmon," *Parabola*, vol. 10, no. 1, Spring 1985, p. 73.

6. Cleary and Cleary, *Blue Cliff Record*, 1:37.
7. Chang, *Original Teachings of Ch'an Buddhism*, p. 141.
8. Cleary and Cleary, *Blue Cliff Record*, 2:365.
9. Ibid., 1:1; see Case 41, my comment.

CASE 20: *Sung-yüan's Person of Great Strength*

1. Yamada, *Gateless Gate*, p. 106.
2. Cleary, *Book of Serenity*, p. 176.
3. Cleary and Cleary, *Blue Cliff Record*, 3:473–482.
4. Shibayama, *Zen Comments on the Mumonkan*, p. 149.
5. Thomas Cleary, *Entry into the Inconceivable: An Introduction to Hua-yen Buddhism* (Honolulu: University of Hawaii Press, 1983), pp. 179–180; Cleary, *Flower Ornament Scripture*, 1:4–5, 215–253.

CASE 21: *Yün-men's Dried Shitstick*

1. Chang, *Original Teachings of Ch'an Buddhism*, p. 269.
2. Cleary and Cleary, *Blue Cliff Record*, 1:237.
3. Chang, *Original Teachings of Ch'an Buddhism*, pp. 266, 285.
4. Ibid., p. 267.
5. Sasaki, *Recorded Sayings of Ch'an Master Lin-chi*, Chinese text p. 2, English text p. 3.
6. Robert Aitken, *The Mind of Clover* (San Francisco: North Point Press, 1984), p. 127.
7. Revised from Aitken, *Zen Wave*, p. 146.
8. Chang, *Original Teachings of Ch'an Buddhism*, p. 267.
9. Dōgen, *Jūundō-Shinki* ("Regulations for the Auxiliary Cloud Hall"); see Tanahashi, *Moon in a Dewdrop*, p. 50.

CASE 22: *Mahākāśyapa's Flagpole*

1. Bimala Churn Law, trans., *Saddamma-Sangaha: A Manual of Buddhist Historical Traditions* (Calcutta: University of Calcutta, 1941), pp. 19–36.
2. Case 6, Wu-men's Comment.
3. Blyth, *Zen in English Literature*, p. 21.
4. Sasaki, *Recorded Sayings of Ch'an Master Lin-chi*, p. 3.
5. See Shibayama, *Zen Comments on the Mumonkan*, p. 163.

CASE 23: *Hui-neng: "Neither Good Nor Evil"*

1. Price, *Diamond Sutra*, p. 45; Suzuki, "The Kongokyo or Diamond Sutra," *Manual of Zen Buddhism*, p. 46.

2. Yampolsky, *Platform Sutra of the Sixth Patriarch*, pp. 126–127.

3. See Sengai's painting of Hung-jen rowing Hui-neng across (Plate 5). In his verse Sengai played with the meanings of *hō*, which in context can be read as Dharma as well as laws of painting. Further, he substituted ideographs meaning "reversed oar" for those meaning "no-law," making fun of Hung-jen's technique with his oars as well as his own draftsmanship. Note that Hui-neng is holding the bowl as he sits happily in the boat.

4. Versions of this account can be found in translations by Philip Yampolsky, Wong Mou-lam, Wing Tsit-chan, Paul and George Fung, and others. The two main versions are the Tun-huang—dating from the ninth century, more than a hundred years after the death of Hui-neng—and the Ming from the late thirteenth century, so called because it was included in the Ming period edition of the *Tripitaka*. The first is a reworked history that reflects the orthodox view of the Southern school of Zen at the time; the second account includes accretions that were part of an oral tradition. See Yampolsky, *Platform Sutra of the Sixth Patriarch*, and Wong, *Sutra of Hui Neng*.

5. Yampolsky, *Platform Sutra of the Sixth Patriarch*, pp. 89–110; also John McRae, *The Northern School and the Formation of Early Ch'an Buddhism* (Honolulu: University of Hawaii Press, 1986), pp. 10–11.

6. Frederick Franck, "Notes on the Kōan," *Parabola*, vol. 13, no. 3, Fall 1988, p. 35.

7. D. T. Suzuki, trans., "On Believing in Mind (Shinjin no Mei)," in *Manual of Zen Buddhism*, p. 77.

CASE 24: *Feng-hsüeh: Equality and Differentiation*

1. This model is an antecedent of the "Five Modes of the Universal and Particular," developed by Tung-shan Liang-chieh, and it can be related to similar schemes worked out by Lin-chi and others. See Powell, *Record of Tung-shan*, pp. 61–63; Yasutani, *Goi, Sanki, Sanju, Jūjūkinkai Dokugo*, pp. 1–55.

2. Part of a sutra dedication, "Daily Zen Sutras," mimeo, Diamond Sangha, Honolulu, n.d.

3. Cleary and Cleary, *Blue Cliff Record*, 3:554.

4. This is the traditional account; actually *The Jewel Treasury Treatise* is probably a later work. See Miura and Sasaki, *Zen Dust*, p. 282, and Dumoulin, *Zen Buddhism: A History*, 1:73 and 80, n. 60.

5. See Shibayama, *Zen Comments on the Mumonkan*, p. 176, and Miura and Sasaki, *Zen Dust*, p. 282.

6. Professor Totsudō Katō doubts that Tu-fu is the original author; Katō, *Mumonkan*, 14:203.

7. Cleary, *Book of Serenity*, p. 422.

8. Cleary and Cleary, *Blue Cliff Record*, 1:10; 2:372, 382, 385.

CASE 25: *Yang-shan's Sermon from the Third Seat*

1. Chang, *Original Teachings of Ch'an Buddhism*, pp. 220–221.

2. Yamada, *Gateless Gate*, pp. 132–133.

3. Charles Luk, trans., *The Śūraṅgama Sutra* (London: Rider, 1966), pp. 119–236.

4. Yasutani, "Introductory Lectures," pp. 38–41.

5. Cleary and Cleary, *Blue Cliff Record*, 1:216–220.

6. Shibayama, *Zen Comments on the Mumonkan*, p. 183.

7. Cleary and Cleary, *Blue Cliff Record*, 2:424.

8. This is Bassui's question; Braverman, *Mud and Water*, pp. 101–104.

9. Shibayama, *Zen Comments on the Mumonkan*, p. 186.

CASE 26: *Fa-yen: Two Monks Roll Up the Blinds*

1. Cleary, *Book of Serenity*, p. 86.

2. Yamada, *Gateless Gate*, p. 140.

3. See Case 41, my comment.

4. Yamada, *Gateless Gate*, pp. 139–140.

5. Aitken, *Taking the Path of Zen*, p. 110.

6. Case 18, Wu-men's Verse.

CASE 27: *Nan-ch'üan: "Not Mind, Not Buddha, Not Beings"*

1. Cleary and Cleary, *Blue Cliff Record*, 1:181.

2. See Appendix I, Lineage Chart III: Generations 36 and 37.

3. Dōgen, *Shinjin Gakudō*; see Tanahashi, *Moon in a Dewdrop*, p. 89.

4. Dōgen, *Shōji* ("Birth and Death"); ibid., p. 75.

5. Dōgen, *Busshō* ("Buddha Nature"); quoted by Kim, *Dōgen Kigen*, p. 124.

6. Cleary, *Entry into the Inconceivable*, p. 188; also Cleary, *Flower Ornament Scripture*, 1:452.

7. Cleary and Cleary, *Blue Cliff Record*, 3:541.

8. Suzuki, *Manual of Zen Buddhism*, facing p. 13.

9. Cleary and Cleary, *Blue Cliff Record*, 1:211.

10. Ibid.

11. Case 8, comment; Case 8, nn. 7 and 8.

12. Arthur Waley, *The Way and Its Power: A Study of the Tao Tê Ching and Its Place in Chinese Thought* (London: Allen & Unwin, 1949); Paul Carus, *The Canon*

of Reason and Virtue: Being Lao-tze's Tao Teh King (Chicago: Open Court, 1945).

13. Waddell, *The Unborn*, p. 5.

14. See Case 41, my comment, for another slant on *te*, set forth there as "merit."

CASE 28: *Lung-t'an: Renowned Far and Wide*

1. Te-shan also appears in *The Blue Cliff Record* (Case 2 and elsewhere) and in the *Book of Serenity* (Case 14 and elsewhere).

2. Price, *Diamond Sutra*, p. 57.

3. Shibayama, *Zen Comments on the Mumonkan*, p. 204.

4. Case 38, my comment; Suzuki, *Manual of Zen Buddhism*, pp. 127–134.

5. Guy Davenport, trans., *Herakleitos and Diogenes* (San Francisco: Grey Fox Press, 1983), p. 22.

6. See Case 13, my comment.

7. Suzuki, *Essays in Zen Buddhism: Second Series*, p. 303 fn.

8. Although Yamada Rōshi does not mention this criticism in his *Gateless Gate*, it was part of his instruction when I worked on the case as a kōan.

CASE 29: *Hui-neng: "Not the Wind; Not the Flag"*

1. See Case 23, my comment, and Case 23, nn. 4 and 5.

2. Cleary and Cleary, *Blue Cliff Record*, 1:98.

3. Distinguish the act of testing yourself against the understanding of others from the act of testing others against your own understanding.

4. Wong, *Sutra of Hui Neng*, p. 22.

CASE 30: *Ma-tsu: "This Very Mind Is Buddha"*

1. Cleary and Cleary, *Blue Cliff Record*, 1:229–230.

2. Alan W. Watts, *The Way of Zen* (New York: Pantheon, 1957), pp. 96–97, 110.

3. Cleary, *Transmission of Light*, p. 3.

4. Yamada, *Gateless Gate*, p. 159.

5. Case 3.

6. Luk, *Śūrangama Sutra*, pp. 97–100; Kapleau, *Three Pillars of Zen*, pp. 54–56.

CASE 31: *Chao-chou Investigates the Old Woman*

1. Sasaki, *Recorded Sayings of Ch'an Master Lin-chi*, Chinese text p. 9, English text p. 16.

2. Shibayama, *Zen Comments on the Mumonkan*, p. 227.

CASE 32: *The Buddha Responds to an Outsider*

1. Cleary and Cleary, *Blue Cliff Record*, 2:413; see also Shibayama, *Zen Comments on the Mumonkan*, p. 230.
2. See Case 27, my comment.
3. Case 27, Wu-men's Verse.
4. Many Zen people practice *shikantaza*, "single-minded sitting meditation," a very rigorous endeavor, though some interpret the practice as "merely sitting." It should be understood that *shikantaza* is not just a matter of being quiet. The term, which is Dōgen's, is discussed in full by Kim in *Dōgen Kigen*, pp. 55–73.
5. Cited by Yamada, *Gateless Gate*, pp. 170–171.
6. Suzuki, *Essays in Zen Buddhism: First Series*, p. 191 and fn.
7. Gard, *Buddhism*, pp. 145–150.
8. Case 22.
9. Blyth, *Zen in English Literature*, pp. 204–205.

CASE 33: *Ma-tsu: "Not Mind, Not Buddha"*

1. "Heart Sutra," Aitken, *Taking the Path of Zen*, p. 110.
2. Tōrei Enji, "Bodhisattva's Vow," trans. Katsuki Sekida, in *Daily Zen Sutras*.
3. Price, *Diamond Sutra*, pp. 29, 41, 53, 65.
4. Suzuki, *Sengai*, pp. 86–87.
5. Ibid.
6. See Wu-men's Preface, my comment.
7. Yasutani, "Introductory Lectures," p. 28.
8. I. A. Richards, "Reconsideration: Walter de la Mare," *New Republic*, vol. 174, 31 January 1976, p. 31.

CASE 34: *Nan-ch'üan: Mind and Buddha*

1. Hoffman, *Radical Zen*, p. 18; Akizuki Ryōmin, *Jōshūroku* [Analects of Chao-chou], *Zen no Goroku*, II:34.
2. Hoffman, *Radical Zen*, p. 119.
3. Chang, *Original Teachings of Ch'an Buddhism*, p. 169.
4. D. T. Suzuki, trans., "Dai-ō Kokushi, 'On Zen,'" *Manual of Zen Buddhism*, p. 146.
5. Case 41, Wu-men's Verse.
6. See Kazuaki Tanahashi, *Penetrating Laughter* (Woodstock, N.Y.: Overlook Press, 1984), p. 15. I have taken liberties with Tanahashi's translation in keeping with the way I first heard the story from Nakagawa Sōen Rōshi.

7. John Blofeld, trans., *The Zen Teaching of Huang Po: On the Transmission of Mind* (New York: Grove Press, 1958), p. 31.

8. Dōgen, *Shinjin Gakudō*; see Tanahashi, *Moon in a Dewdrop*, p. 88.

9. John Clare, "Little Trotty Wagtail," in David Powell, ed., *John Clare: The Wood Is Sweet* (London: Bodley Head, 1966), p. 61.

10. Cleary and Cleary, *Blue Cliff Record*, 1:578.

11. Miura and Sasaki, *Zen Dust*, p. 277

12. Aitken, *Mind of Clover*, pp. 122–123.

13. Kapleau, *Three Pillars of Zen*, p. 278 fn.

CASE 35: *Wu-tsu: "Which Is the True Ch'ien?"*

1. Shibayama, *Zen Comments on the Mumonkan*, p. 246.

2. Lafcadio Hearn, *Exotics and Retrospectives*, vol. 9 of *The Writings of Lafcadio Hearn: Koizumi Edition* (Boston: Houghton Mifflin, 1923), pp. 64–69. I have touched up Hearn's nineteenth-century orthography a bit.

3. Miura and Sasaki, *Zen Dust*, pp. 50, 266.

CASE 36: *Wu-tsu: Meeting Someone Attained in the Tao*

1. Shibayama, *Zen Comments on the Mumonkan*, p. 254.

2. Cleary and Cleary, *Blue Cliff Record*, 3:473, 477, 480.

3. Sasaki, *Recorded Sayings of Ch'an Master Lin-chi*, p. 20. Lin-chi was adapting lines by a still earlier teacher: Ssu-k'ung (Shikū), a disciple of Hui-neng; ibid., pp. 75–76, n. 103.

4. Ch'ang-ch'ing (Chōkei) and Pao-fu (Hōfuku); Cleary and Cleary, *Blue Cliff Record*, 1:154.

5. Ibid., 1:156.

6. Aitken, *Zen Wave*, p. 37, retranslated.

7. Ibid., p. 134.

8. Chang, *Original Teachings of Ch'an Buddhism*, p. 293; modified in light of a translation by Craig Twentyman, unpublished ms., Koko An Zendō, Honolulu, 1990.

9. Words attributed to the Buddha himself; Cleary, *Book of Serenity*, p. 3.

10. Cleary and Cleary, *Blue Cliff Record*, 1:37–38.

11. Ibid., 2:357.

12. Yampolsky, *Zen Master Hakuin*, p. 119.

CASE 37: *Chao-chou: The Oak Tree in the Courtyard*

1. The ideograph translated as "oak" is rendered "cypress" by modern Chinese scholars, "oak" by their Japanese colleagues.

2. Sasaki, *Recorded Sayings of Ch'an Master Lin-chi*, p. 33.

3. Dōgen, *Genjō Kōan*; see Tanahashi, *Moon in a Dewdrop*, p. 69.
4. Chang, *Original Teachings of Ch'an Buddhism*, p. 293.
5. Yamada, *Gateless Gate*, p. 191.
6. Cleary, *Book of Serenity*, pp. 197–198.
7. In this connection, one such teacher quoted the proverb "A good son does not live on his father's money." See Shibayama, *Zen Comments on the Mumonkan*, p. 262.
8. I first heard this story from Nakagawa Sōen Rōshi. See Yamada, *Gateless Gate*, p. 192, for a variant.
9. Shibayama, *Zen Comments on the Mumonkan*, p. 263.
10. Miura and Sasaki, *Zen Dust*, p. 326.
11. Hoffman, *Radical Zen*, p. 270.
12. Wu-men borrowed this verse from Tung-shan Shou-ch'u, who announced "Three pounds of flax" in Case 18; Katō, *Mumonkan*, 15:57.
13. Simone Pétrement, *Simone Weil: A Life*, trans. Raymond Rosenthal (New York: Pantheon, 1976), pp. 39–40.

CASE 38: *Wu-tsu's Buffalo Passes Through the Window*

1. Suzuki, *Essays in Zen Buddhism: First Series*, pp. 363–378 and plates; Kapleau, *Three Pillars of Zen*, pp. 301–311; Senzaki, "Bulls by Kakuan," in Reps, *Zen Flesh Zen Bones*, pp. 165–187.
2. Dōgen, *Genjō Kōan*; see Tanahashi, *Moon in a Dewdrop*, p. 71.
3. Ibid., p. 70.
4. Dōgen, *Kyōjūkaimon* (*Instruction on Receiving the Precepts*); see Aitken, *Mind of Clover*, p. 50.
5. Cleary and Cleary, *Blue Cliff Record*, 1:72.

CASE 39: *Yün-men: "You Have Misspoken"*

1. Cf. Shibayama, *Zen Comments on the Mumonkan*, p. 274.
2. "Hakuin Zenji's 'Song of Zazen'"; see Aitken, *Taking the Path of Zen*, p. 112.
3. Dōgen, *Kyōjūkaimon*; see Aitken, *Mind of Clover*, p. 66.
4. Cleary and Cleary, *Blue Cliff Record*, 2:292.
5. The *Hsin-hsin ming*, attributed to Seng-ts'an. There have been many translations of this poem. The first was Suzuki's version in *Manual of Zen Buddhism*, pp. 76–82.
6. Cleary and Cleary, *Blue Cliff Record*, 1:xxii.
7. Braverman, *Mud and Water*; see the Bibliography for a list of representative works.

8.   Christopher Cleary, *Swampland Flowers: The Letters and Lectures of Ta-hui* (New York: Grove Press, 1977).

C A S E 4 0 : *Kuei-shan Kicks Over the Water Bottle*

1.   This is the traditional story, abbreviated in Chang, *Original Teachings of Ch'an Buddhism*, p. 200.
2.   Ibid., pp. 201–202.
3.   Cleary and Cleary, *Blue Cliff Record*, 3:473, 477, 480.
4.   Blyth, *Mumonkan*, facing p. 261.
5.   Price, *Diamond Sutra*, pp. 44–45; Suzuki, "The Kongokyo or Diamond Sutra," *Manual of Zen Buddhism*, p. 46.
6.   Dōgen, *Kyōjūkaimon*; see Aitken, *Mind of Clover*, p. 94.
7.   Shibayama, *Zen Comments on the Mumonkan*, p. 282.
8.   Yamada, *Gateless Gate*, p. 206.

C A S E 4 1 : *Bodhidharma Pacifies the Mind*

1.   Cleary and Cleary, *Blue Cliff Record*, 1:3; see Lewis Hyde, *The Gift: Imagination and the Erotic Life of Property* (New York: Random House, 1983), especially pp. 23–24. See also my comment to Wu-men's Verse, Case 27.
2.   Cleary and Cleary, *Blue Cliff Record*, 1:3.
3.   Ibid., 1:1–5.
4.   E. Zürcher, *The Buddhist Conquest of China: The Spread and Adaptation of Buddhism in Early Medieval China* (Taipei: Chiao-huang Chou-chü Yu-hsien-kung-k'o, n.d.), p. 22.
5.   Shibayama, *Zen Comments on the Mumonkan*, pp. 286–287.
6.   Blyth, *Zen in English Literature*, facing p. 100.
7.   Kapleau, *Three Pillars of Zen*, pp. 208–229.
8.   Courtois, *Experience of Enlightenment*, pp. 29–30.
9.   Shibayama, *Zen Comments on the Mumonkan*, p. 287.
10.   Cleary and Cleary, *Blue Cliff Record*, 1:5.
11.   Ananda K. Coomaraswamy, "The Bugbear of Literacy," *Am I My Brother's Keeper?* (New York: John Day, 1947), p. 35.
12.   Suzuki, *Essays in Zen Buddhism: First Series*, p. 20.

C A S E 4 2 : *Mañjuśrī and the Young Woman in Samādhi*

1.   *Chu-fo yao-chi ching* (*Shōbutsu Yōjikkyō: A Collection of Abstracts of Stories of the Many Buddhas*); see Kono, *Busshō Kaisetsu Daijiten*, 5:277.
2.   Mañjuśrī is shown in images as androgynous, though perhaps a bit more male than female; see plate 8. For the clearly female Mañjuśrī, see Mayumi

Oda, *Goddesses* (Berkeley: Lancaster-Miller, 1981), p. 14 and opposite plate.

3. Yampolsky, *Platform Sutra of the Sixth Patriarch*, pp. 142–143.

4. Case 1, Wu-men's Comment.

C A S E 4 3 : *Shou-shan's Short Bamboo Staff*

1. Shibayama, *Zen Comments on the Mumonkan*, p. 300.

2. Sōiku Shigematsu, trans., *A Zen Forest: Sayings of the Masters* (New York: Weatherhill, 1981), p. 83.

3. Kuei-sheng (Kishō). Yamada, *Gateless Gate*, p. 219; Shibayama, *Zen Comments on the Mumonkan*, p. 301; Blyth, *Mumonkan*, p. 260.

4. Case 28.

5. Case 40.

6. This Ma-yü is an otherwise unknown figure; not to be confused with Ma-ku, a disciple of Ma-tsu, whose name is also pronounced Mayoku in Japanese. See Sasaki, *Recorded Sayings of Ch'an Master Lin-chi*, pp. 47 and 67–68, n. 20.

7. See Case 35, my comment.

C A S E 4 4 : *Pa-chiao's Staff*

1. Yamada, *Gateless Gate*, p. 224.

2. See Plate 2.

3. Yen-yang (Gonnyō); see Cleary, *Book of Serenity*, p. 241.

4. San-sheng (Sanshō); see Cleary and Cleary, *Blue Cliff Record*, 2:338.

5. Ibid.

6. Hsüeh-yin Tz'u-chio (Setsuin Jikaku); see Katō, *Mumonkan*, 15:178.

7. See Senzaki and McCandless, "The Shōdōka," *Buddhism and Zen*, p. 51.

8. Case 18, Wu-men's Verse.

C A S E 4 5 : *Wu-tsu: "Who Is That Other?"*

1. Wu-men uses an alternative name for Wu-tsu in this case: Fa-yen of Tung-shan (Hōen of Tōzan).

2. Suzuki, *Manual of Zen Buddhism*, p. 134 and plate XI.

3. Shibayama, *Zen Comments on the Mumonkan*, p. 309; Yamada, *Gateless Gate*, p. 228.

4. Dōgen, *Kyōjūkaimon*; see Aitken, *Mind of Clover*, pp. 64–72.

5. Shibayama, *Zen Comments on the Mumonkan*, p. 310.

C A S E 4 6 : *Shih-shuang: "Step from the Top of the Pole"*

1. Cleary, *Book of Serenity*, p. 335.

2. Ching-ts'en (Keijin); see Miura and Sasaki, *Zen Dust*, p. 275.
3. Ibid.
4. Cleary and Cleary, *Blue Cliff Record*, 2:269.
5. Buddhist eulogies are addressed to the deceased.

CASE 47: *Tou-shuai's Three Barriers*

1. Robert Burnett, *The Life of Paul Gauguin* (New York: Oxford University Press, 1937), p. 208 and facing plate.
2. Suzuki, *Manual of Zen Buddhism*, p. 129 and plate 1.
3. Aitken, *Taking the Path of Zen*, p. 110.
4. Cleary and Cleary, *Blue Cliff Record*, 2:365.

CASE 48: *Kan-feng's One Road*

1. Cleary, *Transmission of Light*, p. 82.
2. Cleary and Cleary, *Blue Cliff Record*, 3:490.

Bibliography

SELECTED READINGS FOR THE STUDENT
OF ZEN BUDDHISM

Introductions to Zen Practice

Aitken, Robert. *Taking the Path of Zen*. San Francisco: North Point Press, 1982.

Kapleau, Philip. *The Three Pillars of Zen: Practice, Teaching, and Enlightenment*. Boston: Beacon Press, 1965.

Lives and Teachings of Zen Masters

Arntzen, Sonja. *Ikkyū and the Crazy Cloud Anthology*. Tokyo: Tokyo University Press, 1986.

Blofeld, John. *The Zen Teaching of Huang Po*. New York: Grove Press, 1958.

Braverman, Arthur. *Mud and Water: A Collection of Talks by the Zen Master Bassui*. San Francisco: North Point Press, 1989.

Cleary, Christopher. *Swampland Flowers: The Letters and Lectures of Ta-hui*. New York: Grove Press, 1977.

Cleary, Thomas. *Sayings and Doings of Pai-chang*. Los Angeles: Center Publications, 1979.

Hoffman, Yoel. *Radical Zen: The Sayings of Jōshū*. Brookline, Mass.: Autumn Press, 1978.

Kim, Hee-Jin. *Dōgen Kigen: Mystical Realist*. Tucson: University of Arizona Press, 1987.

Merwin, W. S., and Sōiku Shigematsu. *Sun at Midnight: Poems and Sermons of Musō Soseki*. San Francisco: North Point Press, 1989.

Powell, William F. *The Record of Tung-shan*. Honolulu: University of Hawaii Press, 1986.

Sasaki, Ruth Fuller. *The Recorded Sayings of Ch'an Master Lin-chi Hui-chao of Chen Prefecture*. Kyoto: Institute for Zen Studies, 1975.

Tanahashi, Kazuaki. *Penetrating Laughter: Hakuin's Zen and Art*. Woodstock, N.Y.: Overlook Press, 1984.

———. *Moon in a Dewdrop: Writings of Zen Master Dōgen*. San Francisco: North Point Press, 1985.

Waddell, Norman. *The Unborn: The Life and Teachings of Zen Master Bankei.* San Francisco: North Point Press, 1984.

Wong, Mou-lam. *The Sutra of Hui Neng.* In *The Diamond Sutra and the Sutra of Hui Neng.* Berkeley: Shambhala, 1969.

Yampolsky, Philip B. *The Platform Sutra of the Sixth Patriarch: The Text of the Tun-Huang Manuscript.* New York: Columbia University Press, 1967.

———. *The Zen Master Hakuin: Selected Writings.* New York: Columbia University Press, 1971.

Anthologies of Zen Writings

Cleary, Thomas. *The Original Face: An Anthology of Rinzai Zen.* New York: Grove Press, 1978.

———. *Timeless Spring: A Soto Zen Anthology.* New York: Weatherhill, 1980.

Sheng-Yen, *The Poetry of Enlightenment: Poems by Ancient Ch'an Masters.* Elmhurst, N.Y.: Dharma Drum, 1987.

Suzuki, D. T. *Manual of Zen Buddhism.* New York: Grove Press, 1960.

Kōan Collections

Cleary, Thomas, and J. C. Cleary. *The Blue Cliff Record.* Boulder: Shambhala, 1977.

———. *Book of Serenity.* Hudson, N.Y.: Lindisfarne Press, 1990.

———. *Transmission of Light: Zen in the Art of Enlightenment.* San Francisco: North Point Press, 1990.

Other References

Chang, Chung-yuan. *Original Teachings of Ch'an Buddhism.* New York: Pantheon, 1969.

Corless, Roger J. *The Vision of Buddhism: The Space Under the Tree.* New York: Paragon House, 1989.

Dumoulin, Heinrich. *Zen Buddhism: A History.* 2 vols. New York: Macmillan, 1988 and 1990.

Gard, Richard A. *Buddhism.* New York: Braziller, 1962.

Miura, Isshū, and Ruth Fuller Sasaki. *Zen Dust: The History of the Koan and Koan Study in Rinzai (Lin-chi) Zen.* New York: Harcourt, Brace & World, 1966.

Rahula, Walpola. *What the Buddha Taught.* New York: Grove Press, 1959.

Ross, Nancy Wilson. *Buddhism: A Way of Life and Thought.* New York: Random House, 1980.

Suzuki, Shunryū. *Zen Mind, Beginner's Mind.* New York: Weatherhill, 1970.

EARLIER TRANSLATIONS OF THE
MUMONKAN (WU-MEN KUAN) INTO ENGLISH

Blyth, R. H. *Mumonkan*. Vol. 4 of *Zen and Zen Classics*. Tokyo: Hokuseido, 1966.

Nakamura, Fushiki Hiroji. *Mumonkan: Translated and Annotated*. Mt. Baldy Zen Center, 1972.

Ogata, Sōhaku. "A New Translation of the Wu mon kuan." In *Zen for the West*. New York: Dial Press, 1959.

Sekida, Katsuki. *Two Zen Classics: Mumonkan and Hekiganroku, with Commentaries*. New York: Weatherhill, 1977.

Senzaki, Nyogen. "The Gateless Gate." Unpublished translation and commentary, 1938. Diamond Sangha, Honolulu: Zen Center of San Francisco.

Senzaki, Nyogen, and Paul [Saladin] Reps. "The Gateless Gate." In *Zen Flesh Zen Bones: A Collection of Zen and Pre-Zen Writings*. Rutland, Vt.: Tuttle, 1957.

Senzaki, Nyogen, and Saladin Reps. *The Gateless Gate: Transcribed from the Chinese*. Los Angeles: John Murray, 1934.

Shibayama, Zenkei. *Zen Comments on the Mumonkan*. New York: Harper & Row, 1974.

Yamada, Kōun. *Gateless Gate: Newly Translated with Commentary*. Los Angeles: Center Publications, 1979.

EDITIONS OF THE
MUMONKAN (WU-MEN KUAN) CONSULTED

Harada, Sogaku. *Mumonkan Teishōroku* [Collection of teishōs on *The Gateless Barrier*]. Fukui-ken, Obama-shi: Dai'unkai, 1959.

Hirata, Takashi. *Mumonkan*. Vol. 18 of *Zen no Goroku* [Analects of Zen]. Tokyo: Chikuma Shōbō, 1969.

Iida, Tōin. *Mumonkan Sansui*. [*The Gateless Barrier*: fire by friction]. Tokyo: Morie Shōten, 1959.

Katō, Totsudō. *Mumonkan*. Vols. 13–15 of *Hekiganroku Daikōza* [A complete course of study of *The Blue Cliff Record*]. Tokyo: Heibonsha, 1940.

Shibayama, Zenkei. *Kunchū Mumonkan* [*The Gateless Barrier* explicated]. Tokyo: Kichūdō, 1954.

Yamamoto, Gempō. *Mumonkan Teishō*. Tokyo: Daihōrin, 1960.

Yasutani, Haku'un. *Mumonkan Dokugo* [Musings on *The Gateless Barrier*]. Tokyo: Sanbō Kōryūkai, 1956.

———. *Zen no Shinzui: Mumonkan* [Lifeblood of Zen: *The Gateless Barrier*]. Tokyo: Shunjūsha, 1965.

The Traditional Lineage[1]

I. EARLY TEACHERS

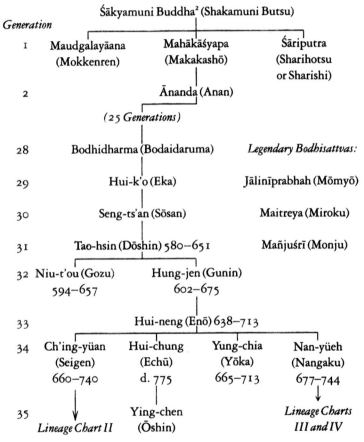

Śākyamuni Buddha[2] (Shakamuni Butsu)

Generation

1   Maudgalayāana   Mahākāśyapa   Śāriputra
      (Mokkenren)   (Makakashō)   (Sharihotsu
                                           or Sharishi)

2   Ānanda (Anan)

          (25 Generations)

28   Bodhidharma (Bodaidaruma)   *Legendary Bodhisattvas:*

29   Hui-k'o (Eka)   Jālinīprabhah (Mōmyō)

30   Seng-ts'an (Sōsan)   Maitreya (Miroku)

31   Tao-hsin (Dōshin) 580–651   Mañjuśrī (Monju)

32   Niu-t'ou (Gozu)   Hung-jen (Gunin)
       594–657   602–675

33   Hui-neng (Enō) 638–713

34   Ch'ing-yüan   Hui-chung   Yung-chia   Nan-yüeh
     (Seigen)   (Echū)   (Yōka)   (Nangaku)
     660–740   d. 775   665–713   677–744

35   Ying-chen   *Lineage Charts*
    Lineage Chart II   (Ōshin)   *III and IV*

1. Japanese pronunciations appear in parentheses. I have used Suzuki, *Chūkoku Zenshū Jimmei Sakuin*, as my authority for lineages and for birth/death dates. I also consulted Y. H. Ku, *History of Zen* (Elmhurst, N.Y.: Dharma Drum, n.d.), and the charts and other backmatter found in Miura and Sasaki, *Zen Dust*; Heinrich Dumoulin, *Zen Buddhism*, vol. 1; Yoshitaka Iriya, *Baso no Goroku* [Analects of Matsu] (Kyoto: Zen Bunka Kenkyūjō, 1984); Cleary and Cleary, *Blue Cliff Record*; Yamada, *Gateless Gate*; Yasutani, *Goi, Sanki, Sanju, Jūjūjinkai Dokugo*; Tanahashi, *Moon in a Dewdrop*; Francis Dojun Cook, *How to Raise an Ox* (Los Angeles: Center Publications, 1978); and Sekida, *Two Zen Classics*.

2. Hajime Nakamura suggests 463–383 B.C. as dates for Śākyamuni. See his *Gotama Buddha*, pp. 13 and 133, nn. 5–9.

II. THE CH'ING-YÜAN LINE

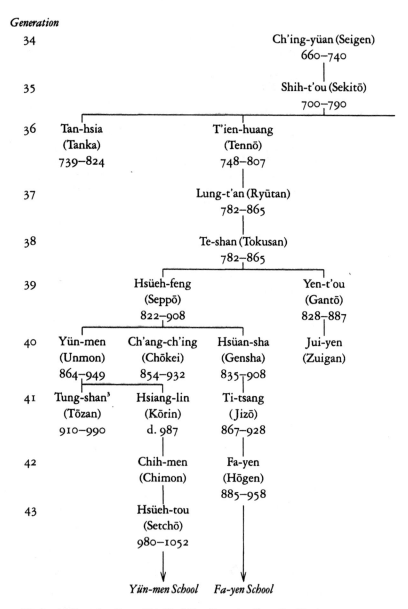

34   Ch'ing-yüan (Seigen)
660–740

35   Shih-t'ou (Sekitō)
700–790

36   Tan-hsia   T'ien-huang
(Tanka)   (Tennō)
739–824   748–807

37   Lung-t'an (Ryūtan)
782–865

38   Te-shan (Tokusan)
782–865

39   Hsüeh-feng   Yen-t'ou
(Seppō)   (Gantō)
822–908   828–887

40   Yün-men   Ch'ang-ch'ing   Hsüan-sha   Jui-yen
(Unmon)   (Chōkei)   (Gensha)   (Zuigan)
864–949   854–932   835–908

41   Tung-shan[3] Hsiang-lin   Ti-tsang
(Tōzan)   (Kōrin)   (Jizō)
910–990   d. 987   867–928

42   Chih-men   Fa-yen
(Chimon)   (Hōgen)
885–958

43   Hsüeh-tou
(Setchō)
980–1052

Yün-men School   *Fa-yen School*

3. Distinguish Tung-shan Liang-chieh (II:38) from Tung-shan Shou-c'hu (II:41).

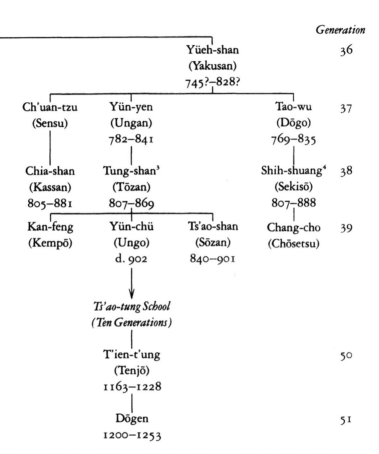

4. Distinguish Shi-shuang Ch'ing-chu (II:38) from Shi-shuang Ch'u-yüan (III and IV:44).

III. THE NAN-YÜEH LINE

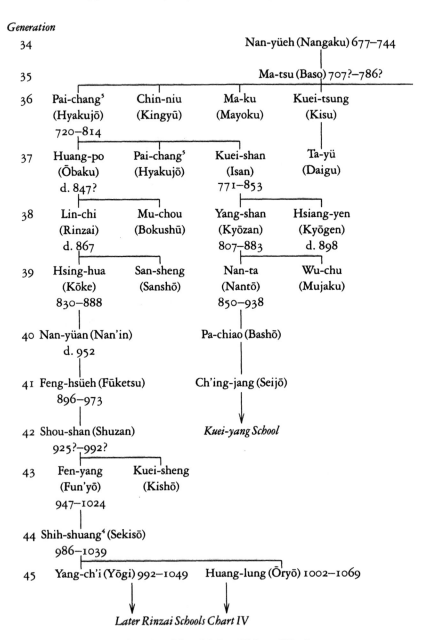

Nan-yüeh (Nangaku) 677–744

Ma-tsu (Baso) 707?–786?

| Pai-chang[5] (Hyakujō) 720–814 | Chin-niu (Kingyū) | Ma-ku (Mayoku) | Kuei-tsung (Kisu) |

Huang-po (Ōbaku) d. 847?

Pai-chang[5] (Hyakujō)

Kuei-shan (Isan) 771–853

Ta-yü (Daigu)

Lin-chi (Rinzai) d. 867

Mu-chou (Bokushū)

Yang-shan (Kyōzan) 807–883

Hsiang-yen (Kyōgen) d. 898

Hsing-hua (Kōke) 830–888

San-sheng (Sanshō)

Nan-ta (Nantō) 850–938

Wu-chu (Mujaku)

Nan-yüan (Nan'in) d. 952

Pa-chiao (Bashō)

Feng-hsüeh (Fūketsu) 896–973

Ch'ing-jang (Seijō)

Shou-shan (Shuzan) 925?–992?

Kuei-yang School

Fen-yang (Fun'yō) 947–1024

Kuei-sheng (Kishō)

Shih-shuang[4] (Sekisō) 986–1039

Yang-ch'i (Yōgi) 992–1049   Huang-lung (Ōryō) 1002–1069

Later Rinzai Schools Chart IV

5. Distinguish Pai-chang Huai-hai (III:36) from Pai-chang Nieh-pan (III:37).

III. THE NAN-YÜEH LINE

Generation

Ta-mei (Daibai) 752–839	Yen-kuan (Enkan) d. 842		Nan-ch'üan (Nansen) 748–834	36
T'ien-lung (Tenryū)	Lu-keng (Rikkō)	Ch'ang-sha (Chōsa) d. 868	Chao-chou (Jōshū) 778–897	37
Chü-chih (Gutei)		Yen-yang (Gonnyō)	Hui-chiao (Ekaku)	38

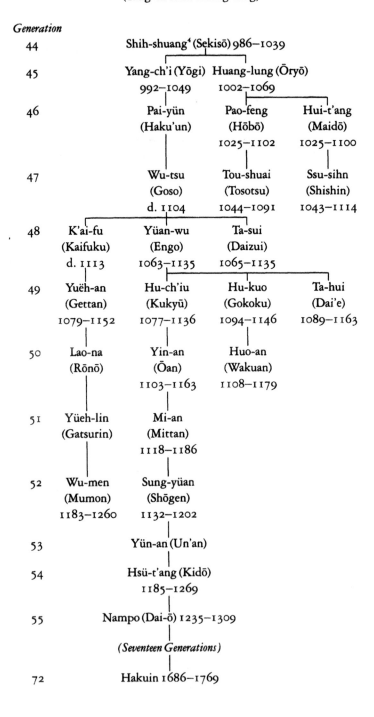

IV. THE LATER RINZAI SCHOOLS
(Yang-ch'i and Huang-lung)

Generation

44   Shih-shuang⁴ (Sekisō) 986–1039

45   Yang-ch'i (Yōgi)   Huang-lung (Ōryō)
        992–1049   1002–1069

46   Pai-yün   Pao-feng   Hui-t'ang
       (Haku'un)   (Hōbō)   (Maidō)
                 1025–1102   1025–1100

47   Wu-tsu   Tou-shuai   Ssu-sihn
       (Goso)   (Tosotsu)   (Shishin)
       d. 1104   1044–1091   1043–1114

48   K'ai-fu   Yüan-wu   Ta-sui
    (Kaifuku)   (Engo)   (Daizui)
    d. 1113   1063–1135   1065–1135

49   Yüeh-an   Hu-ch'iu   Hu-kuo   Ta-hui
    (Gettan)   (Kukyū)   (Gokoku)   (Dai'e)
  1079–1152   1077–1136   1094–1146   1089–1163

50   Lao-na   Yin-an   Huo-an
    (Rōnō)   (Ōan)   (Wakuan)
          1103–1163   1108–1179

51   Yüeh-lin   Mi-an
    (Gatsurin)   (Mittan)
          1118–1186

52   Wu-men   Sung-yüan
    (Mumon)   (Shōgen)
  1183–1260   1132–1202

53   Yün-an (Un'an)

54   Hsü-t'ang (Kidō)
        1185–1269

55   Nampo (Dai-ō) 1235–1309

      (Seventeen Generations)

72   Hakuin 1686–1769

Chinese-Japanese Equivalents

	CHINESE		JAPANESE
Lineage Chart and Generation	(Wade-Giles)	(Pinyin)	
	an-chu	anju	anju
	Ao-shan	Aoshan	Gōzan
	Ch'a-tu	Chadu	Sato
	ch'an-shih	chanshi	zenji
	Ch'ang-an	Changan	Chōan
II:40	Ch'ang-ch'ing Hui-leng	Changqing Huileng	Chōkei Eryō
II:39	Chang-cho Hsiu-ts'ai	Zhangzhuo Xiucai	Chōsetsu Shusai
III:37	Ch'ang-sha Ch'ing-ts'en	Changsha Jingcen	Chōsa Keijin
III:37	Chao-chou Ts'ung-shen	Zhaozhou Congshen	Jōshū Jūshin
	Cheng-tao ko	*Zhengdaoge*	*Shōdōka*
	ch'i	chi	ki
	chia-sha	jiasha	kesa
II:38	Chia-shan Shan-hui	Jiashan Shanhui	Kassan Zenne
	Chiang-nan	Jiangnan	Kōnan
	Ch'ien	Qian	Sei
	Chien-yüan Chung-hsing	Jianyuan Zhongxing	Zengen Chūkō
	Chih-kung	Zhigong	Shikō
II:42	Chih-men Kuang-tsu	Zhimen Guangzu	Chimon Kōso
	ch'in-ch'ieh	chinque	shinsetsu
III:36	Chin-niu	Jinniu	Kingyū
	Ching-ch'ing Tao-fu	Jingqing Daofu	Kyōsei Dōfu
	Ch'ing-jang (see Hsing-yang Ch'ing-jang)		
	Ch'ing-liang	Qingliang	Seiryō
	Ch'ing-shui	Qingshui	Seizei
	Ching-tso-shan	Chingzuoshan	Seizazan

	CHINESE		JAPANESE
Lineage *Chart and* *Generation*	*(Wade-Giles)*	*(Pinyin)*	
	Ch'ing-yüan (line)	Chingyuan	Seigen
I/II:34	Ch'ing-yüan Hsing-ssu	Chingyuan Xingsi	Seigen Gyōshi
III:38	Chü-chih	Juzhi	Gutei
	Chu-ling	Zhuling	Kōrei
	chu-pi	zhubi	shippei
	Chui	Zhui	Sui
	Chung Kuo-shih (Chū Kokushi) (see Nan- yang Hui-chung)		
	chung-sheng	zhongsheng	shujō
	Fa-yen (school)	Fayan	Hōgen
II:42	Fa-yen Wen-i	Fayan Wenyi	Hōgen Bun'eki
	Fan-tan	Fandan	Hantan
	fang-wen	fangwen	hōjō
III:41	Feng-hsüeh Yen-chao	Fengxue Yanjiao	Fūketsu Enshō
	Fu Da-shih	Fu Dashi	Fu Daishi
	Hsi-chung	Xizhong	Keichū
	Hsia-t'ang Ch'ang-lao	Xiatang Changlao	Shōtō Chōrō
III:38	Hsiang-yen Chih-hsien	Xiangyan Zhixian	Kyōgen Chikan
	Hsiang-yü	Xiangyu	Kōu
	hsien	xian	sen
	Hsin-hsin ming	*Xinxinming*	*Shinjinmei*
III:38	Hsin-hsing Yen-yang	Xinxing Yanyang	Shin'yo Gonnyō
III:41	Hsing-yang Ch'ing- jang	Xingyang Qingrang	Kōyō Seijō
IV:54	Hsü-t'ang Chih-yü	Xutang Zhiyu	Kidō Chigu
II:40	Hsüan-sha Hsi-pei	Xuansha Xibei	Gensha Shibi
II:39	Hsüeh-feng I-ts'un	Xuefeng Yicun	Seppō Gison
	Hsüeh-san-lang	Xuesanlang	Shasanrō
II:43	Hsüeh-tou Ch'ung- hsien	Xuedou Chongxian	Setchō Jūken
	Hsüeh-yin Tz'u-chiao	Xueyin Cijiao	Setsu'in Jikaku
	Hu-nan	Hunan	Kōnan
	Hua-shan	Huashan	Kasan
	Hua-yen	*Huayan*	*Kegon*

Lineage Chart and Generation	CHINESE (Wade-Giles)	(Pinyin)	JAPANESE
III/IV:45	Huang-lung Hui-nan	Huanglung Huinan	Ōryō Enan
I:32	Huang-mei Hung-jen	Huangmei Hongren	Ōbai Gunin
III:37	Huang-po Hsi-yün	Huangbo Xiyun	Ōbaku Ki'un
	Hui	Hui	E
III:38	Hui-chiao	Huijiao	Ekaku
	Hui-chung (see Nan-yang Hui-chung)		
	Hui-k'ai (see Wu-men Hui-k'ai)		
I:29	Hui-k'o	Huike	Eka
	Hui-neng (see Ta-chien Hui-neng)		
	Hung-jen (see Huang-mei Hung-jen)		
	Huo	Huo	Kaku
IV:50	Huo-an Shih-t'i	Huoan Shiti	Wakuan Shitai
II:40	Jui-yen Shih-yen	Ruiyan Shiyan	Zuigan Shigen
II:39	Kan-feng	Ganfeng	Kempō
	Kuan	Guan	Kan
	Kuan-tzü-tsai	Guanzizai	Kanjizai
	Kuan-yin	Guanyin	Kannon
	Kuan-yin-yüan	Guanyinyuan	Kannon-in
III:37	Kuei-shan Ling-yu	Guishan Lingyu	Isan Reiyū
	Kuei-sheng (see Yeh-hsien Kuei-sheng)		
III:36	Kuei-tsung Chih-ch'ang	Guizong Zhichang	Kisu Chijō
	Kuei-yang (school)	Guiyang	Igyō
	Kuo-shih	Guoshi	Kokushi
	li	li	ri
	Li-chou	Lizhou	Reishū
	Liang	Liang	Ryō
	Liang-ti	Liangdi	Ryōtei
	Lin-chi (school)	Linji	Rinzai
III:38	Lin-chi I-hsüan	Linji Yixuan	Rinzai Gigen

	CHINESE		JAPANESE
Lineage Chart and Generation	*(Wade-Giles)*	*(Pinyin)*	
	Ling-hsiang	Lingxiang	Ryūshō
	Ling-nan	Lingnan	Reinan
	Ling-yün Chih-ch'in	Lingyun Zhiqin	Rei'un Shigon
	Lo-han (see Ti-tsang Kuei-ch'en)		
	Lo-p'u Lin-chung	Luopu Linzhong	Rakuhō Rinjū
	Lu	Lu	Ro
III:37	Lu-keng Ta-fu	Lugeng Dafu	Rikkō Daifu
	Lu-tsu Pao-yün	Luzu Baoyun	Roso Hōun
II:37	Lung-t'an Ch'ung-hsin	Lungtan Chongxin	Ryūtan or Ryōtan
III:36	Ma-ku Pao-ch'e	Magu Baoche	Mayoku Hōtetsu
	ma san-ching	masanjing	masangin
III:35	Ma-tsu Tao-i	Mazu Daoyi	Baso Dōitsu
	Ma-yü	Mayu	Mayoku
IV:51	Mi-an Hsien-chieh	Mian Xianjie	Mittan Kanketsu
	Ming	Ming	Myō
	Ming (dynasty)	Ming	Min
III:38	Mu-chou Tao-tsung	Muzhou Daozong	Bokushū Dōsō
III:36	Nan-ch'üan P'u-yüan	Nanchuan Puyuan	Nansen Fugan
	nan-t'ou	nantou	nantō
I:34	Nan-yang Hui-chung	Nanyang Huizhong	Nanyō Echū
	Nan-yüeh (line)	Nanyue	Nangaku
I/III:34	Nan-yüeh Huai-jang	Nanyue Huairang	Nangaku Ejō
	nien	nian	nen
I:32	Niu-t'ou Fa-yung	Niutou Fayong	Gozu Hōyū
III:40	Pa-chiao Hui-ch'ing	Bajiao Huiqing	Bashō Esei
	Pa-ling Hao-chien	Baling Haojian	Haryō Kōkan
	Pai	Bai	Haku
III:36	Pai-chang Huai-hai	Baizhang Huaihai	Hyakujō Ekai
III:37	Pai-chang Nieh-p'an	Baizhang Niepan	Hyakujō Nehan
IV:46	Pai-yün Shou-tuan	Baiyun Zhouduan	Haku'un Shutan

	CHINESE		JAPANESE
Lineage Chart and Generation	(Wade-Giles)	(Pinyin)	
	Pan-tan	Bandan	Hantan
	Pao-fu Ts'ung-chan	Baofu Congzhan	Hofuku Jūten
	Pao-tsang lun	Baozanglun	Hōzōron
	Pao-tzu	Baozi	Hōzu
	Pu-tai	Budai	Hotei
	P'u-tien	Pudian	Haden
	Pu-tung	Budung	Fudō
III:39	San-sheng Hui-jan	Sansheng Huiran	Sanshō Enen
	Seng-chao	Sengzhao	Sōjō
I:30	Seng-ts'an	Sengcan	Sōsan
	Shao-lin-ssu	Shaolinsi	Shōrinji
	Shao-ting	Shaoding	Jōtei
	Shen-hsiu	Shenxiu	Jinshū
	Shen-kuang	Shenguang	Shinkō
	Shih-chi	Shiji	Jissai
II/IV:44	Shih-shuang Ch'u-yüan	Shishuang Chuyuan	Sekisō Sōen
II:35	Shih-t'ou Hsi-ch'ien	Shitou Xiqian	Sekitō Kisen
III:42	Shou-shan Sheng-nien	Shoushan Shengnian	Shuzan Shōnen
	Ssu-kung Pen-ching	Sigong Benjing	Shikū Honjō
IV:47	Ssu-hsin Wu-hsin	Sixin Wuxin	Shishin Goshin
	Su-tsung	Suzong	Shukusō
	Sung (period)	Song	Sō
IV:52	Sung-yüan Ch'ung- yüeh	Songyuan Chongyue	Shōgen Sūgaku
	szu-wei	siwei	shiyui
I:33	Ta-chien Hui-neng	Dajian Huineng	Daikan Enō
	Ta-hsiung	Daxiong	Daiyū
IV:49	Ta-hui Tsung-kao	Dahui Zonggao	Dai'e Sōkō
	Ta-kuei	Dagui	Dai'i
	Ta-kung-wang	Dagongwang	Taikōbō
III:36	Ta-mei Fa-ch'ang	Damei Fachang	Daibai Hōjō
	Ta-shih	Dashi	Daishi
	Ta-t'ung Chih-sheng	Dadong Zhisheng	Daitsū Chisō
	Ta-yü	Dayu	Daiyū
	Tai-tsung	Daizong	Daisō

	CHINESE		JAPANESE
Lineage Chart and Generation	(Wade-Giles)	(Pinyin)	
II:36	Tan-hsia T'ien-jan	Tanxia Tianran	Tanka Tennen
I:35	Tan-yüan Ying-chen	Danyuan Yingjian	Tangen Ōshin
	T'ang (period)	Tang	Tō
II:37	Tao-wu Yüan-chieh	Daowu Yuanjie	Dōgo Enchi
	te	de	toku
II:38	Te-shan Hsüan-chien	Deshan Xuanjian	Tokusan Senkan
	Te-shang-tso	Deshangzuo	Toku Shōza
II:41	Ti-tsang Kuei-ch'en	Dizang Guichen	Jizō Keijin
	tien-hsin	dianxin	tenjin
III:37	T'ien-lung	Tianlong	Tenryū
	t'o-po	tobo	takuhatsu
IV:47	Tou-shuai Ts'ung-yüeh	Doushuai Cong- yueh	Tosotsu Jūsetsu
	Ts'ao-hsi	Caoxi	Sōkei
II:39	Ts'ao-shan Pen-chi	Caoshan Benji	Sōzan Honjaku
	Ts'ao-tung (school)	Caodong	Sōtō
	tso-wu	zuowu	samu
	Ts'ui-yen Ling-ts'an	Cuiyan Lingcan	Suigan Reisan
	Ts'ung-jung lu	*Congronglu*	*Shōyōroku*
	Tun-huang	Dunhuang	Tonkō
	Tung-chia	Dongjia	Tōka
II:38	Tung-shan Liang-chieh	Dungshan Liangjie	Tōzan Ryōkai
II:41	Tung-shan Shou-ch'u	Dongshan Shouchu	Tōzan Shusho
	tzu	zi	ji
	wei	wei	bi (mi)
	Wu (the emperor)	Wu	Bu
III:39	Wu-chu Wen-hsi	Wuju Wenxi	Mujaku Bunki
IV:52	Wu-men Hui-k'ai	Wumen Huikai	Mumon Ekai
	Wu-men kuan	*Wumenguan*	*Mumonkan*
	Wu-t'ai-shan	Wutaishan	Godaisan
IV:47	Wu-tsu Fa-yen	Wuzu Fayan	Goso Hōen
III/IV:45	Yang-ch'i Fang-hui	Yangchi Fanghui	Yōgi Hōe
III:38	Yang-shan Hui-chi	Yangshan Huiji	Kyōzan Ejaku
III:43	Yeh-hsien Kuei-sheng	Yexian Guisheng	Sekken Kishō

	CHINESE		JAPANESE
Lineage *Chart and* *Generation*	*(Wade-Giles)*	*(Pinyin)*	
III:36	Yen-kuan Ch'i-an	Yanguan Qian	Enkan Sai'an
II:39	Yen-t'ou Ch'üan-huo	Yantou Quanhuo	Gantō Zenkatsu
	Yen-yang (see Hsin-hsing Yen-yang)		
	Yin-tsung	Yinzong	Insō
	Yin-yüan Lung-ch'i	Yinyuan Longchi	Ingen Ryūki
	Ying-chen (see Tan-yüan Ying-chen)		
	Yü	Yu	Gu
IV:48	Yüan-wu K'o-ch'in	Yuanwu Kechin	Engo Kokugon
IV:49	Yüeh-an Shan-kuo	Yuean Shanguo	Gettan Zenka
IV:51	Yüeh-lin Shih-kuan	Yuelin Shiguan	Gatsurin Shikan
II:36	Yüeh-shan Wei-yen	Yueshan Weiyan	Yakusan Igen
IV:53	Yün-an P'u-yen	Yunan Puyan	Un'an Fugan
	Yün-men (school)	Yunmen	Unmon
II:40	Yün-men Wen-yen	Yunmen Wenyan	Unmon Bun'en
II:37	Yün-yen T'an-sheng	Yunyan Tansheng	Ungan Donjō
I:34	Yung-chia Hsüan-chüeh	Yongjia Xuanjue	Yōka Gengaku
	Yung-chia Ta-shih (Yōka Daishi) (see Yung-chia Hsüan-chüeh)		

Japanese-Chinese Equivalents

JAPANESE	CHINESE	
	(Wade-Giles)	(Pinyin)
buji	wu-shih	wushi
dōjō	tao-ch'ang	daochang
dokusan	tu-tsan	ducan
hōsen	fa-chan	fazhan
kenshō	chien-ch'ang	jianchang
kōan	kung-an	gongan
kusai (shū)	ch'ou	chou
makyō	mo-ching	mojing
Mu	Wu	Wu
rōshi	lao-shih	laoshi
sanzen	tsan-ch'an	canchan
satori (go)	wu	wu
shikantaza	ch'i-kuan ta-tso	qiguan dazuo
shōsan	hsiao-ts'an	xiaocan
teishō	t'i-ch'ang	tichang
zazen	tso-ch'an	zuochan
Zen	Ch'an	Chan
zendō	ch'an-t'ang	chantang

Glossary

Ancestral Teachers (*sōshi*, Japanese). Often rendered "Zen Patriarchs."

Bodhidharma (Sanskrit). Traditional founder of the Ch'an sect, flourished A.D. 520. An archetype of rigorous practice and wisdom.

bodhisattva (Sanskrit). One on the path to enlightenment; one who is enlightened; one who enlightens others; a figure in the Buddhist pantheon.

Bodhi Tree. The tree under which the historical Buddha became enlightened. See *dōjō*.

Buddha (Sanskrit). Enlightened One; Śākyamuni, the historical Buddha (463?–383? B.C.); an enlightened person; the nature of the universe and its beings; any being; a figure in the Buddhist pantheon.

Buddha nature. Essential nature.

Buddha Tao or Way. The path or teaching of the historical Buddha and his successors; Dharma; Buddhism; the Eightfold Path; the Way apparent in the universe.

Ch'an (Chinese). Pronounced "Zen" in Japanese; see *Zen*.

deva (Sanskrit). Heavenly being.

dhāraṇī (Sanskrit). A devotional text read in transliterated form in Far Eastern (and now Western) Mahayana services.

Dharma (Sanskrit). Religious, secular, or natural law; the law of karma; phenomena; Tao or Way; teaching; pure emptiness. "Turning the Dharma Wheel" is lending wisdom and energy to the transformational process of the Buddha Tao.

Dharmakāya (Sanskrit). Law or Dharma Body (of the Buddha); the pure, clear, empty aspect of the universe.

dialogue. *Mondō* (Japanese, question and answer); *shōsan* or *hōsen* (Japanese, Dharma encounter); the exchange between teacher and student, usually in formal teaching circumstances. See *interview*.

Diamond Sutra. The *Vajrachedikā Sūtra* (Sanskrit), a text of the Prajñā Pāramitā literature that stresses freedom from concepts.

dōjō (Japanese). Spot or place of enlightenment of the Buddha under the Bodhi Tree; one's own place of enlightenment; the training hall.

Eightfold Path. The fourth of the Four Noble Truths: the way of practice, beginning with right views of the harmony of all things and of the self as impermanent.

Five Modes of the Universal and the Particular. Aspects of the harmony of the many and the individual, the infinite and the finite, emptiness and form.

Four Noble Truths. The fundamental Buddhist teaching: Anguish is everywhere; the cause of anguish is the inability to accept harmony and impermanence; there is an experience of freedom from anguish; such an experience is found with the practice of the Eightfold Path.

Heart Sutra. The *Prajñā Pāramitā Hrdaya Sūtra* (Sanskrit), a brief summary of Mahayana Buddhism stressing the insubstantial nature of all things.

Hsin-hsin mei (Chinese; *Shinjinmei*, Japanese). "Precepts of the Faith," a long Zen poem attributed to the Third Ancestor, Seng-ts'an (Sōsan).

Hua-yen Sutra. The Chinese version of the *Avatamsaka Sūtra* (Sanskrit), which stresses the innate harmony of all beings.

interview (*dokusan* or *sanzen*, Japanese). The private dialogue of teacher and student during formal Zen practice.

kalpa (Sanskrit). An immeasurably long period of time; aeon.

karma (Sanskrit). Action; cause and effect (distinguished from fate); affinity.

Katsu! or Kats'! (Japanese). A cry in the course of a dialogue or teishō.

kenshō (Japanese). Seeing into one's essential nature and the essential nature of all things.

kōan (Japanese). Universal/particular; a presentation of the harmony of the universal and the particular; a theme of zazen to be made clear.

Kuan-yin (Chinese; *Kannon* or *Kanzeon*, Japanese). One Who Hears Sounds (of the World); the archetypal Bodhisattva of Mercy.

Lotus Land or Pure Land. Nirvana; the afterlife envisioned in the Pure Land schools.

Lotus Sutra. The *Saddharma Pundarīka Sūtra* (Sanskrit), a devotional and metaphysical text presented in allegorical form.

Mahāparinirvāna Sūtra (Sanskrit). A text that recounts the final days of the Buddha's life.

mahāsattva. Noble being; bodhisattva.

Mahayana (*Mahāyāna*, Sanskrit). Great Vehicle; the Buddhism of East Asia, also found in Vietnam; Tibetan Buddhism is also considered to be Mahayana. The practice of saving the many beings.

Maitreya (Sanskrit). The Compassionate One; the future, potential, or inherent Buddha.

Mañjuśrī (Sanskrit). Beautiful Virtue; the archetypal Bodhisattva of Wisdom.

Middle Way. The Way of the Buddha, harmonizing the universal and the particular and other rational opposites; the Eightfold Path.

Mu (Japanese; *Wu*, Chinese). No; does not have; usually the first kōan of Zen practice, from Case 1 of *The Gateless Barrier*.

Nirmānakāya (Sanskrit). Transformation Body (of the Buddha); the unique and varied aspect of the universe.

nirvana (*nirvāna*, Sanskrit). Extinction of craving; liberation found in wisdom. See *Lotus Land*.

Pāramitā (Sanskrit). Perfection.

Path. See *Tao* and *Dharma*.

Prajñā Pāramitā (Sanskrit). Perfection of wisdom.

pratyeka (Sanskrit). Individual; one who seeks enlightenment for the self.

rōshi (Japanese). Venerable master (now a title).

Śākyamuni (Sanskrit). See *Buddha*.

Samantabhadra (Sanskrit). Pervading Goodness; the archetypal Bodhisattva of Great Action (in conveying the Buddha Way).

Sambogakāya (Sanskrit). Bliss Body (of the Buddha); the harmonious aspect of the universe.

Sangha (Sanskrit). Aggregate; priesthood; Buddhist fellowship; kinship of all beings.

satori (Japanese). Enlightenment; the experience or condition of enlightenment. See also *kenshō*.

sesshin (Japanese). To touch (receive and convey) the mind; the Zen Buddhist retreat of five to seven days.

śrāvaka. Hearer; one in the first stage of discipleship.

Sumeru (Sanskrit). Mountain at the center of paradise in the Hua-yen cosmology.

Śūrangama Sūtra. The best-known text bearing this name discusses ways of dispelling delusions, and is of Chinese origin.

sutra (sūtra). Sermon by the historical Buddha or attributed to him; Buddhist scripture.

Tao (Chinese; distinguished from the Tao of Taoism). Way; Dharma; Buddha Way or teaching; the Eightfold Path.

teishō (Japanese). Presentation of the shout; the Dharma presented by the rōshi; the rōshi's public talk.

transmission. Realization of the Dharma and approval of that realization by a true teacher.

Tripitaka (Sanskrit). Three baskets; the traditional categories of Buddhist teaching: the vinaya (precepts), sutras, and śāstras (commentaries).

Tusita (Sanskrit). The heavenly realm of Maitreya.

Way. See *Tao* and *Dharma*.

zazen (Japanese). Seated, focused meditation; formal Zen Buddhist practice.

Zen (Japanese). Focused meditation; harmony of the universal and the particular; the Zen Buddhist tradition.

zendō (Japanese). Zen hall; Zen Buddhist center.

CPSIA information can be obtained
at www.ICGtesting.com
Printed in the USA
LVOW11s1725291117
557960LV00001BA/159/P